MARITIME ADAPTATIONS

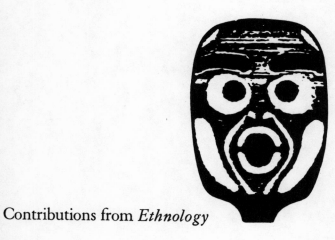

Contributions from *Ethnology*

MARITIME ADAPTATIONS

Essays on Contemporary Fishing Communities

Alexander Spoehr, Editor

UNIVERSITY OF PITTSBURGH PRESS

in cooperation with *Ethnology*

Published by the University of Pittsburgh Press, Pittsburgh, Pa. 15260
Copyright © 1980, University of Pittsburgh Press
All rights reserved
Feffer and Simons, Inc., London
Manufactured in the United States of America

The essays in this volume are reprinted by arrangement with the editors of *Ethnology* and have appeared in the following issues of that journal: "Ethnoicthyology of the Cha-Cha" and "Cognition and the Catch," vol. 6 (October 1967): 405–16 and 417–26; "The Lunar-Tide Fishing Cycle in Northeastern Brazil," vol. 13 (October 1974): 379–92; "Carrying Capacity Analysis of Fixed-Territorial Fishing," vol. 17 (January 1978): 1–24; "Society, Economy, and Shark-Fishing Crews in Rural Northwest Mexico," vol. 15 (October 1976): 377–91; "Pelagic Shark Fishing in Rural Mexico," vol. 18 (October 1979): 325–36; "Sea Tenure in Southern Sri Lanka," vol. 16 (July 1977): 231–51; "The Organization of Coastal Fishing in Tamilnadu," vol. 14 (October 1975): 357–71; "A Comparative Study of Work Groups in an Eastern Canadian Peasant Fishing Community," vol. 12 (October 1973): 393–418; "Action Groups in a Society with Bilateral Kinship," vol. 2 (July 1963): 269–75.

Library of Congress Cataloging in Publication Data

Main entry under title:

Maritime adaptations.

 Essays previously published in the journal Ethnology.
 Includes bibliographies.
 1. Maritime anthropology—Addresses, essays, lectures. 2. Fishing Villages—Addresses, essays, lectures. I. Spoehr, Alexander, 1913–
GN386.M37   301.35'2   79-22486

Contents

Acknowledgments

The editors of *Ethnology* are grateful to the authors of the essays that follow for their cooperation in making this volume possible. As several contributors have changed their institutional affiliations since their articles were first published, the authors and their current institutions are listed below:

Paul Alexander, University of Sydney
Otto Blehr, University of Bergen
Yvan Breton, Université Laval
John Cordell, Stanford University
Shepard Forman, University of Michigan
James R. McGoodwin, University of Colorado
Warren T. Morrill, Pennsylvania State University
Kathleen Fordham Norr, Loyola University of Chicago

The editors of *Ethnology* also express their appreciation to the University of Pittsburgh Press and its director, Frederick A. Hetzel, for making this publication possible.

Introduction

This volume brings together a series of essays dealing with fisheries and fishing communities that have previously appeared in the journal *Ethnology*. The reason for presenting this volume is to make readily available a body of substantive analyses bearing on maritime resources and their utilization. It is the hope of the editors of *Ethnology* that not only anthropologists but a wider audience concerned with the relation of fisheries to technological change and with the increasing pressure on maritime resources exerted by the demands of contemporary society will find the volume useful and of value.

Despite the publication in 1946 of Firth's classic study of Malay fishermen, later issued in revised form in 1966, the study of maritime communities has been slow to develop in anthropology, particularly in comparison with the notable effort expended on comparable studies of agricultural communities. At the present time in anthropology there is an increasing interest in maritime communities and the adaptations they exhibit, including their responses to pronounced technological change. This concern is reflected in the collection of papers on the subject edited by M. E. Smith (1977) and published under the auspices of the American Ethnological Society, as well as by the previously published study of North Atlantic fishermen edited by Anderson and Wadel (1972). The editors of *Ethnology* hope that the present collection will stimulate further anthropological interest in this field of investigation.

It is, of course, true that anthropological studies of man's relationship to the sea cover only a limited part of a large and complicated subject. Marine biologists, oceanographers, fishery technologists, and systems analysts are more prominent in the current literature on man's exploitation of the food resources of the sea than are anthropologists, particularly in view of the ever more sophisticated technology used in capture fisheries, the growing competition among nations for water space, and the acute though still unfilled need for more effective fishery and marine-resource management. From these specialists anthropologists have much to learn. Yet anthropology has a significant contribution to make both to knowledge and to matters of practical policy. Even though public attention has been attracted mainly to the environmental, economic, and political aspects of distant-water, industrialized fishing designed to help satisfy the protein needs of urbanized societies, there are today thousands of coastal fishing communities in the less-developed parts of the world attempting to supply similar requirements of the countries in which they are located. These communities are struggling to survive, with uncertain prospects. Their fate is part of the practical problem of getting protein to the masses of people who need it most. An understanding of such communities and of their responses to technological, economic, and social change is an important task that the anthropologist is professionally equipped to undertake.

As social scientists, anthropologists view technology and technological change as being imbedded in a sociocultural matrix that is just as important to understand as the technology per se. Technological change is one element in a system of human relationships that has cognitive, social structural, economic, political, and ecological dimensions. In capture fisheries, the system tends to vary in complexity with the scale of the communities or societies used as units of observation, as well as with the technology employed. The main point is that progress in the understanding of man's relation to the sea demands greater precision in the analysis of this system and of the nature of the relationships it incorporates. Here anthropology can make both methodological and substantive contributions. Although a theoretically oriented synthesis of fishing and fishing communities is still to be accomplished (Anderson and Wadel 1972:8), there remains a need for analytical field studies to elucidate the specific relationships embodied in maritime adaptations, to clarify patterns of change, and to provide an empirically valid cross-cultural base for generalization.

A few comments are appropriate on the essays comprising this volume. With the exception of Blehr's study of the Faroese community, they deal with communities of small-scale fishermen, although the nature of the market into which their production enters varies considerably. All the communities examined are rural and their inhabitants share many of the characteristics of either a peasantry or in the case of Mexico a form of rural proletariat (granted the imprecision of the terms). These communities are located in the Caribbean, Brazil, west and northwest Mexico, Sri Lanka, south India, eastern Canada, and the Faroe Islands. Within the context of fishing, the specific topics to which the authors address themselves cover a range of subjects: the manner in which knowledge of the marine environment is organized and applied; ecological relationships involved in fishing operations, including the problem of the carrying capacity of fishing grounds; the relationship of work organization and the recruitment of fishermen to community social structure; the impact of technological change; economic factors, including the overcapitalization of fishing enterprises; adaptations of communities through time to changing environmental, economic, and social conditions; and comparisons, contrasts, and relationships between fishing and peasant agriculture.

It is important to emphasiez that although the essays have a common focus on fishing communities, they are directly relevant to problem areas broader than fishing alone. In their own right, they are contributions to human ecology, ethnoscience, economics, social structure, and sociocultural change. Further explication seems redundant, and readers are invited to explore this volume on their own.

—Alexander Spoehr

BIBLIOGRAPHY

Anderson, R., and C. Wadel, eds. 1972. North Atlantic Fishermen: Anthropological Essays on Modern Fishing. Newfoundland Social and Economic Papers No. 5. Institute of Social and Economic Research, Memorial University of Newfoundland. Toronto.

Firth, R. 1966. Malay Fishermen: Their Peasant Economy. Hamden. Rev. of 1st ed., 1946, London.

Smith, M. E., ed. 1977. Those Who Live from the Sea: A Study in Maritime Anthropology. Monograph 62. American Ethnological Society. New York.

MARITIME ADAPTATIONS

Ethnoicthyology of the Cha-Cha[1]

Warren T. Morrill

The term "Cha-Cha" is used by the residents of St. Thomas, Virgin Islands, to refer to the people of French origin living on the island. The two French-speaking communities (Northside and Carenage) were formed in the last quarter of the nineteenth century by migrants from the island of St. Barthelemy in the Departement de Guadeloupe (Lasserre 1961). The present paper is concerned with the icthyological knowledge of the Carenage community. This knowledge is shared to some extent by the people of the Northside community, but fishing is and has been much less important to them because of the emphasis on farming as a subsistence base (Morrill and Dyke 1966). Much of Cha-Cha ethnoicthyology can be understood best as deriving from the particular fishing methods used and the observations which they require or permit. A detailed examination of fishing methods is in preparation, but for purposes of this paper the description will be limited to what is necessary to understand Cha-Cha ethnoicthyology, especially taxonomy, ecology, behavior of marine organisms, and the special problem of toxicity in fish.

FISHING METHODS

The Cha-Cha use three methods of fishing: trapping, seining, and handlining. Each of the three has its special requirements for equipment and for knowledge, not only of the techniques, but of the sea and of marine organisms. The boats used in all three methods are wooden craft of local manufacture; they are never larger than fifteen feet in length and are usually powered with outboard motors. In contrast to the large crews found on St. Barthelemy (Lasserre 1961), the usual fishing crew consists of two men. Occasionally one man fishes alone, but never as a professional fisherman.

Fish Traps

Fish traps are used both by professional fisherman and by Cha-Cha who fish only to supplement family subsistence. The traps are made of wood and metal mesh and conform to the pattern reported for southern Puerto Rico (Wilcox 1900: 25) and for much of the Lesser Antilles (Price 1966). Men who fish only to supplement subsistence set one or two of these traps in shallow waters close to their homes, whereas professional fisherman have five to fifteen traps and set them in waters up to 300 feet in depth. The locations are selected to maximize the species variation in the area, because it is believed that schooling fish will not enter traps. The pattern of species distribution around reefs is known to the Cha-Cha, and the utilization of reef sites insures a predominance of territorial (i.e., nonschooling) species.

Seining

The seines used by the Cha-Cha are made of cotton and have one-inch mesh in the center and two-inch mesh at the ends. They are 600 feet long and eighteen feet deep. Seining requires a shallow bay with a sand or grass bottom, and the essential part of the operation is the location of a school of appropriate size and species in a suitable area. A school of fish will be watched for days or weeks until it moves into a good position for seining. The observation is done by fishermen going back and forth to tend traps, by friends and family, and occasionally by the owner of the seine who is not himself a fisherman. When the school is thought to be in proper position, the fisherman puts out from shore with the seine folded on the transom of the boat. The actual shooting and hauling of the net may be preceded by resting as much as 48 hours in the boat waiting for exactly the right moment. Each species of fish requires a different speed and pace for the seining, and species are identified by schooling and feeding behavior. This method of taking fish has the greatest yield as regards both time and labor, but it is dependent on a great many factors out of the control of the fisherman. It may also result in an embarrassment of riches when the catch is so great that it cannot be sold before some of it spoils. Therefore, seining is not considered nearly as important a technique as either trapping or handlining.

Handlining

The taking of fish by the use of handlines is called "chumming" by the Cha-Cha. There is apparently no French equivalent for this term. Chumming requires a supply of small bait fish belonging to three species referred to as "fry" (see Appendix). These are taken with a circular throw net close to shore after the location and species of a school are determined by observation of the feeding of birds, especially pelicans. When sufficient fry have been taken (10-15 pounds), most are placed in a wooden box, where they are crushed and mixed with sand. The mixture is then thrown into the water at the head of a current which ideally is twenty to thirty feet in width and runs along the edge of a sharp drop in depth at between one and two knots. The mixture of sand and fish ("chum") is carried by the current and attracts large schools of fish. Handlines are then baited with whole fry and allowed to play out in the current. Fish are taken in this way very rapidly and in large numbers, a catch of 150 pounds in two hours not being considered extraordinary. Predators (chiefly kingfish and barracuda) limit the catch in any one location. The feeding habits of the target species are used to determine the presence of predators and their species. The Cha-Cha assert that yellowtail, for example, continue to feed in the presence of barracuda but mouth the bait more gingerly, whereas in the presence of kingfish they stop biting entirely. The difference is attributed to the habits of the predator. The barracuda, a relatively slow swimmer, is easily avoided by healthy yellowtail, which therefore simply become cautious when a barracuda is present. A kingfish, on the other hand, is fully capable of taking any yellowtail which allows it to approach within a body length; hence, when a kingfish is present, the school of yellowtail breaks up and must be attracted again when the predator has left or has been caught by the fisherman. On fifteen of sixteen occasions which I observed, the species of the predator was correctly identified before it became visible. In the sixteenth case, the predator was identified as a kingfish, but it developed that both a kingfish and a barracuda were present.

All three methods are used by all professional fishermen, but analysis of the time spent in each, measured against labor and yield, indicates that the basis of the fishing technology is trapping, in which more poundage is taken per unit of effort and time than in either chumming or seining. If the time spent going to and from the traps and the chumming sites is left out of consideration, the difference becomes even more extreme. However, exclusive dependence on trapping is not possible for a number of reasons. Bad weather more often prevents trap tending than chumming since the traps are further out in the open sea. This is especially true during the hurricane season, when the tending of traps may be impossible for weeks at a time. Chumming is resorted to whenever traps cannot or need not be tended. The vagaries of seining caused by the behavior of schools reduce seining to an occasional activity, which in the case of no fisherman represents a major part of his activity either in the time spent or in the yield per year.

ETHNOICYTHYOLOGY

The traditional anthropological interest in folk knowledge and the more recent interest in ethnoscience have both concentrated on phenomena that are visible to the people of the culture concerned. Heavenly bodies can be observed carefully by large numbers of people over long periods of time; the life cycle of plants from seed to fruit can be observed in its entirety; the weather is sensible to everyone; and the habits of terrestial animals can be observed with no special equipment. Even internal disease has both its external symptoms and the subjective reports of its victims as easily accessible data. Thus in astronomy, botany, meteorology, terrestial zoology, and human pathology, data can be easily collected by everyone in the society, and the knowledge so collected can be codified (however informally) and used to generate testable hypotheses. Folk knowledge of marine organisms offers a different situation. Except for life in very shallow and clear waters, virtually nothing can be known about the inhabitants of the sea except what they look like when (and if) they are caught. The data available are limited in number and kind, and the inferences possible from them appear to be of a different order than those possible about other parts of the environment.

When a culture depends heavily on the products of the sea, one might expect extensive systems of knowledge about these products. Since data about the products are more readily available than those about the processses surrounding the products, one might expect that a fishing people would have an elaborate taxonomy of marine organisms and a limited understanding of the behavior of the organisms and the ecology of their environment. The

Cha-Cha case offers a paradox in that the taxonomy is simple and limited, whereas the knowledge of marine ecology and fish behavior is extensive and detailed.

Taxonomy[2]

Only two levels of icthyological taxonomy are apparent in the Cha-Cha classification. The lowest level, roughly corresponding to the species (and here so called) is represented by 51 items (see Appendix). The higher level, which can be called "family," is represented by three items: "shark," "jack," and "corail" (French for "coral").[3] The Cha-Cha term "shark" includes nine scientifically recognized species, for which eight Cha-Cha specific terms exist. The fishes classified as "shark" share general body morphology, feeding habits with respect to both types of food taken and the method used (scavenging), and value as food (none). They differ from one another in specific body morphology, the depth of water in which they are normally found, and the degree to which they are thought to be dangerous to man. The Cha-Cha depend much more on the habits of sharks to classify them into species than on specific body morphology. The rationale for this is that specific body morphology is too subject to variation by age, sex, general condition, and random (genetic?) variation to be reliable as a classificatory criterion.

The "jack" family includes four scientifically recognized species, for which three Cha-Cha terms exist. All four are members of the scientifically recognized family *Carangidae,* but the family is represented in St. Thomas waters by at least nine species belonging to eight genera. The "jack" share general body morphology, feeding habits, and the fact that all are desirable food fish. They differ in specific body morphology and in feeding habits. It is the latter differences which are used by the Cha-Cha for classification.[4]

The family called "corail" embraces four scientifically recognized families, each represented by several genera and each of these by several species. No attempt was made in the field to identify all the species subsumed under "corail," but 27 were identified, and the total is in excess of this. Whereas under "shark" and "jack" the Cha-Cha have specific names for members of the family, in the case of "corail" they do not. It might be argued, therefore, that this term is, in fact, a species name. However, specific differences are recognized, the various species are thought not to interbreed, and the absence of specific names is justified (in all other cases it is the assignment of specific names that is justified). These fishes are placed in the same taxon because of their uselessness for food and their similar patterns of behavior.

In only one case do the Cha-Cha make finer taxonomic distinctions than are recognized by icthyologists. They classify the spotted goatfish (*Upeneus maculatus*) into three species, distinguished from one another by fine differences in morphology—especially color. These distinctions are unreliable from fisherman to fisherman. All three species are thought to be highly toxic under certain conditions, but all three are highly desirable as food fish.

The taxonomy of marine organisms other than fishes is limited and crude compared to scientific taxonomy. Coral reefs are recognized to be accretions of the exoskeletons of polyps, which are said to be related to "jellyfish." Other taxa are limited to "sponges" (some corals are included here apparently because of similar gross morphology), "worms," "molluscs," "lobsters" (limited to *Panulirus* sp.), "octopus," "starfish," "sea urchins," "conch," and "whelk." A few Cha-Cha identify whelk and conch as members of a larger taxon, but no name exists for it. The term "bug" is used to refer to any small marine invertebrate (including microscopic organisms). A large variety of organisms is subsumed under the term "plants" or "seaweed." Some of these organisms are corals, sponges, or worms (especially of the class Polychaeta).

Compared to scientific classification, the taxonomy of the Cha-Cha is not very elaborate or "accurate." This is not surprising since scientific systematics requires fine techniques of morphological description. The Cha-Cha do not dissect fishes nor count scale patterns or fin-ray distribution; they base their taxonomy on behavioral characteristics rather than morphology. In one sense this is contrary to expectation since the body of a fish is more easily observed than its behavior. In another sense, however, the result is expectable; from the point of view of the fisherman it is the behavior of species that determines the success of his operations. The food value of the catch is also an important factor. This shows clearly in the "lumping" of organisms not used as food and the "splitting" of those which are (e.g., conch, whelk, and octopus).

Behavior

The behavior of fishes and other marine organisms is a subject of great interest to the Cha-Cha and occupies much of the conversational time of the men. This is especially true when they are actually engaged in fishing operations. A one-hour trip to the traps or to catch fry or to chum is filled with commentary on the actions of fishes visible along the route or observed at other times. When men wait for a school of fish to move into appropriate position for seining, they talk of nothing but the actions of this and other schools. The talk takes the form of descriptions of observed behavior, proffered explanations for the behavior, and debate over the soundness of the observations and the conclusions reached from them. While hunters in many cultures avoid discussion of the prey lest such talk prejudice success, the Cha-Cha are conversational monomaniacs fixated on fish. Although feeding behavior is the most important topic of conversation, considerable attention is also paid to reproduction, territoriality, and the "personality" of individuals and species.

Feeding behavior is obviously of importance since chumming is dependent on it entirely, and trap fishing and seining to some extent. (However, the Cha-Cha are also interested in the feeding behavior of fishes which are of no value to them and which they never catch). The predator-prey relationship is of major interest since many of the desired fish are both. Techniques of predation are thought to result from the speed and agility of the predator, the size of the prey, the size of the schools of predators and prey, and the physical conditions of the sea (bottom topography, reef structure, depth of water, turbidity, temperature, etc.). Each species is affected by each of these factors, though the importance of any one factor depends on the particular species and the relative importance of other factors. The Cha-Cha assert, for example, that there is a threshold of turbidity beyond which many predators will cease feeding, the shark being the exception. In turbid waters, therefore, regardless of conditions of temperature, depth, etc., most predators do not feed.

All behavior is affected by the sensory structure of the animal, and the Cha-Cha have knowledge of sensory capabilities and limitations. The importance of lateral line sensitivity, olfaction, taste, and vision are all recognized. The feeding behavior of sharks, for example, is said to begin with detection of arhythmic vibrations at long distances. The shark shifts to mid-distance ranging using olfaction, and makes the final approach guided by vision. These conclusions, based on simple observation, conform rather well with experimental evidence. It is noteworthy that the Cha-Cha do not attribute to fish senses not recognized by icythologists nor do they attribute high intelligence to fish. Their analysis of any item of fish behavior would be accepted by zoologists or psychologists as appropriately restricted and rigorous in method of observation and inference, though it might be incorrect.

The reproduction of fish, while of no immediate practical importance to the Cha-Cha, is a topic of some interest to them. Fish are recognized as being either oviparous or viviparous, and the assignment of method to species conforms with that of icythyologists, except that the distinction between viviparous and ovoviparous is not recognized. The eggs of sharks and rays are identified by size and shape when they wash ashore. The time at which reproductive behavior is initiated is thought to be species specific. Pelagic fishes are thought to initiate breeding in response to seasonal changes resulting from weather changes over large areas. The barracuda, for example, is said to start breeding immediately after the hurricane season (i.e., November). Neritic fishes are thought to breed either in response to specific short-term environmental conditions (e.g., moon phases), or at any time during the year except during the conditions of high turbulence and turbidity which accompany the hurricane season. The frequency with which neritic fish breed is not known, but is thought to be species specific.[5]

Both territoriality and individual "personality" of fish are easily observed by Cha-Cha fishermen since they fish in a limited number of places with considerable frequency. Territorial behavior is thought to be species specific and most closely related to feeding, not reproduction. The fishes which are classified as "corail" are highly territorial from a very early age, the size of the territory and its shape being determined by the topography of the reef. The shape of the territory is thought to be species specific to some extent. Thus some small reef dwellers move up and down over a wide range but have very narrow lateral ranges, while other species reverse this pattern. Fishes which are pelagic as adults may be neritic as fry, and the schooling behavior changes with age. Thus barracuda school until they reach approximately eighteen inches in length (during the third year) and then become solitary and pelagic. Some particularly large barracuda may become highly territorial and can always be found in a certain small bay or near a break in an offshore reef. Like the larger groupers, which occupy particular holes in reefs, they differ widely in personality. One fisherman has had a running feud with two barracuda which haunt a spot favored by the man for chumming. One of the fish appears as soon as the chumming begins, whereas the other waits until the school of yellowtail has gathered and then begins cruising up and down. The fisherman is convinced that he can identify both fish. One of them kills a yellowtail and finishes it before killing again, whereas the other eats only the portion which he takes on the first rush.

Marine Ecology

Many aspects of fish behavior are affected by marine ecology, and Cha-Cha knowledge of this subject is extensive. The dominant ecological feature of the seas around St. Thomas is the coral reef. Both fringing and open-sea reefs are common, though there are no atoll formations. The Cha-Cha recognize the coral reef as a special ecotype in contrast to other parts of the sea. The formation of reefs is attributed to the accretion of polyp exoskeletons, but no hypotheses are made as to whether reefs are emergent or result from subsidence.

The wide diversity of forms present on the reef is explained by ecological-evolutionary factors such as the long time required for reef formation, the complexity of shape (providing a large number of niches), and minor but significant differences in depth, clarity, currents, and sunlight. Inferences about the number of niches in the reef ecosystem, and the relative importance of the factors mentioned above, are based on observation of the distribution and behavior of marine organisms. For example, lobsters live in sheltered areas, but the female moves into the turbulent water when the eggs are ready to hatch; therefore it is reasoned baby lobsters must need more "air" in the water. In addition, turbulent water insures rapid dispersion of the young and reduces predation. Thus, rather than using ecological theory to explain observations of organisms, the observations are used to build theory. The Cha-Cha regard reefs as relatively stable systems with respect to energy flow because of the stability of populations of organisms. Of course, the theory constructed from observation is tested by further observation, but the Cha-Cha do not make explicit the construction of theory and hence do not conceive of observation as a test of theory. Rather they add to theory by producing new *post hoc* explanations, or subtract from theory by dropping existing explanations.

Food chains on the reef are thought to be numerous but very short. Since the organisms involved in one end of the chain are not easily visible to the naked eye, the Cha-Cha conclude that the chain is shorter than it actually is. Nutrients ("chemicals") in the water are used by "bugs" to synthesize food. The bugs are eaten by larger invertebrates or small fishes. These are then taken by predators or "just die" and become detritus eaten by invertebrates or return nutrients to the water.

CIGUATERA

The word *ciguatera* is applied to a form of fish poisoning common to tropical seas throughout the world. It is apparently derived from Spanish *cigua,* a species of marine snail (*Livona pica*) which early New World explorers and colonists thought was the source of the toxin. In tropical areas where fish are an important source of protein, ciguatera is of considerable public-health interest and has been investigated at some length by a number of investigators in several areas (Arcisz 1950; Halstead 1956, 1958; Randall 1958). Only recently, however, has the toxin involved been isolated (Scheuer, *et al.* 1967), and cases of ciguatera poisoning are still treated only symptomatically.

The illness results from the eating of fish whose flesh is toxic. Toxicity is particularly high in certain organs, but all of the flesh is affected. Symptoms appear within a few hours after eating and consist of severe headache, muscular pain and cramps, severe depression, vertigo, loss of motor control, and occasionally hallucinations. Death often results, especially if the victim is a child, is aged, or has a history of cardiac or respiratory disease. When victims recover it is usually after a convalescence of three months to a year marked by frequent relapses, and occasionally permanent motor-nerve damage results. The actual incidence of ciguatera poisoning in St. Thomas is not known, but there are certainly several cases a year as a minimum. All the residents of St. Thomas are acquainted with fish poisoning either by hearsay or by observation, and the Cha-Cha have been familiar with it for a long time. It is common on St. Barthelemy, the island from which the Cha-Cha emigrated, and both there and on St. Thomas the French-speaking population use certain plants in its treatment (Morrill and Morrill).

At least ten families of fish have been implicated in ciguatera (Phillips and Brady 1953). In the St. Thomas area twelve species have been implicated by scientific observers (Arcisz 1950), while the Cha-Cha recognize fourteen species as likely sources of poisoning. What is particularly baffling about ciguatera is the fact that in some areas some species are perfectly safe and in other areas the same species is quite dangerous. In addition there does not seem to be any seasonality in the frequency of attacks (Arcisz 1950: 10). The fishes which are sources of ciguatera resemble each other in that they seem to be primarily inhabitants of reefs rather than the open sea, and that they feed on detritus, benthic algae, or on fish that feed on these substances. Since ciguatera is not species specific, it appears that there are highly localized sources of the toxin. The following have been suggested as possible sources: manicheel berries, jelly fish, marine worms, molluscs, zooanthellae in corals, dinoflaggelates, copper from ship bottoms, and algae. The Cha-Cha see as possible sources only manicheel berries, marine worms, coral polyps, copper, and algae. Each fisherman has his own favorite explanation of the cause of ciguatera, but there is a high degree of agreement on implicated species, on the fact that it is not species specific, and on its seasonal variability. It is instructive to examine the logic by which the Cha-Cha support their arguments about the etiology of ciguatera.

Possible causes of ciguatera are eliminated or made more probable by examination of the corpus of poisoning cases known to the fisherman. One informant (the fisherman generally regarded as the most knowledgeable on the subject) argues that ciguatera must be caused when reef fish eat a certain kind of algae which he claims to have identified. He reasons that it is impossible that manicheel berries are the cause because highly territorial fish which prove toxic are taken in areas where there is no manicheel. Marine worms are unlikely because some fish which are often toxic never eat marine worms or other fish which do eat them. Copper makes some sense as a source because ciguatera is common around wrecks, but not all wrecks have copper bottoms, and some ciguatera is found far from any known wrecks. Algae are the most probable cause because not many species of fish eat algae, only a few of these are taken for food, and these few are heavily implicated.

When the question is raised as to why ciguatera varies areally since it should be expected that the toxic algae would not, the reasoning relies on understanding of reef ecology. Ciguatera is more common on the north and east sides of islands than on the south and west. In addition, its is rare in sheltered bays. Fish which are taken on the south and west or in sheltered areas and which later prove toxic are always piscivorous species. Other areas with a high incidence of ciguatera are near recent wrecks, former anchorages which are no longer active, the mouths of streams, and in areas where there have been recent detonation of explosives.[6] These locations have in common the disruption of the ecology of the reef by physical damage or pollution of the water (including reduction of salinity). Given the fact that the species mix on reefs varies with age, it is reasonable to assume that some algae grow better on old reefs and some algae grow better on reefs which are new or which have been recently disturbed. In effect, the Cha-Cha fisherman is here proposing that the algae are early succession organisms—a view which conforms with that of one of the principal investigators of ciguatera (Randall 1958:248).

Cha-Cha knowledge of and reasoning about ciguatera reveals in capsule form the structure of their icthyological knowledge. The taxonomy reflects a concern with the subject by "splitting" taxa which are strongly implicated in fish poisoning but "lumping" those which are not. The explanations given for ciguatera distribution reveal a sophisticated knowledge of coral-reef ecology and of the behavior of marine organisms. The logic used is essentially inductive in that conclusions are reached on the basis of a large number of prior observations, but hypotheses are not tested by carrying out systematic observation to support or refute their predictions.

NOTES

1. The term "ethnoicthyology" is formed on the model of "ethnobotany," etc. Research for this study was carried out in the Virgin Islands from June to September, 1962. The work was partially supported by a grant from the National Institute of Mental Health (M-6843-A).

2. Analysis of the taxonomy is complicated somewhat by linguistic considerations. Names of fish are sometimes clearly English in both etymology and pronunciation. Other names are clearly French. Some are apparently English in etymology but French

in phonology. For example, "congo" is stressed on the second syllable, and the vowels are closer to French than to English, although the word seems to resemble English "conger" more closely than French "congre." Since all the Cha-Cha fishermen are bilingual, it is difficult to determine how much of the terminology is English because no French equivalent exists, and how much is due to linguistic change. This question can be answered only after study of the terminology used on the islands of St. Barthelemy.

3. It might be argued that there are not three but five families—one being indicated by "fry" and the other a residual category marked by zero. I have chosen not to interpret the data in this way since the Cha-Cha use the term "fry" as a functional and not a taxonomic label and because they specifically deny a taxonomic relationship among species in the residual category.

4. The "horse-eye" jack (*Caranx latus*) is easily identified by differences in specific body morphology as well as in feeding and schooling habits.

5. For several species the breeding season is known through observation of spawning behavior. For others it is assumed that the breeding season could be determined by analysis of feeding patterns of the adult fish. Some species are thought to breed shortly after there is a hatch of hermit crabs.

6. Explosives are used in the clearing of coral from bays to be used as resort beaches. In addition, the underwater demolition units of the U. S. Navy have used St. Thomas as a training area for twenty years.

BIBLIOGRAPHY

Arcisz, W. 1950. Ciguatera: Tropical Fish Poisoning. United States Department of the Interior, Special Scientific Report—Fisheries 27: 1-23. Washington.

Halstead, B. W. 1956. Animal Phyla Known to Contain Poisonous Marine Animals. Venoms: American Association for the Advancement of Science Symposium, Serial Publication 44: 9-27. Washington.

———— 1958. Poisonous Fishes. Public Health Reports 73: iv, 303-312.

Lasserre, G. 1961. La Guadeloupe. Bordeaux.

Morrill, L. A., and W. T. Morrill. Ethnobotany of the Cha-Cha (in preparation).

Morrill, W. T., and B. Dyke, 1966. A French Community on St. Thomas, V. I. Caribbean Studies 5: iv, 3-11.

O'Neill, J. B. 1940. Food Poisoning in the First Marine Brigade, Fleet Marine Force, Culebra, P. R. U. S. Naval Medical Bulletin 36: 629-631.

Philips, C., and W. H. Brady. 1953. Sea Pests. Miami

Price, R. 1966. Caribbean Fishing and Fishermen: A Historical Sketch. American Anthropologist 68: 1363-1393.

Randall, J. E. 1958. Review of Ciguatera. Bulletin of the Marine Sciences of the Gulf and Caribbean 8: iii, 236-267.

Scheuer, P. J., W. Takahashi, J. Tsutsumi, and T. Yoshida. 1967. Ciguatera: Isolation and Chemical Nature. Science 155: 1267-1269.

Wilcox, W. A. 1900. Notes on the Foreign Fishery Trade and Local Fisheries of Porto Rico. Report of the Commissioner, U.S. Commission of Fish and Fisheries (H.R. Document #692, pt. xxv.)

APPENDIX: Fishes Caught and Used by the Cha-Cha

Scientific Names Family	Genus	Species	Cha-Cha Names Family	Species	How Caught	Use	Toxic
Ginglymostomidae	Ginglymostoma	cirratum	Shark	Nurse shark	never	none	
Scyliorhinidae	Carcharias	taurus	Shark	spotted	never	none	
Lamnidae	Isurus	oxyrhincus	Shark	mako	never	none	
Galeidae	Galeocerdo	cuvier	Shark	mako	never	none	
"	Negaprion	brevirostis	Shark	harbor	seine	none	
"	Scoliodon	terrae-novae	Shark	dog fish	seine	none	
Sphyrnidae	Sphyrna	zygaena	Shark	hammerhead	never	none	
Alopiidae	Alopias	vulpes	Shark	thresher	never	none	
"	Urolophus	jamaicensis		spotted sting ray	never	none	
Dasyatidae	Dasyatis	sabina		little sting ray	seine	none	
Aetobatidae	Aetobatus	narinari		leopard ray	never	none	
Megalopidae	Tarpon	atlanticus		tarpon	never	none	
Muraenidae	Gymnothorax	moringa		congo	trap	none	
"	Gymnothorax	funebris		congo	trap	none	
Belonidae	Strongylura	raphidoma		gar	seine, also jumps in boat	food, poor	never
Hemiramphidae	Hyporhamphus	unifasciatus		gar	seine, also jumps in boat	food, poor	never
Exocaetidae	Parexocoetus	mesogaster		flying fish	jumps in boat	food, poor	never
Syngnathidae	Syngnathus	fusus		pipefish	never	none	
Mugilidae	Mugil	cephalus		mullet	seine	bait	
Atherinidae	Hepsitia	stipes		sharkhead fry	cast net	bait	
"	Antherina	harringtonensis		green fry	cast net	bait	
Sphyraenidae	Sphyraena	barracuda		barracuda	seine, line	food, good	often
Holocentirdae	Holocentrus	ascensionis		rouge brullé	trap	none	
Mullidae	Upeneus	maculatus		barbarin rouge / barbarin blanc / queen mullet	trap	food, good	often
Scombroidei	Scomber	scombrus		sotue	line	food, good	never
"	Scomberomorus	cavalla		kingfish	line	food, fair	often
"	Scomberomorus	maculatus		tazade	line	food, good	never
Carangidae	Caranx	ruber	Jack	bonite	seine	food, good	never

| Scientific Names | | | Cha-Cha Names | | How Caught | Use | Toxic |
Family	Genus	Species	Family	Species			
"	Caranx	latus	Jack	horse-eye jack	seine	food, good	never
"	Caranx	hippos	Jack	carang	seine	food, good	never
"	Caranx	bartholomai	Jack	carang	seine	food, good	never
"	Seriola	dumerili		haut-boi	never	none	
Cheilodipteridae	Apogonicthys	stellatus		conch	never	none	
Centropomidae	Centropus	undecimalis		snook	never	none	
Serranidae	Promicrops	itiara		jewfish	trap	food, fair	rare
"	Mycteropera	bonaci		té tore	trap	food, fair	often
"	Mycteropera	venenosa		capitaine	trap	food, fair	often
"	Cherna	americana		capitaine	trap	food, fair	rare
"	Epinephalus	striatus		nassau	trap	food, good	rare
"	Epinephalus	adcensionis		hind	trap	food, fair	rare
Lobotidae	Priacanthus	arenatus		solleille	trap	food, fair	rare
Lutianidae	Lutianus	griseus		gris	trap	food, fair	rare
"	Lutianus	aya		rougé	trap	food, fair	rare
"	Ocyurus	chrysurus		yellowtail	trap, line	food, good	never
Sparidae	Archosargus	unimacculatus		matelote	trap	food, fair	rare
Chomides			Corail		never	none	
Chaetodontidae			Corail		never	none	
Labridae			Corail		never	none	
Scaridae				parrot	trap	none	always
Acanthuridae	Acathus	coeruleus		surgeonfish	never	none	
Chaetodontidae	Pomocanthus	arcuatus		ange	trap	food, fair	never
"	Angelichthys	cilaris		ange	trap	food, fair	never
Balistidae	Balistes	capriseus		old wife	trap	food, fair	never
"	Balistes	vetula		old wife	trap	food, fair	never
Ostraciidae				boites	trap	food, fair	never
Diodontidae	Diodon	hystrix		porcupine	never	none	
Antennariidae	Histrio	histrio		sea-horse	trap	none	always
Haemulidae			Corail		never	none	
Echeneididae				remora	never	none	

Cognition and the Catch:
The Location of Fishing Spots
in a Brazilian Coastal Village[1]

Shepard Forman

Coqueiral is a coastal community of 852 people located at 10°24' south latitude and 37°48' west longitude in the county of Guaiamu in the state of Alagoas in northeastern Brazil. The primary economic activity in Coqueiral is hook and line fishing from log rafts, or *jangadas,* at sea. Constructed entirely of wood and vegetable fiber[2] and made with the simplest of tools, the *jangada* represents the most primitive of ocean-going craft. Still, the advantages of such log rafts are many. Among these we can cite easy construction, low cost, and relative stability, maneuverability and speed. In addition, the utilization of prevailing off-shore winds, the freedom from concerns of anchorage, and the ease with which the *jangada* passes over the low-lying reefs make it an extremely effective craft for the region.

The narrowness of the continental shelf brings the entire range of coastal fishing within the reach of *jangada* fishermen. Variations in the basic design of the rafts permit *jangadeiros* (raft fishermen) to explore virtually the entire range of ocean above the continental shelf over a relatively large area and in all seasons. The rafts vary according to size, method of propulsion, and the accouterments used, all of which depends largely on the area of the ocean in which they fish. The majority of fishermen earn their livelihood by alternating between independent production on their own log rafts and fishing as crew members on *jangadas* belonging to someone else.

The fishermen of Coqueiral share a generalized knowledge of the area of the sea and the aspect of the land which comprise their fishing universe. The possibility of maximizing individual production rests on their ability to locate particular species of fish according to market values in different seasons. Toward this end they have elaborated a complex system of named fishing grounds and landmarks.[3] The location of the fishing grounds by visual triangulation and the knowledge of the distribution of fish within them in given seasons are transmitted over generations. This allows an increasing number of independent producers to locate fishing grounds, thereby maximizing the productive potential of the community. At the same time, secrecy regarding particular spots within the grounds serves as a spacing mechanism which minimizes competition and prevents overfishing by according temporary property rights to individual fishermen.

15

THE COGNITIVE GRID

Coqueiral's fishing universe consists of the ocean extending along approximately twenty miles of coastline, from the village of Jitaí in the north to Joro in the south, and out some twenty miles to the edge of the continental shelf. It also consists of those features of the landscape which are distinguishable from the sea out to this distance. Distance itself is expressed in terms of depth of ocean or of the time it takes to sail there, only occasionally in terms of geographical or nautical miles.

It is within the bounds of this universe that the fishing economy of Coqueiral is worked out. Beyond the edge of the continental shelf is another world, which belongs to the monsters of the sea and to the ships which sail past. It is a world entirely unknown to the fishermen of Coqueiral, and a captain who takes his *jangada* beyond the 200-fathom mark is "tempting the devil."

Within their own world of fishing, however, the *jangadeiros* of Coqueiral have discovered and learned, and they have ordered their knowledge on several levels. The area of ocean plied by the *jangadas* from Coqueiral is first divided into named zones, each running perpendicular to the shoreline for approximately one to two miles and then out to the edge of the continental shelf. The names of these zones (Gurujú, Les-Nordeste, etc.) are taken from the particular area of land on which they front. Between the outer reef, which lies some ten miles offshore, and the edge of the continental shelf, each of these zones is further subdivided into discrete sections, or fishing grounds. These subdivisions are made on the basis of depth and the composition of the bottom, and each is given a name: *restinga, razinho, razo grande, razo,* and *parede,* which is the edge of the continental shelf. Each major zone of the sea is separated by an area, called a *liso,* which is comprised of a plain, sandy bottom which yields few if any fish. Such zoning creates a mosaic-like map with a multiplicity and some duplication of named fishing grounds (see Figure 1).[4] These grounds are identified by their own names and the name of the sea zone in which they are located (e.g., *raso do mar do Gurujú*).

THE LOCATION OF FISHING SPOTS

Particular fishing spots are located within these fishing grounds. They may be jutting rocks, stretches of identifiable reefs, or submerged rocky areas which are frequented by fishermen because they have yielded good catches in the past. All fishing spots are marked and remembered by individual fishermen using a visual system of triangulation which utilizes a series of landmarks which can be seen on clear days from most of Coqueiral's fishing grounds. The landmarks consist primarily of the mountain called Barriga some twenty leagues in the hinterland to the north and of the Pacatuba range in the state of Sergipe to the south. Landmarks are more readily used in the north since the size and proximity of Barriga makes it visible from all of the northern fishing grounds. In the south, on the other hand, the distance of Pacatuba puts it out of the visual range of most fishing grounds north of the zone called Les-nordeste. In addition, the low coastal sandy plain approaching the São Francisco River does not provide a second reference point which can be used for *marcacão,* or "lining up."

When landmarks are used, they may be a grove of coconut palms, a high sand dune, the outline of a familiar plantation, or the steeple of the Guaiamu Church. A fisherman is able to determine his course by "lining up" one landmark behind another in such a way as to constitute directional cues. Thus, to sail to the zone of Barreira do Velho, the steeple of the

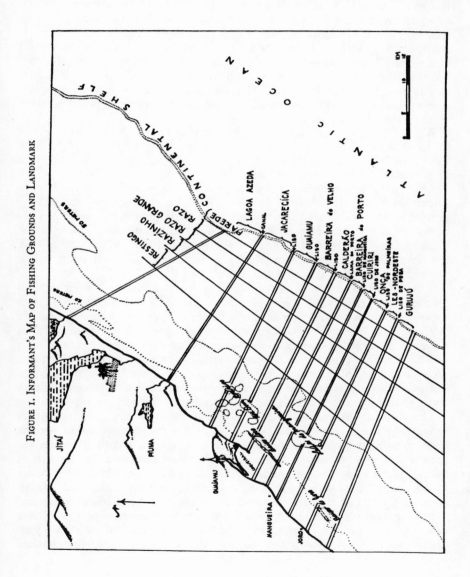

FIGURE I. INFORMANT'S MAP OF FISHING GROUNDS AND LANDMARK

Guaiamu Church must appear about one arm's length from the Coqueiral dunes. Combinations of two such landmarks into sets serve to guide a raft to a given fishing ground. Thus, when the steeple moves to the northeast of the village and nears the house of Dr. Fulano, and Barriga appears to touch on the Barra de Jitaí, a fisherman drops anchor at the edge of the continental shelf in the sea of Barreira do Velho.

Two well-spaced sets of markings are used simultaneously to mark a distinct fishing spot. The *marca de confrontação* is directly on the shore facing the raft. The *marca de altura* is some distance away on a northern or southern shore. For example, one fisherman locates his favorite fishing spot when the Guaiamu steeple meets the "slippery hillside" (*marca de confrontação*), and the hillock of Piuma comes to rest between the second and third hillsides behind Piuma (*marca de altura*). Another favorite spot for first-class species of fish is marked by the Aves do Caboclo da Lagoa Azeda touching on a hillock in Jacarecica (*marca de altura*), while a plantation angles in on Jitaí Lagoon with a small coconut grove showing between them (*marca de confrontação*).

When fishing grounds are out of the visual range of such landmarks, the initial directional cues are taken on the basis of the markings. When the fisherman loses sight of these, he navigates by judging time and distance in accordance with prevailing winds. For example, in the sea zone called A Onça a fisherman loses sight of land after the 50-meter mark. He continues along the same course, however, until he approximates the fishing ground and then drops a plumb line to test the bottom. Onça is located between two *lisos,* or plain sandy areas, and the plumb line identifies the location. The plumb line is recovered and is scrutinized and smelled to note the composition of the bottom. Rocky areas are said to smell sweet, while gravel has a bad odor, and mud smells foul.

It is difficult to assess to what degree sets of landmarks are accurate in placing a raft exactly on a spot previously fished.[5] Fishermen say that if a rocky area is very small they may not locate it again, even on the basis of landmarks. It is possible that landmarks do not put a *jangada* precisely on the same spot but serve, in a more accurate way than plumbing, to place a raft on a similar spot within a general area of the fishing ground. In these areas, fish are not bound to a specific spot, nor is effective production. Rather, it would seem that sets of landmarks bring a fisherman within certain fishing grounds where particular species of fish are caught.

The distribution of fish within fishing grounds is not conceived of as random by the fishermen of Coqueiral but as a function of rather specific conditions, namely depth and composition of bottom. Depth is always expressed in terms of *braças* (2.2 meters), which are measured by a length of fishing line across outstretched arms. The composition of the bottom refers to the general configuration of the ocean floor, whether rock, sand, gravel, or mud. Species of fish are classified according to their market values and located in particular settings.[6] Two distinct fishing patterns prevail. *Peixes de pedra,* or rock-living species with the highest commercial value, are generally caught in deeper waters beyond the 50-meter mark. Second-class

species are primarily caught closer to shore within the ten-mile outer reef above gravel or muddy bottoms.

While the *jangadeiro* is not fully aware of the entire range of phenomena which confronts him, he deduces much about certain aspects of his fishing universe. As a rule his knowledge is connected with the fishing strategy he himself employs, whether fishing for second-class species on the inner grounds or marking spots on the outer grounds for better qualities of fish. He expresses his knowledge in the idiom of a folk understanding of marine ecology.

THE NECESSITY OF FISHING SPOTS

Kottak (1966: 227) has questioned the utility of a system of distinct fishing spots. He notes, correctly, that much of the fishing (in Arembepe) does not depend on the demarcation of small fishing spots but on large zones. Actually, the importance of fishing spots is not related to the entire fishing operation, but is a function of the species of fish being pursued. Marking spots in a specific sense is not necessary for large shoals of fish which travel in mid-water during certain seasons of the year, although it becomes necessary for locating more "sedentary" species which move about singly feeding on the smaller fish which hover around rocks.[7] The system of located fishing spots in Coqueiral concerns itself only with rock-living species inhabiting the fishing grounds beyond the 50-meter mark.

Kottak (1966: 216-217) states that several attributes reminiscent of the "Protestant ethic" are far more important in determining differential success in fishing than familiarity with fishing spots. Youth, good health, sobriety, willingness to take calculated risks, and the ability to command allegiance of a crew are, undoubtedly, characteristics of successful fishermen. However, the information passed on through the system of named fishing grounds and landmarks is essential to becoming an independent producer in Coqueiral. The ability to locate given species of fish within different seasons is necessary if a fisherman is going to learn to distinguish between alternative fishing patterns and fish independently.

Kottak further states (1966: 217) that beyond any utilitarian function the knowledge of fishing spots might have, it is a mechanism by which captains are differentiated from ordinary seamen and justifies their receiving a greater share of the catch. In Coqueiral, however, captains do not receive a greater share of the catch than ordinary fishermen. Moreover, captaincy in Coqueiral is a temporary situation at best. It is a social category rather than an occupational grouping. All captains on other people's rafts want to be independent producers, and most manage to fish on their own rafts during at least part of the year.

The art of "lining up" a specific spot is required, then, if a fisherman is to become an independent producer on his own log raft. Lining up requires an acute sense of vision, the loss of which often forces a fisherman to retire or accept a permanent status as a member of a crew.[8] Most fishermen are able to see land from most points on Coqueiral's fishing grounds, but not everyone can see it in the necessary detail. Moreover, and possibly more important, a fisherman must be able to account for winds and currents in judging the drift not only of his raft, but also of his lines. Finally, he must possess a keen memory in order to keep the fishing spots in his head. It takes time and practice to master this art,[9] which serves, in part, as a mechanism for guaranteeing a temporary crew in a situation where everyone wants to be an independent producer.

THE SECRECY OF FISHING SPOTS

Fishermen speak openly about the fishing grounds, the names used for them, and the seasonal movement of fish within them. The fishing grounds are, thus, common knowledge among all the raft fishermen in Coqueiral. There is, however, very little discussion regarding specific fishing spots which can be marked, and which are held to be far better than others because of their alleged constant yield. These remain the private reserves of fishermen capable of sailing to them. Individual differences exist, therefore, only in terms of the specific fishing spots exploited by particular fishermen, who give them special descriptive names reflecting the set of markings which are used in sailing to them. That all fishermen do not know how to go to a given area is a function of one's ability to mark and remember. The fact that some fishermen know fewer spots than others is a function of secrecy.

A fisherman rarely teaches the art of lining up a specific fishing spot, and a boy's apprenticeship consists largely of curiosity and persistence. While a fisherman is always delighted to have a young apprentice help to augment his catch, he avoids taking him to a preferred spot. When pursuing species of fish of better quality, a crew is not told to what spot they are sailing until they are well out of the harbor.

The zealous guarding of spots as secrets and the attempts of others to find them are constant causes of contention in Coqueiral. Sometimes a fisherman will even follow a raft, whereupon its captain is likely to lift anchor and sail off in anger to avoid revealing his favorite fishing spot. In one of many instances, two brothers-in-law ceased to speak when one revealed the location of a spot which the other had entrusted to him. At the same time, social factors implement the maintenance of secrecy by awarding prestige to the captain who knows many spots and does not divulge them. In a sense, this has an economic basis, since it is the best captain who knows the most fishing spots, and captains are rated according to the size of their catches.

What then is the function of this secrecy? It does not serve to keep the art of lining up in the hands of a privileged class (Kottak 1966: 163). The entire range of shared knowledge of the fishing grounds and landmarks would seem to preclude this possibility. An enterprising fisherman can follow the navigational cues, and once on the fishing spot he has only to look to shore and see how the landmarks fit together.

It is my view that secrecy functions as an ecologically adaptive mechanism with regard to certain aspects of the total fishing operation. It must be remembered that not all aspects of fishing demand the location of specific spots and that not all spots are guarded secrets. In some instances, a fisherman will signal another with a wave of a hat if a particular species of fish is plentiful and is biting. This, however, only occurs on grounds in which second-class species of fish appear in shoals, and which are close enough to be seen from shore and are thus available to all fishermen. On these occasions, a spacing mechanism operates so that lines will not get tangled and fishermen will not interfere with each other's productivity. By the same token, spots beyond the 50-meter mark in the southern waters which cannot be marked are not as avowedly secret as others. Since a fisherman has to plumb and cannot mark the spot visually, he can only approximate the area fished and cannot locate it as precisely. Plumbing, therefore, serves as a natural process of randomization of fishing spots in lieu of secrecy.

It is fishing on the outer grounds for the most valued species in areas which can be localized by landmarks that is characterized by the greatest amount of secrecy. Very little information is vouchsafed regarding specific fishing spots which can be marked and which are held to be far better than others because of their allegedly constant yield. These remain the private reserves of fishermen capable of sailing to them. According to Bottomanne (1959: 128),

The more vessels are amassed, the more they influence each other's catches and the more the acceleration of the decreasing catches per unit is felt . . . smart skippers often try to find their own places. In such cases, the temporary "sole ownership" of *even mediocre* (emphasis mine) fishing grounds may sometimes prove a better source of earnings than the fishing of mass-exploited grounds.

The Ecology of Fishing

The most frequent characteristic of all fisheries is common ownership of the resources of the sea (Bottomanne 1959: 8). However, this is also one of its chief dilemmas (Gordon 1954: 125). In Coqueiral, ready access to the sea on small log rafts is highly conducive to entry into the fishing economy, particularly since the distribution of agricultural land is sharply limited. *Jangada* fishing is a reliable means of subsistence for a large number of independent peasant producers. Approximately 100 different rafts ply the waters around Coqueiral at various times during the year.[10] Yet the lack of motors, of scientific navigational instruments, and of storage and sleeping facilities seriously limits the distance to which they might otherwise go. All fishing is done above the continental shelf, and the size and weight of the catch is thereby limited. Fishing grounds around Coqueiral are limited in extent, and fish populations do not afford an unlimited source of supply despite their tremendous reproductive capacities[11] (Bottomanne 1959: 8; Gordon 1954: 125; Wynne-Edwards 1963: 4). Only approximately 200 square miles of ocean exist for the fishermen of Coqueiral to catch first-class species of fish, and the number of good spots within this area is sharply curtailed by the small number of favorable fishing banks.[12] A general increase in fishing intensity could lead to a general decrease in the yield per individual fishing unit once the optimum level of production has been reached (Bottomanne 1959: 8; Russell 1942: 75; Wynne-Edwards 1962: 5).

While overfishing is perhaps unlikely in view of the rudimentary techniques in use, the more vessels fishing on the relatively few good fishing spots, the less the efficiency of each vessel. Increased demands on the food supply and the intensification of the quest invite the danger of uncontrolled competition and thereby the eventual depletion of certain first-class species of fish which are already caught sparingly.

Any economic activity thus affected by the law of diminishing returns[13] requires a mechanism for the conservation of the stock, maintaining up to a point both the over-all productive capacity of the community and the maximum efficiency of individual units. To go beyond that point would mean over-exploitation to the lasting detriment of the fishermen themselves.[14] Any decrease in the productive efficiency of peasant producers who already function with so small a margin of profit would probably decrease their earnings below the cost of operation and thereby put them out of business. We can assume, therefore, that independent production in Coqueiral is being maintained at least at a steady state. We can hypothesize that the mechanism by which this is accomplished can be found in the elaborate system of spacing based on named fishing grounds and landmarks by which the fishermen of Coqueiral conduct their daily economic activities. Secrecy of fishing spots within these grounds serves to minimize competition by affording temporary property rights to individual fishermen. The massing of rafts on particular fishing spots would certainly decrease the size of the catch for each unit, and competition would compel a fisherman to return frequently and early to a favorite spot that might otherwise be fished out by someone else.

SUMMARY

A complex system of named fishing grounds and landmarks exists and knowledge of it is transmitted transgenerationally. In this way, the economic structure of the village is maintained and allowed to expand, even though at a slow rate. Fishermen are always learning to be independent producers, even though they are never directly taught. This increases the dangers of overcrowding and overfishing. Free access to sea resources and common knowledge of all fishing spots could encourage over-exploitation through excessive competition. The system of named fishing grounds and landmarks exists as a long-range device for maximizing catches according to seasonal and market variations while at the same time allowing particular fishing spots to remain secret for the immediate economic benefit of individual fishermen. By spacing rafts within the area, the daily productive efficiency of individual units is kept high, while overall production for the village is maintained.

NOTES

1. Research in the field in 1964-65 was supported by an NDEA-Related Fulbright-Hays award, #FH-4-44. The writing of this manuscript as part of a doctoral dissertation at Columbia University was supported by a National Institute of Mental Health Predoctoral Research Fellowship, #1-F1-MH-19, 158-01A1 (BEH). I am indebted to Professors Charles Wagley and Marvin Harris and to my colleagues Stanley and Suzanne Regelson for reading and commenting on an earlier version of this paper.

2. *Jangadas* are made from a light balsa-like wood known as piuba (*Apeiba tuberbou*), or, simply, *pau de jangada* (jangada wood). The term *jangada* was applied to indigenous rafts by the Portuguese who saw similar craft called by this name on their voyages to the East (Camara Cascudo 1957a: 61). Metal is not used in the construction of rafts since rusting facilitates rotting.

3. Similar systems of named fishing grounds and landmarks and the secrecy of particular spots are reported for the entire northeast coast of Brazil (Camara Cascudo 1957a: 22-25, 1957b: 5-6; Forman 1965; César de Magalhães 1966: 2; Kottak 1966: 163-164). However, these phenomena seem to be far more generalized among fishermen the world over. According to a personal communication from Dr. E. Lowe Pierce, Department of Zoology, University of Florida, "This type of position finding is an old method with fishermen and it is also probably an even older custom not to reveal your best fishing spots to your fellow competitors."

4. The map is an informant's conception of his fishing universe. The names were written in by the author. While all informants interviewed agreed on the names of the fishing grounds as outlined in Figure 1, names and locations of fishing spots within these differed according to informants.

5. Carl O. Schweidenbank, Marine Biology Laboratory, Woods Hole, Massachusetts, states in a personal communication: "I believe that you will find that they (the fishermen) are correct in using visual marks for fishing in any given spot. We have found that fixed objects on shore are much better and certainly more accurate than radar or fathometers. We have used this method ourselves . . . in dredging for certain species of fish in different localities." Dr. Marta Vannucci of the Oceanographic Institute, Universidade do São Paulo, reports in a personal communication that experiments with fishermen in the waters around the island of Fernand de Noronha indicated that they were able to return to the same location time and again with a surprising degree of accuracy.

6. Fish are not believed to be sedentary, and their habitats are clearly associated with seasonal and even daily climatic variations. Some attention is given to feeding habits. The same species of fish is known to be found at widely varying depths and above both rocky and gravel bottoms. Fish are known to migrate over great distances, and species associated with fresh water are sometimes found in ocean areas. Fishermen relate this latter phenomenon directly to the silting up of the bay in the winter months by the waters from the rivers to the south.

7. According to Schweinbank (personal communication), "Particular species of fish frequent certain spots. For instance, Tautog (*Tautoga onitis*) like to hover behind rocks where there are slight whirlpools caused by the currents, and dart after their food as it comes by. Also, I believe that some of these fish hover in any given area because there also might be more oxygen where there is turbulence."

8. Kottak (1966: 217) suggests that loss of vision is an ideological rationale which justifies retirement owing to old age and still allows old sea captains to command the respect of younger fishermen. However, such justification is not necessary in Coqueiral, where old men are rewarded for retiring with sizable pensions.

9. E. Lowe Pierce, in a personal communication, states: ". . . you have to align your points quite precisely and remember just how they are aligned. It takes practice to become expert at this—but with practice you can mark a spot well."

10. The minimum importance that Kottak (1966) attributes to distinct fishing spots in Arembepe may well be due to the relatively few vessels (c. 35) which fish from that port in an expanse of ocean equal to that utilized by more than 100 vessels in Coqueiral.

11. Unfortunately, no studies of marine ecology have been carried out along this stretch of coastline, and fish populations are unknown.

12. "Many coastal fisheries afford relatively few good fishing spots, depending as they do upon advantageous reefs or banks . . . since such natural advantages for fishing are often scarce, the more vessels there are fishing, the less the efficiency of each vessel" (H. Gordon Scott, quoted in Bottomanne 1959: 127).

13. Bottomanne (1959: 12) writes: "Development of the fishing industry is largely a

race with the decrease in productivity per unit, which prevents them . . . from accumulating much wealth." Any general increase in fishing causes a decrease in catches per fishing unit.

14. There is evidence to indicate that where ownership of fishing equipment has become concentrated in the hands of single companies or a few individuals the phenomenon of secrecy disappears and resources are "fished out" (Forman 1966: 23-24).

BIBLIOGRAPHY

Bottomanne, C. J. 1959. Principles of Fisheries Development. Amsterdam.

Camara Cascudo. 1957a. Jangada. Rio de Janeiro.

—— 1957b. Jangadeiros. Rio de Janeiro.

César de Magalhães, J. 1966. Jangadas e jangadeiros. Fatos e Fotos 28: 2-9.

Forman, S. 1964. The Location of Fishing Spots in a Brazilian Coastal Community. Unpublished manuscript.

—— 1966. Jangadeiros: The Raft Fishermen of Northeast Brazil. Ph.D. dissertation, Columbia University.

Gordon, H. S. 1954. The Economic Theory of the Common Property Resource: The Fishery. Journal of Political Economy 62: 124-142.

Kottak, C. P. 1966. The Structure of Equality in a Brazilian Fishing Community. Ph.D. dissertation, Columbia University.

Russell, E. S. 1942. The Overfishing Problem. Cambridge.

Wynne-Edwards, V. C. 1962. Animal Dispersion in Relation to Social Behavior. New York.

The Lunar-Tide Fishing Cycle
in Northeastern Brazil[1]

John Cordell

The canoe fishermen who work the estuaries and mangrove swamps of the Brazilian coast are one of the most economically borderline peoples in Latin America. With the expansion of large-scale commercial fishing, the relative market value of third-class species such as mullet and catfish netted by traditional fishermen has rapidly declined. Moreover, their share of the total catch in inshore waters has been reduced through cut-throat competition with better equipped nylon net entrepreneurs and groundfish trawlers. The result is that canoe fishing specialists have had to gradually turn away from the market to marginal fishing, subsisting largely on the crabs and shellfish they can gather in the mangrove swamps.

In some outlying areas, however, marginalization has not yet run to this extreme and the remnants of a previous, highly viable, canoe fishing adaptation may be found. One such area is in southern Bahia along the Valença delta or *beirada*.

The purpose of this paper is to describe how canoe fishing functions as a man-environment system in its traditional estuarine setting. I do not intend so much to reconstruct a tradition that is fast disappearing as to provide a sense of what is being lost through marginality. In this connection, the question of the adaptive value of fishing lore takes on a special significance. The intricate knowledge of how to locate fish carries a formal elegance that helps transcend the spectre of poverty in swamp neighborhoods and may also explain how canoe fishermen have been able to survive the encroachment of outside entrepreneurs as long as they have.

PERCEPTION OF THE FISHING GROUNDS

To understand what the *beirada* fishing universe is like we must take care not to assume that it contains the same unknowns and enigmatic qualities attributed to the ocean in Western or non-seafarers' folk beliefs. These preconceptions appear in fisheries theory usually as an exaggerated concern with the uncertainties and risks fishermen are up against. As far as locating fish is concerned, there is a tendency on the part of economists to discount important intuitive aspects of environmental decision-making; the assumption is that fish must be sought blindly (Christy and Scott 1965: 88). In general, there is little appreciation of how, and to what extent, fishermen make use of environmental clues to predict the behavior and movement of different species.

It would be quite misleading to assume that canoe fishermen face a kind of "separate" reality when they are dealing with their fishing environment. On the contrary, fishermen do consistently know where the fish are, and it is this widely shared knowledge, not simply the fact that they are using a common property resource, that makes fishing competitive. In this respect, canoe fishing is somewhat unique among inshore traditions. The decision of where to fish each day is made largely on the basis of pre-determined information about the environment (Andersen and Wadel 1972: 154). The source of this information is fishermen's perception of the cyclical regularities of the tides which affect both the mechanical operation of fishing methods and the distribution of species within the estuary. To net fish successfully in these waters, one must above all master the art of timing the tides.

The most characteristic aspect of an estuarine fishing environment like the *beirada*, is that it is a region of steep and variable gradients in environmental conditions (Emery and Stevenson 1957: 673). Two processes are responsible for this: tidal currents and active sedimentation. Together they act to produce remarkable depth and substrate changes over a short distance. The principles of estuarine zoning have been carefully taken into account in the way canoe fishermen classify their fishing grounds. Three main subdivisions are recognized: *boca da barra, canal,* and *mangué* (see Map 1). These terms correspond respectively to the mouth (tidal inlet including sandbanked

Map 1.   Three Main Subdivisions of Estuarine Fishing Grounds

headlands), main body, and head of an estuary as defined by biologists. Two additional terms designate fishing areas used during the summer season: *a costa* (a long beach fronting the village of Guaibim) and the *mar perto* (the inshore reef areas fringing the island of Tinhare between the villages of Morro and Garapua). The existence of these grounds outside the estuary and the network of waterways accessible to fishermen as far south as the villages of Boipeba and Barra de Cavalho give an impression of the considerable extent of the canoe fishing grounds. As a result of trip time differences involved in fishing this territory, fishermen distinguish between the inner grounds (*beirada do canal*) and those to the south, their home port of Valença (*beirada do sul*). Since the estuary forks both eastward and westward from the island of Cairu, the southern fishing territory is subdivided into a *beirada leste* and a *beirada oeste*.

While the above terms enable one to refer to all major parts of the fishing ground, a second set of terms is used to mark off physiographic zones within these areas. Shores are *costeiros,* and the areas of shoreline exposed at low tide are *baixos*. *Riachos* are tidal creeks and rivers forming the brackish water portions of the estuary, *enseadas* are shoals within the mangrove swamp, and *coroas* are tidal flats. *Ilhas* are tidal flats which have been covered with mangrove vegetation.

Most of the bottom materials in the estuary are unconsolidated muds and sand. Mud is usually characteristic of the upper reaches of the estuary, the region of reduced current action, where sand is found near the mouth and channels. *Costeiros* in the northern *beirada* are normally rock strewn. The tidal flats which line and fill parts of the southern *beiradas* consist mostly of mud. Their surfaces are intertidal and thus periodically exposed to air and then covered with water. A large proportion of the prism of water that covers the flats at high tide travels via large channels, called *esteiros*. Minor channels vein the bottom of the estuary and may act as either tributaries or distributaries. These are known as *regos* and along their sides are natural levees which may rise to a foot or more.

These bottom features within the different physiographic zones of the estuary constitute the basic micro-environmental units from the standpoint of the distribution of fishing methods. Since most net fishing requires fishermen to leave their canoes and seine along the bottom, the pattern of substrate zoning and composition is known with great accuracy. Depth changes are similarly known to a fine degree.

Superimposed on the mirco-environmental framework of fishing is the influence of the tide. It is the most important ecological factor in the estuary not only because of its effect on animals, but because of the way it affects the positioning of fishing techniques. The periodic changes in sea level produced by the tides sub-divide the estuary into zones having nearly horizontal boundaries. The height of these zones varies with their distance from the tidal inlet. Like most estuaries with a gradual deepening from head to mouth, the tidal range decreases going away from the entrance. Thus, at the mouth of the Valença estuary, the tide range is relatively great (from 1 meter on the average at neap tide to 2.5 meters at a spring tide), but in the mangrove areas the neap and spring ranges are reduced by about half. The tide sweeps strongly in and out, invading the seaward end of the flood plain, but has a much less pronounced effect on the foreshores and in the tidal creeks and rivers. The tidal currents in the Valença estuary range from six knots at the mouth to three knots at the head at spring tides, while at neap tides the range is from three knots at the mouth to less than one knot at the head.

Several other points about currents in the estuary deserve mention as a background for understanding the fishing system. First, towards the bottom and sides of the channels, the current speed is reduced by frictional drag. The fastest currents are therefore found at the surface and at mid-stream. Also, there are counter-currents which result from irregularities in the shape of the estuary, and in the case of canoe fishing, from multiple tidal inlets. Where these currents cross in a channel, eddies are set up which considerably reduce the strength of current. Fishermen identify these areas as *reversas*. Finally, in the southern hemisphere the earth's rotation deflects inward flowing sea water counterclockwise. This results in stronger flood currents on the right-hand side of an estuary (looking down estuary) and stronger ebb currents on the left-hand side. This distinction is recognized in the vocabulary of fishing by the terms *canal de vazante* (flood channel), and *canal de enchente* (ebb channel).

Prior to the recent introduction of nylon gill nets, estuarine canoe fishing utilized thirteen different methods. It will not be necessary here, however, to launch into an elaborate discussion of fishing technology. From the range of methods available, most are viewed by fishermen as subsidiary in terms of cost and production to the large drag net (*rede grande*) and encircling net (*calao*). We must now consider what it is about these categories of nets that serves as a basis for environmental specialization. In this connection, the limiting variables are current strength, depth, and substrate. Depth and substrate considerations give rise to a distribution of these nets in micro-environments that is both lateral and vertical. Thus, some nets are located higher on shore (*artes de terra*) while others are situated lower down (*artes de fora*). At the same time, they may be submerged or floating.

Depths in the estuary range from surface to twenty meters in the deepest holes which lie in the direction of the northern tidal inlet. Although the estuary, viewed overall, becomes shallower from mouth to head, the depth range in a transect at any given point is fairly constant. This means that at least some environments with depths appropriate for net fishing can be found at almost any point. By the same token, fewer environments with depths suitable for shallow water nets will be found as one approaches the tidal inlets, and fewer environments for deep-water nets will be found in the inner reaches of the estuary. Finally, the distribution of techniques in a wedge of water is always such that nets of different categories do not overlap and compete for the same space.

The role of current conditions in the zoning of fishing methods adds an element of complexity to the distribution that emerges from depth and substrate considerations. The same current may impede the efficiency of one technique, increase the efficiency of another, or preclude altogether the use of a third. Techniques set low on shore may be quite safe during a neap tide, but on a spring tide will be moved to higher ground because the currents lower on shore would sweep them away. Similarly, techniques set at a neap tide in the outer estuary may not be able to withstand a spring tide in the same location, and will be moved inward. On the other hand, daily tide level changes often dictate both where and when a technique may be used. These restrictions are especially true for the large nets which must be operated against the tidal flow, with catches removed at turntide.

By all indications, the risk of loss or damage and the difficulty of handling heavy gear under incompatible tide conditions is enough to compel fishermen to closely observe the following restrictions in planning their fishing operations:

1. Gill nets, trot lines, and fish traps which are anchored and may drift slightly in the channels work best at neap tide when currents are weakest.

2. Barricade devices and fish corrals work best at any tide but neap, since they require considerable current and depth changes to snare fish at locations high on shore and in the tidal creeks.

3. The dragged nets and encircling nets do not function well at either spring or neap tide since they require medium velocity currents, and these only come at rising and falling phases during the tide cycle.

It should be noted, however, that these restrictions are not as limiting as they first appear. Because of the way the shape of the estuary conditions current action, a spring tide in its inner reaches is more like a neap tide in its outer reaches, and vice versa. The result is that fishermen can use most of their techniques on a daily schedule throughout the tidal cycle, as long as the choice of fishing spots conforms to the particular current regime on any given day.

TIMING THE CHOICE OF FISHING SPOTS

Choosing a fishing spot is largely a matter of timing— putting together information on tides, techniques, and fishing areas so that there is a good chance of locating a school of fish. To make this decision, fishermen need to know as finely as possible the details of tide sequences and spatial configuration of the fishing grounds. This knowledge defines the micro-environments for all techniques, but the tide cycle serves also as a calendrical device to mark off major fishing events and catalogue information on production.

Contrary to what one might expect, a fishing spot is not thought of as a purely spatial point. Rather, its existence is always relative to the different phases of the lunar month which in turn are recognized as the source of tide level changes. The way canoe fishermen classify the effect of lunar periodicity of tides is depicted in the polar diagram (Figure 1). By their system of reckoning, names are given to each day in the 28 day lunar cycle which mark the corresponding water level changes. An important feature of this system is that the moon's phases are regarded essentially as boundary markers for the semi-monthly ebb and flood of the tides, rather than as names for specific days in the cycle.

This taxonomy is founded on two principles: (1) the difficulty of visualiz-

Figure 1.   Fishermen's Classification of the Fluctuations by Lunar Phases

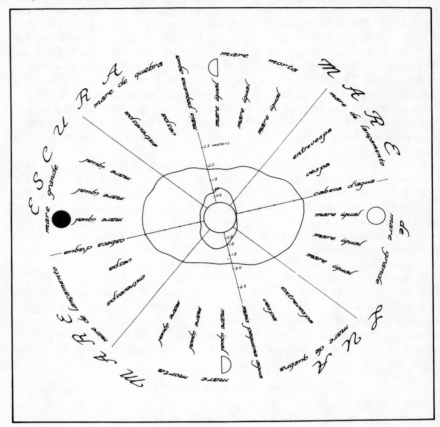

ing finer changes within each lunar phase as precisely corresponding to de-
grees of water level change, and (2) the fact that the greatest rise and fall
in tides does not come exactly on the days of the new and full moon. Instead, there is generally an interval of one or two days between full moon
and the greatest range of the tide, and a like interval is found between the
first and third quarters of the moon and the smallest tides (Marmer 1926:11).
Thus, a set of terms (*mais pequena agua, cabeca d'agua*) exists to denote
the days of smallest and greatest tide range.

Finally, the entire lunar-tide calendar is sub-divided by a set of terms indi-
cating when the moon is moving from first to third quarter through full
(*mare de lua*) and from third to first through new (*mare escura*). The significance of these terms is the way they partition the lunar month according
to the duration and intensity of light available for night fishing. Moonlight is
critical for navigation purposes and, what is even more important, may influence certain aspects of fish behavior such as migration and ability to see

nets in the water. This topic will be explored in a later section of the paper. Here, however, the point is that the choice of fishing spots can be shown to vary, not only with the tide cycle, but with the lighting conditions associated with phases of the moon. The fact that this is an important consideration in choosing where to fish is revealed by the way the fishermen group the tide cycles into darker and lighter periods in their calendar.

The lunar-tide classification thoroughly maps the repetitive fortnightly rise and fall in tidal height and current. However, there is another interesting dimension in the tides which fishermen recognize in planning trips. This is the relationship between lunar transit and the timing of the daily tide-change sequences from one phase of the tide cycle to the next (e.g. from spring to neap). Thus, just as fishermen watch the lunar phases which define the boundaries of tide changes, they also keep close track of the moon's position in the sky each day. This series of changes is recorded by a set of expressions (see Table 1.) which identify the position of the moon on the horizon relative to land or sea, depending on whether it is first seen at sunset or sunrise, and if so, where. These expressions are *passagem de lua, sol por lua, lua em terra,* and *lua no mar.* In this order, roughly translated, they mean whether the moon is beginning a new passage, whether it is fully exposed to the sun, whether it is over the land or over the sea.

At first these expressions seem to duplicate the information already given by the lunar-tide calendar (*passagem de lua* necessarily corresponds to a new moon, *sol por lua* is a reference to the full moon, *lua em terra* to first quarter, and *lua no mar* to last quarter). However, the observations of moon transit/ tide change conveyed in these expressions provide a variety of relevant information which could not be arrived at by simple reckoning of phases and tides. The terms refer to the sequential variation in daily tides over a lunar month that results from a constant retardation in the moon's passage (Marmer 1926: 12-13). Thus, each day as the lunar cycle progresses, there is a fifty minute retardation in the interval between high and low waters. This means that each week the time of a particular daily tide will be advanced

TABLE 1

Tide Sequence According to Moon's Transit

Tide Cycle Phase	Lunar Phase	Time of Moonrise	Daily Tide Sequence 1st Hi Water	1st Lo Water	Moonlight Duration	Position Terms
Spring	New	Dawn	Noon	Dusk	————	passagem de lua
Spring	Full	Dusk	Midnight	Dawn	12 hours	sol por lua
Neap	1/4	Noon	Dusk	Midnight	(increasing) 6 hours	lua em terra
Neap	3/4	Midnight	Dawn	Noon	(decreasing) 6 hours	lua no mar

nearly six hours over the week before. Thus, when fishermen see the moon over the meridian in a particular phase, they may be certain that six hours later the tide will be halfway through its semi-diurnal cycle. For instance, when a spring tide occurs with a full moon, the moon will rise at dusk and the first high tide of the day will occur shortly after midnight. From his initial lunar position observation, a fisherman will be able to time the daily tide phase sequences for approximately a week.

At this point one may wonder why canoe fishermen bother with such minute details. The answer, I think, follows not only from the previous discussion of how tides govern the use of techniques, but also from a consideration of how a fishing trip must be planned. The lunar position terms, together with observations of phases indicate changes in moonlight and thus whether night fishing is feasible. Moreover, fishermen must know what specific sequence of tide changes will occur during the part of the day they set aside for a trip. Timing a fishing trip properly is seen as even more crucial when one considers the location of the fishermen's home base relative to the estuary.

The main fishing neighborhoods are situated on a river eight kilometers from the mouth of the estuary and four kilometers from the main net casting channels. Most of the river is closed in by mangrove swamps which reduce the wind available for sailing. The pronounced effect of the tide on the river thus becomes the main bond between fishermen in their non-motorized canoes and the fishing grounds. So that the tide will not be working against them each day, fishermen must rely on the lunar-tide system to solve three essential timing problems: (1) getting out to the fishing grounds on a favorable tide; (2) once out, finding a tide compatible with the micro-environment suitable for their nets; and (3) getting back home without running into adverse currents. The sequence of tide changes that will allow smooth fishing must therefore be in keeping with the semi-diurnal tidal rhythm and there are only two full sequences daily. Consequently, most fishing trips are timed to take place over six-hour periods: beginning at some point on an ebb tide (depending on the distance of the fishing spot), and ending on the subsequent floodtide. The changes in daily tide levels are generally observable by the relationship of water height to the base of the mangrove swamp. However, in some cases tides can be predicted from lines of stakes driven into the mud across the inter-tidal zone at various points along shore. It should be noted that there are six terms for daily tide changes (*preamar, descanso degua, vazante, baixa-mar, virada,* and *enchente*), reflecting the fine breakdown in timing choices.

More than once during my stay in the *beirada,* a fishing captain whose crew did not assemble in time to leave on an appropriate tide would refuse to leave at all rather than having to compensate later for the timing error. Perhaps, though, the utility of the lunar-tide system can only be appreciated by trying to imagine oneself in a predicament that may result from poor timing. A fishing crew may easily be caught becalmed at the mouth of the estuary on a spring ebb tide of up to five knots and have to row home with a valuable load of fish about to spoil.

Having defined the categories of timing elements in fishing, it is now possible to show how they are built into the notion of a fishing spot, or *pesqueiro*. The first thing to consider is that *pesqueiros* are the minimal micro-environmental units of fishing, but depending on their location in the estuary, they are only activated at certain times during the lunar cycle. *Pesqueiros* always fall within more inclusive types of physiographic zones, and are usually referred to as belonging to a specific shoreline (*costeiro*) which in turn is subsumed under one of the major sub-divisions of the fishing grounds (*beiradas*). Over 400 fishing spots are known and frequented by Valença fishermen and each has a name, ordinarily taken from a coastal landmark such as a plantation which it may front.

Fishing spots are found continuously along the shores of the estuary, but are actually distributed in discrete clusters. This is because each spot is always defined with reference to the phase of the lunar-tide cycle (neap, spring, light or dark tide) when it may be used. However, since a fishing spot may accommodate a range of techniques, three further factors act to partition it into what are called *lancos* or water spaces for casting nets: (1) fortnightly current changes (*morta, lancamento, quebra, grande*), (2) daily tide level changes, and (3) the position of the particular water space relative to the slope of the shore. Thus, a water space may be an area reserved for shooting nets, for setting trotlines, or for construction of a fish corral, but because of the different zoning and current considerations which apply to each, they do not overlap. *Lancos*, like *pesqueiros*, have distinctive names taken from their boundary markers, such as bottom type (e.g., *bugaial*, a type of gravel, *tabatinga*, a clay) or their position on shore relative to other *lancos* (e.g., *lanco de fora; dentro; meio; cima; baixo*). In any case, the overall effect of timing considerations is to subdivide *pesqueiros* according to an order of technical priorities in which they and the *lancos* they contain are thought of by fishermen as geographical points within the lunar month.

By eliciting the characteristics of several hundred fishing spots, I was able to derive the pattern whereby, at least in theory, fishermen shift the focus of their activity during the tide cycle. This pattern was then compared with the locational data on actual fishing trips, and the correspondence between boat positions and tidally activated fishing zones proved extremely close. Moreover, the fishing pattern as shown by trip frequencies is striking in the way all groups of specialists consistently tend to concentrate in the same general locations from one tide level to the next. At neap tide the concentration is on the *costeiros* at the northern end of the estuary; as the tide begins to rise (*lancamento*) people move into the main body of the estuary (*o canal*), in from the mouth. At spring tide, activity shifts to the southern *costeiros,* and finally as the tide begins to fall (*quebra*), fishermen move back up the estuary into the main channels. Canoe fishing, in other words, moves in a circuit of logistic areas which are activated periodically by a tide cycle which has a differential impact along the course of the estuary.

ADAPTIVE USE OF FISHING KNOWLEDGE

In the *beirada,* learning how to reckon moons and tides goes hand in hand with learning how to fish, until the necessary relationships between timing and production have been mastered. A sufficient number of locations must be cognitively marked in this way for a fisherman to be able to work throughout the tide cycle and at different seasons. The continuity and viability of the fishing tradition depends on successfully transferring this environmental lore to new generations of fishermen.

It is difficult to conceive the backlog of trial and error experience that must have preceded the codification of fishing knowledge into the present orientation system. Yet to some extent this process is repeated each time a man is recruited to fishing. In other words, the system is always being modified and updated by new experiences and events which arise in the course of fishing to shape future plans.

However, it is one thing to understand the basic principles of environmental variability but another problem entirely to apply them by consistently selecting sites which yield good catches. In deciding where to fish, the production history of individual fishing spots becomes a vital point of reference. Because of the cyclical framework of the fishing environment, no production event is considered to be unique. Instead, memories of more or less abundant catches are stored in the lunar-tide reference system as a series of events set in spatial context. For instance, when a good catch is recorded twice in the same spot at the same time in the tide cycle, this is taken by fishermen as evidence of a casual link between moons, tides, and fish behavior. Later this is recalled in making subjective probability assessments of production potential in deciding where to fish.

The significance of ordering environmental data in this fashion across generations raises a critical question about canoe fishing: what is the actual economic value, if any, of such a system of orientation in predicting the location and concentration of fish? Is adaptive use being made of this body of knowledge by conferring a productivity advantage on those who inherit it over those who do not? Or, does the tide exert such a restricting influence on estuary fishing that the system of orientation is maladaptive for individuals and the fishing population as a whole? To answer this question one would need, along with time-series data on production, some independent biological measures of the relative abundance of fish at different points during the tide cycle, through different seasons, and at different fishing locations, including those deactivated for fishing as the tide changes. This way, in theory, it would be possible to see what advantages or disadvantages in terms of production are involved in long-term use of the orientation system, but still leaves the problem of understanding why lunar-tide lore should be predictive of fish behavior.

Despite these complexities, it is still possible to evaluate this aspect of canoe fishing, based simply on a consideration of some of the adaptive tendencies which seem inherent in the way the system works. First, it is necessary to think of the question of adaptation in terms of differences in production potential among fishermen. *Beirada* fishermen may be easily ranked in this regard, since they have clear ideas as to whom is good at fishing and why. Holding efficiency of equipment constant, factors of age, experience in fishing local waters, eyesight, endurance, drinking habits, and a host of related impressions enter into these informal rankings. Most importantly is the special knowledge confined to fishing captains to *fazer o lanco certo* (properly time a net-cast). This in turn implies the ability of a fisherman to bring his knowledge of production history to bear on the choice of where to fish. Since, as I have shown, the influence of the tide is variable from *costeiro* to *costerio*, a fisherman has a lot to consider in making this decision. It is not surprising, then, that the basis for productivity ranking among fishermen is mainly the finer ability of experienced fishermen over new recruits to simplify the range of locational alternatives specified by the lunar tide system. It is from this standpoint that environmental knowledge begins to take on considerable economic value.

It is at least an intriguing possibility to ask whether the very precise work routines established by certain fishing captains are adaptive in the sense that they are based on some of the same environmental principles that determine fish behavior. If this could be demonstrated, it would mean that the sustained large catches by some captains are not just based on fishermen's luck.

Unfortunately, very little is known about estuarine species on this part of the Brazilian coast and not much work has been done in marine biology that is relevant to our question. Korringa (1957: 921) points out that biologists have been inclined to underestimate the importance of tidal rhythms to marine animals. This, he adds, is possibly because the tides are not considered that biologically important to us. Generally speaking, the lunar-tide system incorporates several variables which are known to be important elements in fish behavior, especially migration and spawning.

The first point to mention in this connection concerns the salinity of the tide range. Since the *beirada* estuary is fairly large, with several deep inlets, there is a fairly stable salinity gradient from head to mouth. This gradient will move backwards and forwards with the tides. On a flood tide the salinity will increase along the length of the estuary, and the salinity at any one point will depend on the extent to which sea water travels upstream. On a spring tide the sea will penetrate further into an estuary than on a neap tide, and so will cause a more widespread increase in salinity. There is actually very little fresh water runoff into the estuaries so the brackish water conditions conducive to mangrove formation are found mainly along the inner reaches of the estuary, with sea water penetrating far up the tidal creeks.

The distribution of fish according to their salinity tolerances (ability to osmoregulate) will conform to this gradient. The significance of this conformity from the standpoint of fishing is that the abundance of fish populations will change relative to this gradient (Hedgepeth 1957: 702). Thus, preliminary work on the comparative productivity of various regions in estuaries indicates that productivity is probably lowest in the transition between marine and fresh water regions in the same gradient. Assuming this finding is indicative of the productivity pattern in all estuaries with stable salinity gradients, zones of the *beirada* estuary may be at least tentatively ranked in terms of fishing potential. This task is fairly straightforward since the estuary, again like most estuaries with deep channels and sheltered middle reaches, has very nearly vertical salinity gradients. True brackish water conditions (that is, the zone of transition between marine and fresh water and therefore the zone of lowest productivity) should be found only in the mangrove swamps. This means that as the tide rises, its isolhaline zone bulges upstream and when the tide falls, the bulge is reversed to point downstream. In terms of the logistic pattern of canoe fishing defined by the lunar-tide system, this alternation would virtually eliminate the zones of least productivity. At neap tides, when fishing is concentrated in the outer estuary, it is well away from the zone of transition even though it moves somewhat out from the mangrove swamps. At rising and falling monthly tide phases, the main channels become the foci of fishing, and similarly they lie beyond the zone of transition or least productivity. Finally, at spring tides, fishing moves up into the inner estuary but still does not fall within the zone of transition, since the mangrove swamps are well innundated with sea water which pushes the zone far inland. It is possible to suggest, then, that canoe fishermen may benefit by not being in the areas of least productivity potential during the tide cycle. In this sense, there may be some adaptive value in adhering to the lunar-tide system.

The current which accompanies the tidal wave may be of considerable significance in relation to the way fish move in an estuary (Green 1968: 274-291). By its means, creatures having little or no powers of resistance may be carried inshore. This is important to the migrations of the young stages of animals and plants on which larger fish feed. The retreating tide in an estuary may carry them out to sea and the advancing tide may convey young stages from the sea to the estuary or from lower to higher shores. Estuaries are rich in invertebrate life and support large populations of fish which primarily feed on the invertebrates. Thus, the flounder (*linguado*) and guppy (*morea*) are important predatory animals appearing in the Valença estuary, and the behavior of the invertebrates on which they feed, especially certain larval plankton forms, may be governed almost entirely by the current regime (Green 1968: 96). In a second sense, then, the lunar-tide system might be interpreted as having some adaptive functions, since the logistic pattern of fishing may take advantage of the differential distribution of the organisms that fish feed on during the tide cycle.

Finally, there is the variable of lunar periodicity to consider. Canoe fishermen mentally tag all their catches in terms of the moon's phases (e.g., *mare de lua, mare escura,*). At the same time, it is assumed that moonlit nights are categorically poor for some types of fishing—sardine fishing for example. Presumably, on moonlit nights, these fish can see the nets and so are vulnerable only on moonless nights. Still, there are other fishing routines that simply must conform to the proper phase of the lunar cycle, which may be either light or dark. It should be noted that these occasions relate principally to the spawning activities of species such as catfish and bluerunner.

The widespread utilization of estuaries as nursery grounds is one of the features that distinguishes them from other marine environments (Hedgpeth 1957: 700). Thus, not only do many of the motile invertebrates and vertebrates found in estuaries come in with the tide and leave on it, but there is ample evidence that cycles other than daily and annual rhythms are involved

(Korringa 1957: 917). This does not necessarily mean there is a direct causal link between the moon's phases and the reproductive behavior of fish such as those which spawn in the *beirada*. In fact, it is entirely possible that these animals are sensitive to both the tide cycle and the moonlight rhythm.

In any event, it is this aspect of lunar tide knowledge that most seems to aid fishermen in making large catches. The spawning cycles they recognize seem to run so closely parallel to the lunar cycle that it is difficult not to attach considerable adaptive significance to the system of orientation. On these grounds I do not think it is too farfetched to suggest that ultimately the lunar-tide system has been perfected as an index of spawning periodicity. It is as though the purely mechanical considerations dictating the positioning of techniques put fishermen onto habits of fish concentration similarly influenced by the tidal level change.

CONCLUSIONS

Catches in the *beirada* often consist of large quantities of estuarine spawning fish. Therefore, it would not seem too bold to characterize canoe fishing as basically an economic adaptation which relies on the fishermen's ability to trace and capitalize on fish spawning behavior. This is accomplished by organizing environmental knowledge of moons and tides into a system for choosing fishing spots that also seems to be a fairly accurate index of the migration of estuarine species. The lunar-tide calendar is closely adhered to by all traditional fishing captains on this part of the Brazilian coast. As a culturally shared four-dimensional mental map of the fishing grounds, it synchronizes boat movements, the choice of fishing methods, and the availability of fishing spots according to bi-weekly and daily tide fluctuations. The cumulative effect of following this system has been to stabilize the fishing community as a whole in an ecologically adaptive, moderately competitive economic routine. The cyclical shift from inner to outer fishing grounds that results from the tide changes also tends to work again over-fishing. It should be noted that over-fishing would not, in any case, be a very real possibility, given the small fishing population using the *beirada* waters and the fact that many pelagic schools enter the estuary during their ocean-spanning migratory cycles. The real danger to canoe fishermen is not that their system is economically inefficient or maladaptive due to the peculiarities of estuary fishing, but that government agencies and/or private investors will introduce over-efficient catching systems into these areas before expansion capabilities can be realistically evaluated.

NOTE

1. Research for this article was done in 1970-71 in Valenca, Bahia. I am indebted to the following institutions for fellowship support: the Anthropology Department and International Studies Committee of Stanford University, the National Institute of General Medical Sciences, and the Woods Hole Oceanographic Institution. I would also like to thank Bernard Siegel and Charles Drucker for reading an earlier draft of this paper and Kip Nigh who drew the lunar-tide calendar (Figure 1).

BIBLIOGRAPHY

Anderson, R., and C. Wadel, eds. 1972. North Atlantic Fishermen: Anthropological Essays on Modern Fishing. Newfoundland Social and Economic Paper No. 5. Memorial University of Newfoundland.

Christy, Jr. F. T., and A. Scott. 1965. The Common Wealth in Ocean Fisheries. Resources for the Future Foundation. Washington.

Emery, K. O., R. E. Stevenson, and J. W. Hedgepeth. 1957. Estuaries and Lagoons. Treaties on Marine Ecology and Paleoecology, ed. J. W. Hedgepeth, pp. 673-683. Memoir 67, Vol. 1, Geological Society of America. Washington.

Green, J. 1968. The Biology of Estuarine Animals. University of Washington.

Hedgepeth, J. W. 1957. Estuaries and Lagoons (pt. 2). Treatise in Marine Ecology and Paleoecology, ed. J. W. Hedgepeth, pp. 700-702. Memoir 67, Vol. 1, Geological Society of America. Washington.

Korringa, P. 1957. Lunar Periodicity. Treatise on Marine Ecology and Paleoecology, ed. J. W. Hedgepeth pp. 917-921. Memoir 67, Vol. 1, Geographical Society of America. Washington.

Marmer, H. A. 1926. The Tide. New York.

Carrying Capacity Analysis
of Fixed-Territorial Fishing[1]

John Cordell

Overfishing has seldom been evaluated as an actual or potential problem in anthropological studies of traditional fishing. Rather, there has been a tendency for anthropologists to assume, along with fishery biologists, that over-exploitation of local coastal waters is unlikely where fishing communities are small and isolated and where fish species have a wide distribution and can feed on planktonic larvae. Additional support for this view stems from evidence that in certain maritime traditions there are internal checks on fishing pressure in the form of conservation measures designed to insure the longevity of valuable species (cf. Johannes 1976; Klee 1976). As in other traditional economies where human population density is low, we might expect most fishing communities to exist at levels well below carrying capacity (cf. Harpending 1974: 229-243). This situation may change abruptly, however, when technical innovation occurs or when outside market demands increase, as in the case of the Miskito Indians of Nicaragua (cf. Nietschman 1974).

Rarely does a fieldwork situation provide the opportunity to examine precisely the overfishing question. Necessary multispecies time-series data on catch and effort are hard to obtain even under the most ideal research conditions. Fishery development theory similarly is lacking in means to estimate the expansion potential of traditional fishing as technical advances are introduced. Many studies make passing reference to the biological concept of carrying capacity to interpret change or stability within the production system. The carrying capacity concept itself, however, has come under increasing criticism; it has been erroneously formulated on the basis of exponential rather than logistic models of growth, and threshold definitions are ultimately subjective in that they depend on highly variable ethics concerning the optimal allocation of resources (cf. Johnson 1974; Street 1969).

Here I would like to suggest a somewhat different line of inquiry from that which is normally taken in carrying capacity analysis, especially as applied to fixed-territorial coastal fishing. Given the difficulty of measuring population pressure and resource deterioration in many coastal marine settings, an alternative is to inquire how fishermen perceive and talk about the carrying capacity or expansion potential of their system.

Using the example of a small-scale inshore fishing system in Brazil, this paper takes up the problem of how population build-up may be controlled by territorial access limitations. These limits are expressed in the criteria which fishing captains use to decide where to fish each day.

A strictly biological approach to the problem of carrying capacity may well prove to be impractical and unrealistic in most cases of small-scale fishing. Yet I found the concept itself to be meaningful to fishermen. My purpose here is to illustrate how lunar-tide complexities set restrictions on fishing pressure, thus providing the context for the failure of technical innovation.

The Common Property Myth in Coastal Fishing

Probably the foremost problem in the management of the world's sea fisheries is their susceptibility to "overcapitalization" (Marr 1976: 39). This tendency is usually attributed to the "common property" character of marine resources, to which everyone is presumed to have free access. The yield of any fishery resource is finite, so under conditions of unlimited entry of production units, the total catch will be divided among more and more vessels until individual profits begin to decline. Overcapitalization does not inevitably lead to biological overfishing. However, it will occur if the degree of fishing intensity at which the fishery as a whole becomes unprofitable approximates the level of intensity necessary to prevent a fish stock from reaching maximum weight in a given age class.

The common property theory has proven applicability in industrial-scale, open-ocean fishing. Traditional inshore fishing, however, may present an interesting exception to the common property theory. Recent studies in maritime anthropology have shown that various forms of proprietary rights have evolved in certain small-scale coastal fisheries (Forman 1970, 1966; Nietschmann 1974; Cordell 1974; Johannes 1976; Klee 1972).

Boats must be free to follow fish as they move. Yet fish behavior is not random; most species periodically concentrate to feed or spawn, or migrate in schools. As fishermen learn to capitalize on the patterned behavior of fish, they incorporate this knowledge into "systems of orientation"; essentially calendrical devices which enable them to map out the distribution of sites through which fish pass at predictable intervals. Thus fishermen are presented with opportunities to establish temporary territorial rights which may be converted to long-standing territorial claims.

From the standpoint of resource control and competition, coastal fishing would seem to be transitional, in both a logical and evolutionary sense, between inland and open ocean production settings. In many coastal fisheries the fishing grounds are restricted enough and located close enough to home base to allow fishermen a daily observational check on one another's activities. Tabs are kept on the whereabouts of competitors so that estimates may be made of changes in fish concentration. The fishing grounds may be sufficiently enclosed in river-estuary systems, reefs and lagoons, shoals, banks, etc. so that fishing spots can be treated as unique locations with precise boundary markers for the different methods used (Cordell 1974; Nietschmann 1974; Grossinger 1975).

Realistically, however, one wonders how the fieldworker, often a single investigator, can go about evaluating a complex carrying capacity issue posed by a possible overfishing situation. Time series data on dynamics of fish populations and fishing pressure are usually only obtainable through costly and elaborate biological surveys. Even under conditions where catch and effort data are available and reliable, fishery biologists point out that it is almost impossible to obtain the necessary information on spawning stock/recruitment relationships (Marr 1976: 41).

The primary danger in traditional fishing, however, is not internal human population pressure, but the fact that entrepreneurial agents may introduce over-efficient catching systems before knowledge of expansion potential is available. In fishing communities that have utilized the same stocks for years without depletion, the occurrence of naive modernization may rapidly generate an overfishing situation. Thus we are still critically in need of a method to gauge the expansion potential of local fishing waters where production is geared to low harvest rates but is subject to sudden intensification.

CARRYING CAPACITY IN FIXED-TERRITORIAL FISHING

Ideally, carrying capacity estimates should enable us to evaluate the nutritional adequacy of existing man/marine resource ratios, and by extension, the threat or reality of overcrowding in a given area. In recent years, this mode of analyzing the maximum population level that a given area can support, depending on its potential for food production, has been the focus of much debate in human ecology.[2] Despite valid criticisms of its limited utility as an explanatory device, with certain modifications I have found the concept to be a valuable aid in investigating problems of fishery modernization, providing more refined estimates of population pressure than simple density measures.

Most carrying capacity studies have been concerned with the risk and danger of overpopulation in traditional economies, most often in areas with related landscape deterioration (Allen 1949; Carneiro 1960: 231). Roughly what these studies do is calculate how much food families consume or need to consume, the average yield of land, and the area required to support various levels of population. The production system is then further analyzed to determine the quantity of resources needed to (a) feed the population, and (b) keep the population fully employed at present levels of output, and at current employment levels (supply function of labor), assuming the narrowly defined traditional technology remains constant. Finally, the required levels of resources are compared with available levels to define the limits of overpopulation.

Carrying capacity analysis has been extensively employed to study population pressure in shifting cultivation and other systems of agriculture, but there is only cursory information in the ethnographic and fisheries literature on the overfishing question in a traditional context. As I have indicated, it may be that traditional fishing is not susceptible to overfishing if technology remains constant. On the other hand, in the absence of precise time-series data on fishing pressure, it is always possible to argue that overfishing is a real danger, but that it does not occur because of regulatory social mechanisms. Thus, in an otherwise compelling study of raft fishing in northeastern Brazil, Forman (1970: 65) reasons: ". . . . secrecy regarding particular spots within the grounds serves as a spacing mechanism which minimizes competition and prevents overfishing by according temporary property rights to individual fishermen."

Forman's analysis raises another critical point in regard to carrying capacity which is seldom considered by fishery planners. This concerns the fixed-territorial nature of many inshore fishing grounds. Boats may be equipped with sails, or even motorized, yet fishermen characteristically frequent the same configuration of territories which must be shared and which are ranked according to variables such as ease of accessibility from home port, past production history, and weather conditions. Thus, whether or not a full-fledged system of property rights has developed, inshore fishing is likely to have definite spatial limitations. In this case, the initial restriction on expanding fishing operations may be favorably located waterspace, and secondarily the availability of fish stocks. To enter the fishery under such circumstances, any new production unit would have to contend with the fundamental matter of gaining access to waterspace and the fishing system would be vulnerable to competition along these purely spatial lines.

In light of these considerations, I would like tentatively to propose here that the key to avoiding overcapitalization and to conserving many coastal fisheries lies in recognizing their fixed-territorial nature, and restricting entry accordingly. With gear-upgrading innovations, fisheries may develop so rapidly that for management purposes there is not enough time to acquire the relevant catch and effort data. Furthermore, if the fixed-territorial limits are initially well defined, then an elaborate biological survey, at least for inshore waters, may prove in the long run unnecessary.

Though by no means intended as a substitute for catch and effort data, there are some simple interview techniques which I have used in previous fieldwork which may have a bearing on the carrying capacity issue. I have found that much revealing information can be elicited from the ethnobiology realm by taking a closer look at the identifying characteristics of fishing spots. In the search for some indirect indices of carrying capacity, this procedure assumes that traditional fishermen have a fair impression of the expansion potential of their production system and that the relevant dimensions are reflected in their decisions of where to fish each day. I now proceed to document the pattern of change in Brazilian canoe fishing in which the production expansion capacity of local inshore waters was put to a critical test.

The Developmental Cycle of Canoe Fishing

The fishing-plantation area in question lies in the coastal lowlands of southern Bahia, Brazil (Map 1) and is known locally as the *beirada*. Its inhabitants are *beiradeiros* or "shore dwellers." The *beirada* forms a type of geologically submerging coast, which consists of a narrow plain cut by tidal creeks and rivers. These open onto an extensive system of estuaries flanked by mangrove swamps. Following the river and estuary shoreline, there are small scattered communities of marginal fishermen who now work mainly for a subsistence living. They customarily fish from dugout canoes operated by eight-man crews, though today a wide variety of subsidiary methods, such as traps and trotlines, are utilized. Fishermen also forage for crabs and shellfish in the mangrove swamps. The port of Valenca, located somewhat inland on the Una River about 60 miles down the coast from Salvador, Bahia, is the heart of the canoe-fishing tradition. Valenca has several competitive fishing neighborhoods which I visited in 1970-71.

Most fishing traditions in this part of Brazil retain some interesting adaptive features from earlier periods of essentially noncommercialized, noncompetitive growth (cf. Forman 1970, 1966: 16). Through technical change and outside entrepreneurial activities, however, these traditions are gradually breaking down and many fishermen are being forced into poverty. Throughout my stay in Valenca I was faced with the problem of understanding a group of people whose system of livelihood seemed to have outlived its usefulness and would soon disappear. People continued to fish, though less for the market than for home consumption, and less with larger nets than with secondary techniques which they could operate with a low upkeep as independent producers. Many fishermen were out of work and tended to congregate along the waterfront speculating that the summer fishing season the following year would bring a catfish spawning run up the estuary, in which case all might be well again.

The economic slump in fishing, however, did not appear to be a temporary condition due to a chance off-season in production. Instead, it coincided with recent efforts by fishery planners to upgrade the traditional catching system with

Map 1. Location of Valenca Canoe-Fishing Tradition

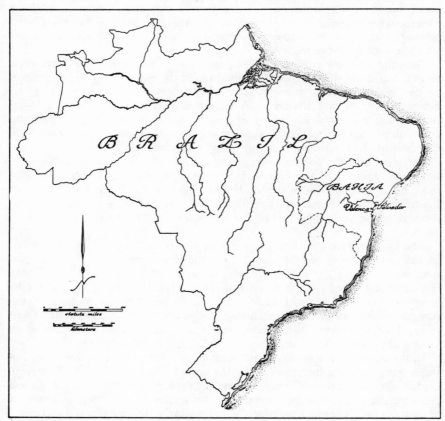

nylon nets. Because of its single-minded emphasis on gear efficiency, this innovation was doomed to failure. No one bothered to ask how the traditional fishing system worked in its estuarine environment, how production was organized in local communities, or what impact intensified fishing would have on marine resources. It is no surprise then, that the modernization attempt ultimately proved incompatible with the expansion possibilities of net fishing. The first limitation was purely mechanical, having to do with the fixed-territorial aspect of net fishing. Canoes without motors could seldom venture out beyond the estuaries. Second, the tides along this part of the coast act greatly to restrict fishing in terms of the number of suitable locations for nets each day. I will elaborate on this point in the following section. Let it suffice now to summarize, that over a ten year period too many nylon nets were added, and too few waterspaces were available to accommodate them in the local estuary.

Worse still, in the context of these unrecognized range limitations, was the mistake made in the manner of introducing the new nets. They were originally intended for purchase by traditional fishing captains. Nearly all captains rejected the innovation, not out of any inherent conservatism, but because they could not meet the loan repayment schedules. Consequently, the nylon nets fell into the hands of wealthy middlemen (factory bosses, plantation owners, and local merchants) who could afford to speculate in fishing. Numerous fishermen were already indebted to the entrepreneurs and so were drawn into an easily exploitable pool of cheap labor.

Over the next few years a highly competitive nylon-net fishing enclave grew up in the midst of the traditional community. In the ensuing struggle for control of the fishing grounds, the previous balance between production units and fishing territories was shattered. A tremendous amount of cut-throat competition was generated and much equipment was destroyed in costly disputes over fishing rights. Economic warfare crippled the industry in general and members of the traditional community in particular.

Pressured by the effects of overfishing, traditional captains were increasingly lured into high risk strategies with their equipment against better financed nylon-net specialists. Since the traditional fishermen did not have sufficient capital to continue fishing on this basis, many captains were forced to dismiss their crews and move their base of operations to the tidal creeks of the mangrove swamp.

The type of developmental cycle I have briefly documented for the canoe-fishing system might best be described by the term "marginalization." Beginning with a period of essentially nonmarket-oriented expansion, the fishing system then entered a stage of growth characterized by increasing control by entrepreneurs who brought capital and technical advances to part of the community. As this period of speculation ended and catches declined, fishermen reverted to subsistence production, reflected by expansion in utilization of swamp areas and almost exclusively specialized to crab gathering.

In the course of my fieldwork I attempted to reconstruct the major events in this miniature boom-bust cycle, and this brought to light a series of carrying capacity issues concerning adaptive response to modernization. The first of these concerns the traditional system prior to innovation. As a baseline for interpreting change, it seemed necessary to show what, if anything, was "adaptive," that is, what tended to keep the intensity of fishing within tolerable bounds in its traditional culture-environmental setting. What were the mechanisms governing the relationship of production units to available resources which tended to make fishing reliable as a long-term occupation? What sort of production expansion was characteristic of the traditional system and how did innovation in the form it took alter this pattern? In the light of the state of economic stagnation at the time of my research, the system had been unable to withstand innovation, but how could this incompatibility be formally shown in the absence of an elaborate biological survey of fish stocks and production?

LUNAR-TIDE FISHING SPACE

With regard to the *beirada* fishing grounds (Map 2), it is difficult to speak of production potential inherent in local waters, since pelagic fish schools enter the

Map 2. BEIRADA FISHING GROUNDS

estuaries at various points in their migratory cycles. Fishermen's ability to capitalize on these migrations, particularly spawning runs, depends to a great extent on their knowledge of lunar-tide periodicity. Through careful observation of the tide cycle they are able to cue in on the movement of different species on a daily basis. At the same time the variable influence of the tide along the course of the estuary determines the selection and positioning of all their fishing methods on a strictly mechanical basis. To net fish successfully in *beirada* waters one must above all master the art of timing the tides.

Superimposed on the microenvironmental framework of fishing the tides is the most important ecological factor in the estuary. The periodic changes in sea level produced by the tides subdivide the estuary into zones having nearly horizontal boundaries. The tide sweeps strongly in and out of the estuary, invading the seaward end of the floodplain, but has a much less pronounced effect on the foreshores and in the tidal creeks and rivers.

The effect of fortnightly current changes in the zoning of fishing methods adds an element of complexity to the distribution that emerges from depth and substrate influences. The same current may impede the efficiency of one technique, increase the efficiency of another, or preclude the use of a third altogether. Fishing gear set low on shore may be quite safe during a neap tide, but on a spring tide must be moved to higher ground or the currents lower on shore will sweep it away.

The risk of loss or damage and the difficulty of handling heavy gear under incompatible tides is enough to compel fishermen to observe closely the following set of priorities:

1. Gill nets, trotlines, and fish traps which must be anchored and set to drift in the channels work best when currents are weakest at neap tide.

2. Barricade devices and fish corrals work best at any tide but neap tide, since they require considerable current and depth change to snare fish high on shore and in the tidal creeks.

3. Dragged nets and encircling nets do not function well at either spring or neap tide since they require medium velocity currents and these only come at rising and falling phases during the tide cycle.

The limitations on techniques always hold, but never for all areas of the fishing grounds at once. Because of the way the shape of the estuary influences current action, a spring tide in its inner reaches is more like a neap tide in its outer reaches, and vice versa. The result is that fishermen can use most of their techniques on a daily schedule throughout the tide cycle, as long as the choice of fishing spots conforms to the particular current regime on any given day.

Choosing a fishing spot is then largely a matter of proper timing—putting together information on tides, techniques, and fishing areas so there is a good chance of locating a school of fish. Contrary to what one might expect, a fishing spot is not thought of as a purely spatial point. Rather, its existence is always relative to the different phases of the lunar month. By their system of reckoning, names are given to each day in the 28 day lunar cycle which marks the corresponding water level changes (Cordell 1974: 379-391).

It is important now to consider how these timing elements are built into the notion of a fishing spot, or *pesqueiro* (Figure 1). The first point to bear in mind is that *pesqueiros* are the minimal microenvironmental units of fishing, but depending on their location in the estuary, they are only activated at certain times during the lunar cycle. *Pesqueiros* always fall within more inclusive types of physiographic zones, and are usually referred to as belonging to a specific shoreline (*costeiro*) which is in turn subsumed under one of the major sub-divisions of the fishing grounds (*beiradas*). Over 400 fishing spots are known and frequented by Valenca fishermen and each has a name ordinarily taken from a coastal landmark.

Fishing spots are found continuously along the shores of the estuary, but are actually distributed in discrete clusters. This is because each spot is always defined with reference to the phase of the lunar-tide cycle (neap, spring, waxing, or waning tide) when it may be used.[3] However, since a fishing spot may accommodate a range of techniques, three further factors act to partition it into what are called *lancos*, or water spaces for casting nets: (1) fortnightly current changes, (2) daily tide level changes, and (3) the position of the particular water space relative to the slope of the shore. Thus, a water space may be an area reserved for shooting nets, for setting trotlines, or for construction of a fish

FIGURE 1: Subdivisions of a Fishing Spot

Water Spaces	"Enseada"	"Lancinho"	"Bugaial"	"Tabatinga"
Position Relative to Shore	intertidal	high	mid	low
Depth in Meters	1 - 3	3	3 - 6	6 - 9
Fortnightly Tide Zones	spring	spring neap	neap waxing waning	waxing waning
Daily Tide Zones	high ebb low flood	high ebb low flood	ebb flood	low high
Techniques Used	fish corrals lift nets	beach seine	purse seine gill net	purse seine trot line
Bottom Composition	sand clay	mud	gravel	clay

corral, but because of different zoning and current considerations which apply to each, they do not overlap. *Lancos*, like *pesqueiros*, have distinctive names taken from their boundary markers, such as bottom type (e.g., *bugaial*, a type of gravel; *tabatinga*, a clay), or their position on shore relative to other *lancos*. In any case, the overall effect of timing considerations is to subdivide *pesqueiros* according to an order of technical priorities in which they and the *lancos* they contain are thought of by fishermen as geographical points within the lunar month.

By eliciting the characteristics of several hundred fishing spots, I was able to derive the pattern whereby, at least in theory, fishermen shift the focus of their activity during the tide cycle. This pattern was then compared with the locational data on actual fishing trips, and the correspondence between boat positions and tidally activated fishing zones proved extremely close. Moreover, the fishing pattern as shown by trip frequencies is striking in the way all groups of specialists consistently tend to concentrate in the same general locations from one tide level to the next. At neap tide the concentration is on the *costeiros* at the northern end of the estuary; as the tide begins to rise, people move into the main body of the estuary in from the mouth. At spring tide, activity shifts to the southern *costeiros* and finally, as the tide begins to fall, fishermen move back up the estuary into the main channels. Canoe fishing, in other words, moves in a circuit of logistic areas which are activated periodically by a tide cycle that has differential impact along the course of the estuary.

TERRITORIAL COMPETITION

We have now seen how the fishing grounds are sufficiently enclosed in a river-estuary system, so that fishing spots have come to be treated as unique locations with precise boundary markers for the different methods used. But to find out how fishermen implement their claims, and the implications this has for competition, it is necessary to focus once again on the lunar-tide system.

I have indicated how decisions about where to fish are taken on the basis of timing and zoning considerations contained in this system. Timing and zoning have separate functions, however, when it comes to competition for fishing territories which are at a premium. Taking zoning principles into account first, one can see that they establish a pattern of specialization on the fishing grounds by spatially dissociating fishermen using different methods. This happens because no two classes of nets compete for exactly the same type of micro-environment. The result is a "boat-spacing" effect. On the other hand, timing principles act to confine fishermen using the same nets to a series of logistic areas which must be shared from tide phase to tide phase. Superimposed on the zoning effect, tide-timing gives rise to a concentration of boats and emerges as the conflict-conducive aspect of the fishing pattern. On a strictly mechanical basis, timing principles tend to negate the boat-spacing effect of micro-environmental specialization by reducing the number of alternative fishing spots fishermen using identical nets have to choose from. Relative to the extent of the fishing grounds, the range of spots fishermen actually can work, after preliminary timing and zoning considerations have been applied, is surprisingly small. Restriction on choice options may be illustrated by listing the lunar-tide criteria used to eliminate parts of the fishing grounds which are not viable alternatives for a particular point in the tide cycle. The process is shown below for a typical fishing captain, who would ordinarily be selecting a fishing spot out of a total of 246 *pesqueiros* (or 1,470 possible *lancos*), on the basis of zoning considerations alone.

Lunar-tide Elements	No. Variants	Total No. Net-casting spaces	Reduced Fishing Spot Choices
1. Lunar Phase	(2) dark tide, moon tide	$\dfrac{1470}{(2)}$	735
2. Tide Cycle Phase	(4) neap, waxing, spring, waning	$\dfrac{1470}{(2) \times (4)}$	183
3. Lunar Position	(4) time of moonrise:dawn dusk, noon, midnight	$\dfrac{1470}{(2) \times (4) \times (4)}$	45
4. Daily Tide Levels	(3) high, flood, ebb	$\dfrac{1470 \times (2)^*}{(2) \times (4) \times (4) \times (3)}$	43

* There are actually six times during the 24 hour daily tide cycle when it is possible to use encircling nets. This is because high, flood, and ebb tides (the three variants) occur twice daily. Accordingly, all the net casting spaces are activated twice daily.

When timing considerations are introduced (each category contains a number of variants), the total range of fishing spots is eventually reduced to that group appropriate for a specific net at a certain time of day. Thus, moving through the list given above in flow chart fashion, we see that ultimately a fisherman is in theory free to choose from a range of only 43 alternatives from his total known set of 1,470 *lancos*. When the actual choice of where to fish is made, this set of alternatives is further reduced in terms of criteria of weather, production history, etc. It is therefore easy to see how a number of specialists using the same gear might compete for the same fishing spot, and even the same *lanco* on a given day, despite the fact that zoning considerations tend to keep specialists using different methods out of one another's way.

Because nets depend on the right combination of daily and monthly tide conditions to function efficiently, and without risk to equipment in terms of loss or damage, net fishing is subject to territorial competition on a daily, even hourly basis. Only one properly timeable daily fishing opportunity is really thought to exist in most net-fishing locations. Furthermore, opportunities to shoot a net are customarily held on a first-come, first-serve schedule. This puts net fishermen in a competitive position similar to fishermen on the open ocean, with no means short of beating their competitors to the most productive fishing areas, and "not moving for no one," once there (cf. Anderson and Wadel 1972: 612).

Though fishermen must share a so-called "common property" resource, they exercise definite temporary territorial claims to net-casting areas. Serious trouble may occur in net fishing because the stakes are high (catfish landings of several hundred dollars per boat are not uncommon), timing restrictions are acute and there is considerable pressure on available fishing spots. The average ratio of all net captain owners to total available net fishing waterspaces works out to be roughly one-sixth. When other fishing-spot choice criteria are applied after the initial lunar-tide breakdown, the range of choice fishermen need to operate their nets effectively is critically reduced. The opportunity to monopolize waterspace temporarily for net casting is thus in great demand in canoe fishing. Yet temporary ownership rights are difficult to establish and to enforce without disputes. What usually happens to create confusion is the arrival, simultaneously, of several boats in a fishing spot when there is evidence of a large school and only one properly timeable *lanco* in the area. When no one has a clear-cut prior claim, fishermen may draw lots to choose who will be the first to cast his net. Once an order of priorities is established, a tide marker, usually a pole stuck in the bank, is used to dictate the sequence of exploitation rights (not more than one tide-level change is allowed per boat). Sometimes this works, but often a boat will not close its net and draw in the catch in the time specified by the tide sequence. If the next boat in line begins its operations regardless, the two nets may become fouled. Or a boat captain may ignore the normal procedure in drawing lots and insist on casting his net, thereby forcing his competitors to accept a *fait accompli*.

This strategy, however, seldom goes unchallenged. On fishing spots with several *lancos*, net crews may work simultaneously. As I have indicated, *lanco* boundaries theoretically enable boats to keep a safe distance from one another. Where fish are concerned, however, there are no such limits, and fishermen tend to depart somewhat from predetermined water space as the need arises to secure a satisfactory catch. As a result, the crew working on one *lanco* may be cut out of the waterspace otherwise reserved for it by a crew working on an adjacent *lanco*. Still another possibility is that the best *lanco* on one fishing spot will overlap somewhat with that of another spot located immediately upstream or downstream. In this case, *lanco* boundaries may be correctly observed by the boats involved. What frequently happens, however, is that the crew working upstream takes too much time in hauling its net and in the process interferes with a downstream crew, even though the two begin operating at different tide levels. Such infringements, although they may appear trivial, nevertheless generate much hot debate and occasionally end in serious long-term disputes.

PERCEPTION OF CROWDING IN FISHING STRATEGIES

Possible timing conflicts like the above, which are of a purely ecological nature, provide much of the background for competition in canoe fishing. Without forcing the issue at this point, there are at least two things about canoe fishing which imply its vulnerability to population pressure under the impact of nylon nets. The conversion of a segment of the traditional fishing community to more efficient gear took place within the context of the spatial limitations inherent in following the lunar-tide routines which are adaptive to estuary fishing. Under this system, large otherwise potentially fishable areas are ruled out by adverse currents so that a "massing effect" of net specialists is created where spots are available. The number of actual choice alternatives is further reduced because not all spots defined as appropriate by lunar-tide reckoning are thought to offer equal potential for fishing. Instead, they are rank-ordered by considerations such as daily weather, distance from home port, and past history of production.

The second limitation in expanding fishing operations (without somehow simultaneously increasing the range of boats), concerns the fixed-territorial aspect of the fishing grounds. Because canoes as they are presently outfitted are unsuitable for ocean travel, all fishing activity is confined to the local river-estuary system. The lack of ice to preserve the catch and the scarcity of fish-marketing alternatives outside the town of Valenca itself further reinforce transportation limits that set the boundaries of fishing waters. Any addition of production units to the fishery, therefore, has had to be accommodated within a fixed territory.

The modernization trend in canoe fishing did not alter either of the above systemic or range restrictions. It involved only the application of a new and purportedly more efficient catching system. The new gear, however, did not displace traditional methods. It merely increased the total number of production units competing for use of the fishing grounds through the addition of several hundred new nets distributed among some 70 new crews and canoes. It is necessary to ask if the environmental base of fishing was adequate to absorb such a large and relatively sudden increase in fishing units.

As noted earlier, there is little possibility of excessive predation in these waters, since the estuary is periodically replenished by open ocean stocks. Fishing pressure, rather, would appear to be controlled by the number of fishing opportunities which may be appropriately scheduled to coincide with the arrival of fish at different phases in the tide cycle. Therefore, one way to evaluate population pressure on the fishing grounds would be in terms of numbers of production units (canoes rigged for net fishing) as against the numbers of available net-fishing spaces in contention. In this formulation, the notion of a carrying capacity threshold in fishing may be retained. However, it would be expressed simply in terms of the concentration of boats compared to the total configuration of fishing spaces (*lancos*) activated each day by lunar-tide reckoning. If the maximum permissible boat concentration/fishing space ratios were exceeded, then the stage might be set for unavoidable cut-throat competition, though not necessarily with implications of overfishing. To evaluate the impact of nylon nets, we must know whether fishermen still had the margin of choice they needed to make satisfactory decisions of where to fish. Or, had this decision become increasingly hazardous owing to scarcity of preferred water spaces?

To begin to get some idea of the expansion capacity threshold for net fishing in the sense of territorial access possibilities, I first calculated from my data on fishing spots (*pesqueiros*) how many net shooting spaces (*lancos*) were in theory available at the beginning of each of the four phases in the tide cycle (spring, neap, waning, and waxing). These calculations included only water spaces available for the main competitors: crews using a large traditional encircling net and dragged net, and the nylon beach seine and drift net. On the average 980 *lancos* were theoretically open for fishermen using these methods to choose from each day during the tide cycle. This figure can be taken as representing the maximum possible boat load the tidally activated fishing territories could support each day. By the same token, if all such water spaces were occupied whenever they were available by a separate fishing crew, this can be considered the "optimal" distribution of boats from the standpoint of minimizing territorial competition and maximizing access to the fishing grounds.

Having determined *lanco* possibilities, I proceeded to record the total number of actual fishing trips by both traditional and nylon net specialists to compare with the above "boat load" threshold. This was done for each phase of the tide cycle during a summer month (November), and in winter (August). Not all net crews in question made trips at all tide phases surveyed. On the average, 57 were tracked each day at the summer check and 79 in winter.

Figures on trips compared with water spaces available are summarized in Table 1. Before these data can be properly evaluated, it is important to note the basis for several discrepancies in the production unit/fishing space ratios. First, not only were there more boats fishing in winter (taking advantage of spawning runs up the estuary), but also fewer net-fishing areas were available to accommodate them. The winter shortage is due to the elimination of the northern ocean beach, neap-tide fishing grounds (see Map 2), along with portions of the spring-tide fishing grounds at the southern tip of the estuary. Rough water and unfavorable winds make travel to these areas difficult.

Second, there are absolutely fewer fishing spaces at neap and spring tide phases than when the tide is in its intervening waxing and waning stages. Spring tide, moreover, is the least well-supplied phase of all in terms of fishing space. These differences are very likely due to a distance factor. Both spring and neap-tide grounds are more distant than falling and rising phase grounds, which are centered on the main body of the estuary in the north. Farther away from home port, one might expect to find fishing spaces less concentrated than close in. In any case, relative distance must be considered by fishermen in deciding where to fish. Fewer boats worked the more distant neap and spring-tide grounds, at least on the days when trips were recorded, and fishermen generally recognized fewer appropriate water spaces for their nets in these zones. Variations in the number of lunar-tide correspondences thus reflect the total range limitations on nets caused by the variable action of the tides over the estuary.

TABLE 1
Boat Concentration/Fishing Space Ratios

Tide Phase	Spring Outer Southern Grounds	Waning Tide Inner Grounds	Neap Tide Outer Northern Grounds	Waxing Tide Inner Grounds	Averages
SUMMER					
Net Fishing Spaces	945	1270	915	1510	1160
No. Boat Trips	46	66	47	69	57
Boat-Load Fishing Space Ratios	1/21	1/19	1/19	1/22	1/20
WINTER					
Net Fishing Spaces	610	930	655	1065	820
No. Boat Trips	71	82	69	84	79
Boat-Load Fishing Space Ratios	1/9	1/10	1/9	1/12	1/11

At first glance, today's ratios of boats to available water space might indicate that there is still ample room for increasing the number of production units in fishing. Obviously, however, the maximum carrying capacity of fishing, if it is defined as complete utilization of water spaces, is unrealistic. This would allow no flexibility in choosing where to fish, and the tendency of fishing to concentrate in certain areas, of weather to change abruptly, and of boats to shift destination accordingly, makes some margin of flexibility in choosing fishing spots imperative.

I do not intend to attempt to determine an exact boat load figure which would signify the carrying capacity threshold of canoe fishing on the basis of choice margins. The point is, however, when criteria for rank-ordering fishing spot alternatives are introduced, such as weather, distance, and fishermen's desire to monopolize net casting areas, existing choice margins are really not generous (there are 57 sets of 21 nonoverlapping, noncompetitive fishing spot choices for summer net crews in contrast to 79 sets with eleven alternatives each for winter crews).

Nevertheless, it is possible to judge somewhat more conclusively the adequacy of alternative choice margins to enable net crews to avoid competitive encounters on the fishing grounds. One important consideration here is that competitive pressure over net territories has lessened in the ten year period since the first nylon nets were adopted. Many of these nets are no longer in use, and there has been a corresponding trend in specialization away from traditional net fishing. Present boat loads may thus be viewed as the natural outcome of earlier economic choices made by fishermen to ease competition.

A second consideration in evaluating expansion capabilities concerns the relative distance of fishing spots. As I have suggested, there are numerous reasons this factor may be used as an important ranking criterion in the way fishermen reduce alternative choices. It is often necessary to negotiate difficult tide changes in getting to and from the fishing grounds. Generally, the farther away from home port a spot is, the more difficult it becomes to time the optimal ordered sequences of fishing events—departure on an ebb tide, claiming a *lanco* before competitors arrive, net casting, and getting fish back to market on a flood tide at peak selling hours before they spoil in the sun.

If distance is indeed as critical as I assume in determining where fishermen go, then one would expect the outer limits of the fishing grounds not to be as heavily fished as the inner grounds. Yet, in the trips I recorded there is only a slight difference in boat leads, despite the considerable distance interval (roughly three hours rowing under sail) which separate inner and outer grounds. The outermost fishing areas activated at neap and spring tides are even further away in terms of time. Thus, even the slightly reduced boat loads on the outer neap and spring-tide grounds may be significant in interpreting canoe-fishing expansion potential. In these areas, fishing opportunities are fewer relative to other tidally activated zones. Their correspondingly reduced boat loads may thus represent an adjustment to minimum conditions for preserving the fishing spot choice margins needed for noncompetitive fishing. That is, the maximum number of production units that can be supported effectively by the range of Valenca waters may be limited by the tide phases when fishing spots are minimal, i.e., spring and neap tides to which the outer grounds are attached.

One source of evidence bearing on this possibility lies in the incidence of disputes over fishing rights. In questioning fishermen on this subject, I was able to record where and when disputes had taken place. If we look at the pattern of disputes occurring both before and after innovation with nylon nets, an interesting correlation with tide phase limitations is found. Disputes are itemized in terms of their chronological markers and locations in Table 2.

What these findings indicate is that competition for fishing spots and ensuing disputes occur more often on the least accessible fishing grounds, within the tide phases theoretically offering the fewest available fishing opportunities, relative to the demand for noncompetitive fishing space.

A final estimate of the degree of crowding in canoe fishing may now be made by asking what fishermen themselves consider to be a reasonable margin of choice, and whether this can be exercised. It proved impossible to count preferred locations and compare these data with boat loads to obtain precise measures of crowding since "preferred" sites are never fixed for more than a few hours. When they decide where to fish, captains always have fixed points of reference. They always return to the same considerations in the procedure used to rank-order options. In this fashion, trip destinations are predetermined but fishermen are able to switch to alternate locations as they receive fresh information on the way out to the estuary. Options are selected by anticipating the kinds of fresh information they may have to consider, such as a sudden change of weather.

While conducting some exploratory interviews on this question, I found that fishermen were considering factors other than timing, weather, and distance in ranking their options. Practically above all else, they tried to anticipate the chances of run-ins with competitors, and conversely, where their friends would be fishing—people they might rely upon for favors such as a tow back from the fishing grounds. In their probability calculations, fishermen were most of all concerned with the chances of having a spot to themselves. The question now is how to evaluate the relative weights of the various ranking criteria fishermen

TABLE 2
Location of Disputes

	Waxing and Waning Inner Grounds		Spring and Neap Outer Grounds	
	Summer	Winter	Summer	Winter
1950–1960 (Prior to Nylon Nets)	3	9	4	16
1960–1970	5	12	18	59
1971 (Fieldwork Period)	1	–	–	3

were using. In particular, how strongly did their expectations of competition and crowding affect their choices?

In setting up an interview to elicit these considerations, I assumed that fishing strategies would be planned according to perception of crowding, just as fishermen anticipated other factors to be operating. If the fishing grounds were indeed overcrowded due to "preferred" site scarcity, it seemed reasonable to expect this to show up in the kinds of fishing spot options selected. That is, depending on the value placed on certain of their characteristics, spots would either be rejected as unsuitable or left as options. The point was to determine whether anticipated competitive encounters were sufficient grounds for reducing alternatives, all other things being equal.

The first step in this process was to determine the range of fishing spots a captain had in view before the following day's fishing. My intention was to get fishermen to be explicit about the relative advantages and disadvantages of various spots, without forcing them to simplify among them. Ultimately, this procedure yielded a body of preliminary information concerning the process whereby certain fishing spots are eliminated from the total range being taken into account according to lunar-tide reckoning.

After this initial breakdown, it was possible to sort out the types of considerations which occurred most frequently to narrow down fishing alternatives. Below is a list of these:

1. Distance from home port.
2. Size of fish which could be caught.
3. Variety of fish which could be caught.
4. Whether day or night fishing would be possible.
5. How abruptly the daily tide would rise and fall in a specific location.
6. Whether the weights and tow lines on a fisherman's net were long enough to match the depth range of the *lanco*.
7. How many other net crews might be going for the same *lanco*.
8. Relationship with captains in charge of other net crews that might be encountered—i.e., whether past relations had been co-operative or competitive.
9. Possible wind changes on the way out to the *lanco*.
10. History of the previous catches on the *lanco*.

Having obtained both a realistic range of spots and decision criteria, the next step was to encourage fishermen to narrow their choices, much as they would do naturally in planning a fishing trip. As before, I had them discuss the advantageous and disadvantageous characteristics of the spots they were considering. However, this time they were asked to rank each fishing alternative on all the criteria obtained previously. From these orderings, four factors emerged as almost equally critical in differentiating spots: relative distance, the number of identical net crews which would likely be trying to work the same spot, wind changes that either impede or facilitate navigation, and memories of previous catches.

Having established these principles, a final series of interviews was conducted with five traditional and five nylon-net fishing captains. Each fisherman was asked to name his range of preferred sites for the following day's trip and differentiate each according to the above four criteria. This was done on three consecutive days for a spring-tide and rising-tide phase to cover fishing plans for inner and outer grounds. As fishermen verbalized their choice simplification procedure, their considerations for a criteria preference scale was formed. For traditional fishermen, all other things being equal, perceived competitive possibilities emerged as the foremost criterion for ranking options, followed by distance, production history, and wind changes. While nylon-net fishermen perceived crowding as a factor, it was only third in importance behind distance and memory of previous catches.

Too few fishermen were interviewed on this topic to draw any wide-ranging conclusions about the role of anticipated competition in motivating fishing strategies. If pressure on prime water space were not much of a problem, however, it is doubtful that it would have entered so consistently into captains' plans. The fact that nylon-net fishermen seem to be paying less attention to expected boat concentrations may be due to the fact that they stand less to lose in equipment in a competitive encounter than the traditional captains. Nylon-net captains do not own their equipment, and thus may be more prone to risk-taking.

SUMMARY

In a small-scale coastal fishing system like the one just described, the carrying capacity issue may appear in several forms, disguised as an economic slump, an increase in competition, or an escalation of disputes arising at sea or on land which are carried over into fishing. The carrying capacity issue came to light in Brazil as I examined how fishing captains plan their trips to different parts of estuary fishing grounds. In any given year, a wide range of catches is possible compared with previous years. Catches may paradoxically increase for a short period and then begin an abrupt decline. When modernization occurs, this catch fluctuation is even more likely, as competition for prime production areas increases. A fishery with customary permanent or temporary territorial rights may revert to the status of common property, a trend which is detrimental to the whole industry. Thus, the first task of carrying capacity analysis is to distinguish actual population-induced welfare reduction from ordinary economizing behavior under conditions of temporary resource scarcity. However, both situations make it necessary to alter the strategy of production. Where population pressure is truly manifest, peoples' conception of the distribution and availability of a resource may change radically. Here I have outlined a way to evaluate the carrying capacity of a fixed-territorial fishery indirectly by focusing on fishermen's perceptual change of resource and territorial availability. Information on this topic is readily accessible through analysis of the daily decision-making procedure used to select fishing spots.

The second goal of this carrying capacity study, where the lack of proper biological surveys forced me to seek alternative measures, is to examine fishermen's own conceptions of the sources of fishing pressure, its tolerable limits, and its consequences. Carrying capacity represents an ideal threshold, but I have found that fishermen in Brazil definitely seem to operate and organize production in terms of what might be called an ethnoecological model of resource use. Even under their own traditional methods, they regard both overfishing and cut-throat competition as a situation which may well develop given the proper incentives. The incentive most to be avoided is any outside factor which will disrupt the flow of authority over fishing territories and their customary means of recruitment of manpower to fishing. Controls on the opportunity structure of fishing are consciously and deliberately exercised by traditional captains who own chunks of lunar-tide fishing space. The knowledge of how to exploit fish stocks and the use of fishing equipment is passed on to only a few apprentices who will become really proficient net-casting specialists. In the Brazilian case, prior to the introduction of nylon nets, competition was directly curbed by fishing property rights which had evolved over generations along with a strict ethic of co-operation in all activities surrounding production. Moreover, the cyclical shift of activity from inner to outer grounds resulting from tide-level changes provided some relief to fish stocks native to the local estuaries which would otherwise be exploited on a continual basis.

With certain modifications along lines I have suggested, the biological concept of carrying capacity may be retained to help visualize the limits to fishery expansion. In the case of canoe fishing in Bahia, traditional fishermen themselves did much toward stabilizing their production system. The critical point here is the time depth of their adaptation. Through an extended period of trial and error, it was possible for fishermen to interpret expansion limits and set the intensity of fishing accordingly. In planning their economic strategies as if there were always a potential overfishing situation, they had established temporary territorial claims which insured that only a gradual expansion of fishing operations took place. Thus, the opportunity structure of traditional fishing, and by extension the population as a whole, was able to grow at a resource harvest rate which was compatible with continuing resource availability within a fixed location. Trouble only came to canoe fishing when the previously adaptive ratio of production units to available water space was disrupted by the unregulated entry of a competitive group of nylon fishing entrepreneurs.

APPENDIX*

Fish Taken in Valenca Waters

Local Name	Scientific Name	English Name
Agulha		
Agulhão bandeira	*Istiophorous albicans*	Sailfish
Agulhão verdadeira	*Tylosurus marinus*	Billfish
Amoreatim	—	—
Aracanguira	*Alectis ciliaris*	Threadfish
Aramaçã	—	—
Arraia duas bocas	—	Ray
Arraia fita	—	—
Arraia jamanta	*Monfa biuostris*	Devilray
Arraia jereba	—	Ray

Arraia pimenta	—	Ray
Arraia pintada	*Aetobatus narinari*	Ray
Arraia verdadeira	—	Ray
Badejo	*Acanthistus brasilianus*	Sea bass
Bagre amarelo	*Tachysurus luniscutsis*	Catfish
Bagre arituí	—	Catfish
Bagre arituaçú	—	Catfish
Bagre baguri	*Genidens genidens*	Catfish
Bagre bandeira	—	Catfish
Bagre bôca mole	—	Catfish
Bagre	*Tachysurus barbus*	Catfish
Bagre sapo	—	Catfish
Baiacú	*Lachtophrys trigonus*	Common trunkfish
Baiacuara	—	—
Baiacú de espinha	*Cyclichtys spinosus*	Puffer ?
Baiacú-ferreira	—	—
Baiacú-mirim	—	—
Barbeiro	*Acanthurus bahianus*	—
Barbudo	*Polynemus virginicus*	Goatfish ?
Beijuperá	*Rachycentrou canadus*	White grunt
Bicuda	*Sphyraena* sp.	—
Bobó	—	—
Bomhomen	—	—
Botó	—	—
Budião	—	—
Cabeçudo	*Caranx hippos*	Crevalle jack
Cação agulhão	—	Shark
Cação baiacú	—	Shark
Cação bico doce	*Justelus canis*	Smooth dogfish shark
Cação canexa	—	Shark
Cação cauacú	—	Shark
Cação estrella	—	Shark
Cação lixa	*Nebrius cirratum*	Shark
Cação Lustroso	—	Shark
Cação mambimba	—	Shark
Cação panã	—	Shark
Cação sombrero	*Sphyrna tudes*	Hammerhead shark
Cação sucurapoia	—	Shark
Cação-tintureiro	*Galeocerdo cuvier*	Tiger shark

Cação-viola	*Rhinobatus percelens*	Guitar fish
Cambuba	—	—
Camurupim	*Tarpon atlanticus*	Tarpon
Caranha	—	—
Carapeba	*Diapterns rhombeus*	—
Carapau	*Cloroseombrus chrysurus*	—
Carapicum	*Encinostromus californiensis*	—
Canapum	*Promicrops itaiara*	Jewfish
Cascudo	*Plecostomus* sp.	—
Caramura	—	Eel
Chumberga	*Caranx srysos*	Bluerunner
Clariosa	—	—
Curimã	*Mugil cephalus*	Striped mullet
Dentão	*Lufjanus aga*	Snapper
Dourado	*Coryphaena hippurus*	Dolphin fish
Durmioco	—	—
Enchova	*Pomatomus saltutrix*	Bluefish
Galo (verdadeiro)	*Vomer setapinnis*	Moonfish
Gato	—	—
Guaçani	—	—
Guaribebé	—	—
João de ar	—	—
João Duro	—	—
Jabú	—	—
Juruna	*Elops lacerta*	Ten pounder
Linguado	*Paralychthys brasilienis*	Flounder
Maçambí	—	—
Manjuba	*Anchoviella hubbsi*	Anchovy
(vermelha)	—	Anchovy
(lirio)	—	Anchovy
(cara de cachorro)	—	Anchovy
(de roda)	—	Anchovy
Margarida	*Diplecturm formosum*	—
Mariuá	—	—
Merete	*Promiorops ?*	Small jewfish
Mikim	—	—
Mirorô	—	—
Mirorô-mirim	—	—
Mirucaia	—	Thimble-eye mackerel
Mucutuca	—	Eel

Mucutucuçú	—	Eel
Navalha	—	—
Obarana	*Elops sauras*	Ladyfish
Olho de miguel	—	—
Olho de vidro	—	—
Pampo (espinha-mole)	*Trachinotus glaucus*	Pompano
Papa-terra	*Menticirrhus martinisensis*	Kingfish
Piampara	—	—
Piaú	*Leopovinnus* sp.	—
Parú	*Pomacanthus para*	Spadefish
Penima	—	—
Peixe Porco	*Balistes vetula*	Triggerfish
Peixe-pena	—	—
Pegador	—	—
Pescada amarela	*Cynoscion acoupa*	Sea trout
Pescada aratanha	*Bairdiella ronchus*	Ground drum
Pescada branca	*Cynoscion leiarchus*	Sea trout
Pescada camina	—	Sea trout
Pescada de dente	—	Sea trout
Pescada perereca	—	Sea trout
Pescada sete bouchas	—	Sea trout
Pescada savage	—	Barracuda
Pipira de lixa	—	—
Pirira clariosa	—	—
Pira boca	*Lobotes surinameusis*	Tripletail
Premetara	—	—
Rabo Aberto	*Ocynrus chrysurus*	Yellowtail
Redondo	*Peprilus paru*	Harvest fish
Rico manda	—	—
Robalo branco	*Centropomus ensiferus*	Snook
Robalo caramuri	—	Snook
Robalo camurupi	—	Snook
Robalo ripa	—	Snook
Roncador	*Boridia grossidens*	Grunt
Sabão	—	—
Sardinha verdadeira	*Sardinella aurita*	Smooth sardine
Sauara	—	—
Saúna	—	—
Saramonete	—	—
Sardinha mulata	—	Sardine
Sardinha de água clara	—	Sardine
Sororoca	*Scomberomorus commersoni*	King mackerel

Taínha	*Mugil brasiliensis*	Mullet
Taínha bandeira	—	Mullet
Taínha pratibú	—	Mullet
Tapa	*Eropus crossatus*	—
Tapa redonda	—	—
Tirirí		
Treme-treme	*Narcine brasiliensis*	Red gurnard
Traeira	—	
Vermelho	*Lutjanus aya*	Lane snapper
Voador	*Exocoetus evolans*	Flying fish
Xangô	—	
Xaréu	*Caranx* sp.	Jack

* Note: The list contains a fair number of locally named species which either have no accepted English equivalents or for which I was unable to obtain a scientific classification. Where correspondences are given, however, they were taken from *Glossario de nomes dos peixes:portugues, ingles, sistematico. Boletim de Estudos de Pesca* 4:11-40.

NOTES

1. I express my appreciation to the American Philosophical Society for a grant-in-aid which made this research possible. Also, I thank Charles Frake and Charles Drucker for their comments on an early draft and Sally Stevenson, who drew the figures.
2. The utility of the usual form of carrying capacity analysis to predict population pressure has been criticized on a number of grounds: (1) diminished welfare can be the result of various processes, not simply population growth (Street 1969:104-107; Bender 1971:40). The a priori assumption of the model is that production functions are fixed or that the populations considered do not optimize under conditions of scarcity; (2) that existing consumption levels accurately represent the nutritional status quo of the population; (3) that no universally applicable carrying capacity measure can be derived since the ethics of land-use vary cross-culturally and through time (Johnson 1974).
3. On Charles Frake's suggestion I have adopted the terms "waxing" and "waning" to refer to the tide changes between spring and neap which coincide with the intervals of lunar passage. For the period between new moon and first quarter, for example, Brazilian fishermen use the term *mare de quebra*. The period between first quarter and full they call *mare de lancamento*. So far, I have been unable to find recognized English nautical equivalents for the Portuguese.

BIBLIOGRAPHY

Allan, W.   1965.   The African Husbandsman. New York.
Anderson, R., and C. Wadel (eds.)   1972.   North Atlantic Fishermen: Anthropological Essays on Modern Fishing. Newfoundland Social and Economic Papers, No. 5, Institute of Social and Economic Research. Memorial University.
Bender, D. R.   1971.   Population and Productivity in Tropical Forest Bush Fallow Agriculture. Culture and Population, A Collection of Current Studies, ed. S. Polgar, pp. 32-45. Carolina Population Center, Monograph No. 9, University of North Carolina.
Carneiro, R.   1956.   Slash and Burn Agriculture: A Closer Look at its Implications for Settlement Patterns. Man and Culture, ed. A. Wallace, pp. 229-234. Philadelphia.
Cordell, J.   1974.   The Lunar-Tide Fishing Cycle in Northeastern Brazil. Ethnology 13: 379-392.
Forman, S. O.   1966.   Jangadeiros: Raft Fishermen of Northeastern Brazil. Unpublished Ph.D. dissertation, Columbia University.
————   1970.   The Raft Fishermen. Bloomington.

Grossinger, R. S.   1975.   The Strategy and Ideology of Lobster Fishing on the Back Side of Mt. Desert Island, Hancock County, Maine. Unpublished Ph.D. dissertation, University of Michigan.

Harpending, H.   1974.   Genetic Structure of Small Populations. Annual Review of Anthropology 3: 229-243.

Johannes, R. E.   1976.   Exploitation and Degradation of Shallow Marine Food Resources in Oceania. The Impact of Urban Centers in the Pacific, ed. R. W. Force and B. Bishop, pp. 47-72. Pacific Science Association. Honolulu.

Johnson, A.   1974.   Carrying Capacity in Amazonia: Problem in Theory and Method. Paper presented at the 73rd Annual Meeting of the American Anthropological Association, Mexico City.

Klee, G.   1972.   The Cyclic Realities of Man and Nature in a Palauan Village. Unpublished Ph.D. dissertation, University of Oregon.

———   1976.   Traditional Time Reckoning and Resource Utilization. Micronesia 12: 211-246.

Marr, J. C.   1976.   Fishery and Resource Management in S.E. Asia. Resources for the Future Program of International Studies in Fishery Arrangements. No. 7, Washington.

Nietschmann, B. O.   1974.   When the Turtle Collapses, the World Ends. Natural History 83: 34-43.

Street, J. M.   1969.   An Evaluation of the Concept of Carrying Capacity. The Professional Geographer 21: 104-107.

Society, Economy, and Shark-Fishing Crews in Rural Northwest Mexico[1]

James R. McGoodwin

In this paper I explore aspects of social and economic organization in Teacapán, Sinaloa, a rural-mestizo community on Mexico's northwest coast. Like many of Mexico's small rural communities, Teacapán is neither closed, corporate, peasant, nor traditional; rather, it is open, wage dependent, has modern inclinations, and is trying to adapt to the radical changes occurring in the nation at large.

In this century, particularly during the past 25 years, many Mexican communities have become separated from traditional patterns of social and economic life. A large number have emerged from semi-isolation, becoming more involved with the life of the nation. Many have lost direct access to natural resources, continuity of tradition, and have been transformed into societies of culturally impoverished rural proletarians, peoples who emulate the values of the modern world while enjoying few of its comforts and many of its miseries. Teacapán is one such community.

My studies have focused on an activity which affects the lives of more than half of the total populace of Teacapán: shark fishing. Of particular interest has been the problem of selecting shark-boat crewmen, since this form of employment offers the highest wages and some of the steadiest work available in this poor, wage-dependent milieu (see Table 1). By determining who is chosen for the town's best job, and why, important aspects of Teacapán social and economic life are revealed.

Three categories of information are presented in order to facilitate an understanding of the crew choices of Teacapán's shark-boat owners: first, the owner's stated preferences, which suggest value orientations guiding their decisions but which also contain potentially misleading information; second, a description of the ethnographic setting, or situation, in which the choice behavior occurs; and third, an analysis of the boat owner's empirical choices which underscores the important value orientations motivating them.

Teacapán has a personal society, which I define as one in which every adult is personally acquainted with every other to a high degree.[3] It also has a highly kin-articulated society. Nevertheless, Teacapán's pattern of interpersonal organization, particularly in regard to ramifications of local kinship in economic life, departs significantly from those patterns commonly associated with more traditional, rural-peasant societies.

TABLE 1
Wage-Labor Incomes in Teacapán and Region[2]

Type of Work	Daily income in pesos (1 peso = $0.08 U. S.)
(1) Shark-fishing crewman	50.00 – 75.00
(2) Skilled (equipment operator, master construction worker, etc.)	40.00 – 55.00
(3) Unskilled	
a. Heavy work (mostly in fishing and agriculture)	25.00 – 35.00
b. Light work (most jobs in town)	20.00 – 30.00

THE SHARK-BOAT OWNER'S ACCOUNTS

When shark-boat owners were asked about their employee preferences, initial responses struck me as indefinite or ambiguous and did not permit an immediate understanding of the essential criteria motivating them. Viewed retrospectively, their accounts contain both important clues and some misleading information. The modal responses were "family members" and *"bien conocidos"* (literally, "well-known people"). The latter response seemed at first trivial since nearly all adults in the town are well known to all others. Later, I learned that *bien conocido* in local parlance implies a person of long-standing residence who also has numerous locally-residing relatives.

As the research continued, many informants stressed the importance of kinship in the organization of the local shark-fishing industry. Mention of a particular crewman usually prompted the detailing of his many relatives also employed as shark fishermen, and it was common to hear crewmen greeting one another with terms of kin address. During the early phases of this study it seemed natural enough to suppose that certain ramifications of local kinship might underlie the local shark-fishing organizational structure. The informants promoted this view by stressing that the most important people in their lives were their families; relatives and close friends were placed next in importance, while the bulk of the remaining was portrayed as untrustworthy.

However, as the ensuing study reveals, kinship *per se* is not the organizational basis of local shark fishing despite the insistence of many informants to the contrary. Members of bilateral societies often use the terms "family" and "relative" synonymously, while anthropologists conversely find these terms to represent highly contrastive entities.

Other accounts were more disparate, but likewise contained important clues. "Someone I do not have to pay" was elicited a few times, as was "someone who takes orders without complaint." Many accounts were artfully humorous, but perhaps too salty for mention here. The only rule-like, concensual preference elicited was that shark-boat crewmen must be old enough to work, and male, but that did not narrow the field very much.

ETHNOGRAPHIC SETTING: SOCIETY AND ECONOMY

Situated at the mouth of an estuary's emptying into the Pacific Ocean, Teacapán is located about 70 miles south of Mazatlán, the dominant urban center in the region (Map 1). The town's settlement pattern is nucleated; nearly all 2,597 inhabitants are crowded into eleven small blocks. The people of the town and surrounding region are all Spanish-speaking, rural-mestizo Mexicans and comprise a culturally homogeneous, residentially stable population. Although this region is within the confines of Old Mesoamerica and once had a large indigenous population, no Indians are presently in evidence; Sinaloa today is one of Mexico's least Indian states (Spicer 1964; Beals 1932; Scott 1967-1971; Marino Flores 1967).

The Local Society

The town has no self-identified social or economic classes. Wealthy local individuals have poor relatives living in the town and vice-versa. This great cultural homogeneity, as Balán (1970) observed of a rural-mestizo, open community in Mexico's interior, is not conducive to the crystallization of classes. Local wealth differentials and the competition for scarce resources create a social environment of considerable conflict and tension which suggests a tendency towards a poor quality of interpersonal relations.

The major social and economic changes of this century have converted Teacapán's people from rural peasants to rural proletarians. Their vulnerability and exposure to the rapidly changing nation continually forces them to reassess their own values and adjust to new ones imposed from outside their community.

For most families, total household incomes barely cover subsistence needs; the situation is considerably worse in the region's surrounding villages and hamlets. Onslaughts of insects, poor and scarce drinking water, the absence of sewerage or plumbing facilities, and insufficient medical care combined contribute to an unusually high incidence of chronic, endemic, infectious and parasitic diseases. Most houses are simple thatch and daub, yet even the more permanent houses of the town's affluent families are relatively bare and austere.

The local society is personal, even though everyone does not interact face-to-face on a daily basis. But however personal, the society is not highly integrated; rather, it is atomistic in both the psychological and empirical senses of the descriptive paradigm discussed by Rubel and Kupferer *et al.* (1968) and especially Honigmann (1968: 234). Local orientations stress individualism, self reliance, caution in dealings with others, and living *sin compromisos* (without obligations), which Foster (1967: 139) also finds to be a central value guiding

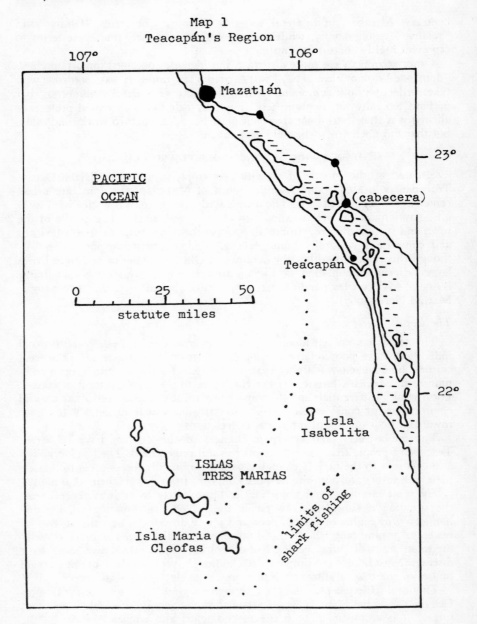

Map 1
Teacapán's Region

interpersonal relationships in the open, rural-mestizo community of Tzintzuntzan, Mexico. In social organization, Teacapán manifestly lacks supra-household, institutionalized, collective activities; households are the important structural units of the society as well as focal points of socialization, social life, and individual security. In much the same manner as the Middle American Indian households described by Hunt and Nash (1967: 257), Teacapán's households each function as small, independent, competitive economic firms. As Reina (1966: 222) and Wagley (1949: 17) observe, household membership, regardless of its importance in individual welfare, usually denotes an existence of dependency, subjugation, and labor exploitation among the household's subordinate members.

Teacapán also lacks an effective leadership structure. Politically it is a dependency of the *cabecera* (head town) of the *municipio* (similar to a county within a state in the United States) of which it is a part. It is an open society having none of the autonomy or integrative institutions characteristic of closed, corporate, rural-peasant communities in Middle America (see Hunt and Nash 1967: 259; Wolf 1957). Since the town's public offices are not actively sought, most of the important civil posts are filled by short-term appointees from the *cabecera*.

Religious involvement is practically insignificant in daily life. There are no religious sodalities or other institutions which involve large numbers of persons in religious affairs. Only about 2 per cent of the total population attends Sunday Mass in the town's small Catholic church. The important fiestas are those of the Mexican nation, secular affairs where a few concessionaries sponsor money-making enterprises, the cost of which relegate most to the status of mere onlookers. There were gala, community-wide fiestas until the late 1950s which featured religious rituals, feasts, and a variety of traditional folk dances and games. Today's fiestas, however, seem more oriented toward entertaining a growing number of visitors from regional urban centers.[4] Similarly, other traditional beliefs, *brujería* (witchcraft) and *ojo* (evil eye) for example, now seem regarded as signs of backwardness or ignorance. "We may be poor and somewhat common," many will say, "but we are a modern people."

Interpersonal Relations, Ascribed and Achieved

The important ascriptive ties are co-residents of households, bilateral kinsmen, affinal kinsmen (especially the close lineal relatives of the in-marrying tie), and ritual kinsmen (especially peers, or socio-economic near equals).

Lineal and co-lineal bilateral kinsmen are the most ascriptive social ties. Local behavioral norms prescribe respect and mutual assistance among such persons, while actual behavior often deviates widely from this ideal. Breaches of respect protocol, and especially requests of financial assistance, are common sources of ill feeling among close, bilateral kinsmen. Complaints that kinsmen exploit their affiliation by taking excessive liberties in visiting and loitering about the household, especially when unemployed, are frequently voiced. Structurally, the bilateral descent system is not conducive to the formation of alliances of economically-co-operating groups of kinsmen. As Murdock (1949: 61; 1960), Pospisil and Laughlin (1963: 187), and others observe, kindreds in bilateral systems are ego centered, overlap endlessly, and can rarely function as well defined collectivities. Hence, it is not surprising that there are no corporate kin groups in Teacapán. Large gatherings of bilateral kinsmen are rare; the only important exceptions are saint's day observances, or funeral services for an elderly ancestor.

While the local society ascribes a social tie entailing some obligations among close kinsmen, at the same time kinsmen residing in different households may be competitors for the same, scarce resources. Hence, it is not surprising that close bilateral kinsmen are often regarded as among one's most potentially problematic ties. It is fortunate for Teacapán's employers that the society reckons descent bilaterally, thus allowing a greater freedom of choice in the selection of laborers than would be enjoyed were the local society organized according to lineage principles.

Affinal kinship in Teacapán's social life is less ascriptive and less important than bilateral kinship; local behavioral norms prescribe only a modicum of obligatory courtesy among affinally-related persons. In reality, many affinal relationships are marked by strain and discourtesy; some are actively disavowed, even though the society at large still ascribes the tie. Ideally, post-marital residence is neolocal, but in practice most are ambilocal. Therefore, marriage often disrupts the composition and functioning of the spouses' respective households; one usually loses a member valuable in providing income or performing household chores, the other often gains an unwelcome, new member. Further, many marriages are initiated without parental consent (as following elopement or outright abduction), and few are subsequently formalized in any way except civil registry. Divorce and family abandonment are also common. Teacapán marriage, as observed by Diaz (1964) in another mestizo-Mexican town, often defines opponents while providing no machinery for solidarity.

Ritual kin relationships (*compadrazgo*) are highly variable in nature. *Compadre* ties among peers are initiated cautiously, since ideally these obligate the participants to nearly sacred obligations of mutual respect and aid. Employer-employee dyads among peers are avoided, since these might negate the inherent presumption of interpersonal equality. Over a lifetime, a large number of both the peer and vertically phrased interpersonal ties are established. Nevertheless, at any given time most men will name only one *compadre*, invariably a peer, whom they regard as their special ally, while the rest of their ritual kinsmen are regarded simply as persons who once helped them to fulfill ritual obligations to the Catholic Church. Therefore, the *compadrazgo*, a mechanism facilitating formal relationships in societies prescribing few other institutionalized ties, is a factor urging neither social cohesiveness nor integration in Teacapán. This pattern is much like that described by various researchers interested in rural, Middle American, atomistic communities (Spielberg 1968; Sayres 1956; Foster 1967: 79-85; Mintz and Wolf 1950: 196).

A final category of achieved, yet institutionalized, social relationship is the *amigo de confianza* (trusted friend) or simply *mucho amigo* (great friend), which is very similar to the institutionalized *camarada* found by Reina (1959) in a rural, Guatemalan Indian community. Among Teacapaneños who stress the importance of this tie, it is described as a special sort of personal liking, loyalty, and alliance. Although such ties are most important among males, particularly adolescents, five years' observation convinces me that most are transitory. Teacapán's "great friends" often infuse these relationships with continual accusations of disloyalty or expressions of possessiveness, a burden few relationships can long endure. Also, most such ties are activated for practical, mutually beneficial reasons, and they quickly dissolve when their usefulness has passed.

Most of Teacapán's enduring "great friend" and "trusted friend" ties are between spatially distant individuals, persons living in different towns or even nations. This pattern is very similar to that observed by Piker in rural Thailand (1968: 200-204).

Overall, Teacapán's pattern of interpersonal relations is much like that reported by Foster (1967) in rural-mestizo Tzintzuntzan, Mexico; most of the really significant ties are dyadic and achieved. In this same vein, Lynch (1959: 12-13) observes that "in a community where most men are kin, a man must live by the friends he makes."

Local Economy

In this century Teacapán's economy has evolved from one in which individual subsistence depended upon open access to natural resources to today's dependency upon wage labor. The typical Teacapaneño, as Harris (1971: 261) would say, "pays for the priviledge of staying alive by selling his labor." Casual visitors in this region, often impressed by its natural beauty and wont to romanticize a life spent close to nature, usually do not realize that most fishermen are not catching fish to eat nor are most men laboring in the fields raising their own food; rather, both are working to secure national currency, which they must trade for life's necessities.

Most of the town's population is landless; fewer than 10 per cent of the adult males own land. Of the community's *ejidal* land, much is taken up by house sites, while most of the remainder permits only marginal agricultural activity. Nearly all of the region's best lands are latifundia, either privately owned by a handfull of local individuals, or held by agro-corporations; both types sporadically employ large numbers of day-wage laborers. Poorer lands, such as those fringing the estuaries, briny lagoons, and mangrove swamps, comprise nearly all of the region's small holdings—both *ejidal* and lands owned by the town's few independent small farmers.

The alienation of the population from regional land resources results from a number of changes occurring in this century, particularly during the last two decades. First, land ownership has never been widespread, although land access once was. Prior to the revolution begun in 1910, nearly all of the region's land was part of a large hacienda. This hacienda, which specialized in cattle grazing, allowed the region's *peones* the use of small garden plots. The revolutionary conflict scattered and decimated much of Teacapán's population. In the revolution's aftermath, three local individuals were able to seize the hacienda's best lands, while its poorer, marginal lands became the substance of various governmental land redistribution programs. However, phenomenal population growth has long since exhausted the government's capacity to make available any more of these marginal lands.

More significant, however, has been a great change in regional modes of production and marketing. The former agrarian economy emphasized subsistence gardening and swidden cultivation, cattle grazing, and an orientation toward local and regional markets; today's agrarian economy emphasizes capital intensive, mass production which is oriented toward national and international markets. Whereas the pre-revolutionary hacienda permitted the region's *peones* to grow crops on small plots of fairly good land, today's small plots are usually on marginal land, much of which is subject to periodic flooding of brackish water. Therefore, continuity of primary individual subsistence upon small plots is a risky or practically impossible undertaking.

It is also ironic that primary individual subsistence upon marine resources is likewise a marginal activity, especially since estuarial marine life has been the mainstay of the regional diet and economy since pre-historic times (Scott 1967-1971). Although cataclysmic flooding has always caused wide fluctuations in local marine resources, other recent changes which are all by-products of advanced technological growth in the nation have been more significant in alienating the local people from these resources.

Beginning in the early 1950s, motorized boats and larger, more durable nets were extensively employed in the estuaries and resulted in a general impoverishment of the marine-ecological system over the ensuing decade. Continuing pressure through present times has never permitted any substantial recovery of these resources. Consequently, estuarial commercial fishing is now relegated to a marginal enterprise, and individual subsistence fishing is no longer relied upon to provide the mainstay of the local families' diets. Aggravating the estuarial ecological imbalance is the increasing use of chemical fertilizers and pesticides in regional agriculture, much of which eventually washes into the estuaries and does further damage to marine life.

Of greater consequence, however, has been the recent growth of large, complex, and technologically sophisticated urban-based fishing enterprises in northwestern Mexico. Although these operate on the high seas, their activities hasten the decline of estuarial marine life, because of the interconnected nature of open sea and inland-water ecological systems; shrimp, for example—the Teacapaneño's most important marine resource—must spend part of their life cycle in the open sea, part in estuaries. In addition, the urban-based organizations are able to dominate the seafood markets, and they have also been extremely effective politically, convincing governmental agencies to restrict harvesting in the estuaries, the Teacapaneño's traditional fishing territories, in the name of resource management and governmental supervision of northwest fisheries' growth. Since the early 1960s, Teacapaneños have risked fine and imprisonment for fishing in certain formerly dependable waters.

Wage Labor

The town's wage-labor force is almost exclusively male; there are no marketing activities nor craft specializations of the type which economically involve women in other rural, Middle American communities.[5] Of the total population, about 750 are working-age males (14-60 years): 44 per cent of these work predominantly in fishing, 42 per cent in agriculture, and 14 per cent have town-oriented and miscellaneous occupations. Only 23 per cent of the male labor force is independent or self employed. This minority comprises the owners of boats, land, or other business enterprises. The remaining 77 per cent of the male labor force is wage dependent. Most workers are relatively unskilled and poorly educated; the average adult educational level is slightly under three years. Although there is no institutionalized career pattern, occupational specializations in fishing or agriculture evidence generational depth. Regional wage-labor rates are comparatively high for rural Mexico (Table 1), but this fact is mitigated by the sporadic or seasonal nature of most work; in a year's time most laborers have a variety of short-term jobs. Hence, it is common to see men loitering about, with apparently little to do, since at any given time there is a surplus of available laborers relative to the availability of wage work.

Most laborers seek work among a multiplicity of local *patrones*, or employers, (the 23 per cent of the town's adult males who are independent by virtue of their ownership and control of income-producing assets). Employer-employee dyads entail highly explicated agreements, usually personal in nature, and incorporating elements of paternalism and exploitation on the part of the employer, dependency and subordination on the part of the employee. An employee's dependent status is often reinforced through debt peonage, a mechanism whereby most local employers assure the availability of their laborers. But however exploitive, local employers prefer to hire individuals whom they have enjoyed harmonious working relationships with over an extended period of time. Most laborers favor this personal type of arrangement over wage work on the region's corporately-owned landholdings, which hire labor impersonally and seldom extend credit to workers not actively employed.[6]

Shark Fishing

Teacapán's shark-fishing industry began in the early 1940s, when the Allied Powers began to offer high prices for shark-liver oil; prior to this time, fishing on the open sea was a minor activity. During these boom years, a number of Teacapaneños became specialists in shark fishing, acquiring its basic skills, technology, and capital. The local industry dwindled following the war but has now made a total recovery, based upon the marketing of diverse products: shark's fins, hides, meat, liver oil, and fishmeal. Two factors which promoted the industry's resurgence were the general decline in estuarial fishing and the completion during the 1960s of an all-weather road linking the town with the *cabecera*. The newly paved road facilitated not only the marketing of shark products but also the intensification of the town's involvement with the rest of the nation, and with tourism. Along this coast, where nearly all commercial fishing on the high seas is large scale and government controlled, Teacapán's shark-fishing industry is a rare example of relatively simple, small scale, individual free enterprise. Each boat owner is a lone entrepreneur in competition with all others; the local industry is neither a collective nor a co-operative enterprise, but rather a large number of people all engaged in the same activity. This situation may be short lived, however, due to national-government plans to bring coastal shark fishing under strict control.

Nineteen men, all household heads, own Teacapán's 28 shark-fishing boats. The boats range from simple, motorized dugout canoes to sturdy, seaworthy launches, the latter comprising a majority of the crafts. A typical launch has a wooden hull, measuring approximately 30 feet in length by 10 feet through the beam, and is equipped with a powerful diesel engine. These vessels represent a considerable investment, about 75,000 *pesos*, or 6,000 U.S. dollars. None carry communications equipment, lifesaving gear, or any navigational equipment except simple compasses, even though some voyages extend as far as 80 miles from the mainland coast (Map 1).

Most shark boats require three crewmen. Although their tasks overlap considerably, crew members can be differentiated as follows: the *jefe* (boss) is responsible to the owner, and is in command at sea; the *marinero* (seaman) is a general laborer and seaman; and the *pavo* (literally, a parasite or sponger) does proportionally more of the shark fishing's dirty work, such as rendering the liver oil. Thus, the crewmen are organized hierarchically, although they are paid similar fractional shares of the production, with differential bonuses stipulated for unusually productive voyages. Most shark-fishing skills are quickly learned; the only notable exceptions are efficient butchering and experienced seamanship. The essential attributes of a crewman are that he have a local reputation for being hard working, fearless, and able to work co-operatively with other crewmen while confined to a small space for long periods of time.

Many townspeople consider the occupation to be prestiguous not only because it pays well, but also because it is associated with individual daring and a unique local identity as an *hombre del mar* (man of the sea). While most insist that the job is neither as hard nor as monotonous as agricultural work, nearly all agree that it is far more dangerous.

Shark-fishing activities normally occur around *Isabelita*, a small island situated about 20 miles from the mainland coast, and nearly 50 miles by sea from Teacapán (Map 1). A primitive work camp on this island is the fishermen's home throughout most of the long fishing season. Occasionally, fishing activities take them far from their island camp and into the vicinity of the *Islas Tres Marias*, particularly south of *Isla Maria Cleofas*, which is situated near the northern rim of the deep, Middle American Trench.

About once a month a fishing crew returns to Teacapán to hand over its catch. For a few days there is a chance to enjoy town life, but since the boat owners want to keep their craft as productive as possible during the season, crewmen must soon return to sea and their island camp. Separation from their homes, families, and friends for much of the year is the most lamented aspect of their profession. This factor combined with the activity's hazards explains the high wages.

SHARK-BOAT CREWMEN: THE EMPIRICAL CHOICES

The hiring decisions of Tecapán's shark-boat owners differ considerably from hiring decisions in larger, complex societies, where abstract credentials often supplement an employer's lack of personal knowledge of prospective workers. Not only do these boat owners have a high degree of personal familiarity with nearly every adult in the town, on the average they each also have over fifteen lineal, co-lineal, and affinal kinsmen already working as boat crewmen in local shark fishing. Therefore, relative to the usual number of necessary hirings (three), most boat owners have a large number of qualified ascriptive ties they can choose if they so desire.

In the first part of this analysis, I will examine choices which seem motivated strictly by economic imperatives. Of Teacapán's 75 shark-boat crewmen, six are boat owners working in their own boats. Since considerable prestige accrues to boat owners who manage their operations from town, whom crewmen refer to as "men who do not work," it would seem that only relatively poor boat owners would work in their own boats, in order to avoid paying a wage to a hired crewman, while relatively affluent boat owners having sufficient incomes from other sources would not work in their own boats. Table 2 shows a comparison of the boat owners' relative affluence with whether they work in their own boats. While the measure of relative affluence used is rough, the latter part of the foregoing hypothesis seems confirmed; affluent boat owners do not work in their own boats.

The other category of choice motivated by economic imperatives is hired co-residents. Technically, a co-resident's income accrues to his household. In actual practice boat owners pay their co-residents far less than competitive wages, and many pay their young, unmarried co-residents nothing at all. Twenty co-residents were hired, and considering the fact that only one eligible co-resident did not work in his household head's boat, choosing co-residents seems fore-ordained solely by economic considerations. As a result, informant preferences which were presented earlier, such as "our families" or "someone I do not have to pay," now seem more meaningful, since one's self and one's co-residents are those types of laborers.

The foregoing analysis has accounted for 26 of the 75 hired crewmen (the six owners who work in their own boats, and the twenty hired co-residents). But the analysis becomes more socially significant by examining the choices of the 49, non-resident crewmen; these each command about the same wage, so their

TABLE 2
A Comparison of Relative Affluence With Working in One's Own Boat

Number of owners working in their own boats	Number of owners not working in their own boats	Affluence Points, or Relative Affluence[7] (1 = lowest, 8 = highest)
1	1 (female)	1
2	3	2
3		3
	3	4
	3	5
	2	6
		7
	1	8

TABLE 3
A Summarization of Non-resident Choices

Crewman's relationship which boat owner will acknowledge	Number Chosen	Percent of Total
none	38	78%
ritual kinsman	6	12%
affinal kinsman	4	6%
bilateral kinsman	1	2%

Total   49

hirings are not primarily motivated by economic imperatives. From Table 3, which summarizes choices of non-resident crewman, a significant fact emerges; ascriptive categories of persons seem to be avoided: 78 per cent of the non-resident crewmen are no ascriptive relation of their employers. Also, two of the four non-resident affinal kinsmen hired are so geneaologically distant that their ascriptiveness is questionable (a FBWB and MZHMBS). Finally, considering all nineteen boat owners have a relatively large number of ritual kinsmen, the fact that only six were chosen affirms the notion that ascriptive categories of persons are not preferred; indeed, all hired ritual kinsmen are the subordinate members of vertically-phrased ties, participants in ritual-kin relationships which are much less ascriptive than such ties among peers.

The underlying rationale of accounts from other informants now seems clearer; "somebody who will take orders without complaint" is not likely to be one's highly ascriptive social ties, particularly not one's close kinsmen. The hiring of these could complicate the employer-employee relationship by bringing to it pre-existing obligations, emotional sentiments, and perhaps the necessity for contradictory role playing. Hiring a close kinsman might also incur the resentment of other kinsmen who would have welcomed the job, and if a close kinsman were dismissed, one still would have to deal with him in kin-interactional contexts. Finally, close kinsmen would be likely to resent their retention through debt peonage. Hiring a hard working, well known, "no relation" avoids the necessity for coping with any of the foregoing, potentially conflict-laden, situations.

One other aspect of the hiring choices deserves mention. All but one of the 75 crewmen were born in Teacapán. In other words, nearly all are *"bien conocido,"* persons of long-standing residence who have many locally residing relatives. Conspicuously absent among the hired crewmen are the town's more recent arrivals, a minority of disparate families, practically all of whom are involved in agriculture and who live mostly around the town's periphery; such persons are not *"bien conocido."* Therefore, while boat owners do not prefer to hire their own kinsmen, they do prefer the kinsmen of the other boat owners, since each boat owner does have an average of fifteen kinsmen working as shark-boat crewmen. Occasionally, one of Teacapán's relative newcomers is given a job in town, such as butchering and salting shark meat or rendering liver oil, but these newcomers are not subsequently promoted into work aboard the boats. In this sense, the overall hiring pattern suggests a tendency toward mutual group identity and solidarity among the town's shark-boat owners.

CONCLUSIONS

The foregoing analysis reveals a structural pattern underlying the choice of Teacapán's shark-fishing crews. The choices can be accounted for by two rules, hypothesized as the major motivational criteria guiding the hirings: first, minimize labor's cost; and second, avoid hiring ascriptive categories of persons. The preceding analysis, therefore, quantitatively underscores the importance of that guiding precept in interpersonal relations: living *sin compromisos* or without obligations.

When informants stressed the importance of kinship in organizing local shark fishing they were often merely paying lip service to local myths of kin fealty, making politic statements for the benefit of their co-residents and visiting kinsmen who were present while interviewing took place. In that situation it would have been a breach of etiquette to assert that one exploits his children or prefers not to hire his relatives. As Lynch (1959:12-13) describes the nature of interpersonal relationships in a similar situation, "relatives are important, but the importance is often relative."

It is also informative to compare these findings with those of two other ethnographers who have studied boat-crew recruitment in rural, bilateral societies. Among the rural fishermen of South Thailand, Fraser (1966) finds that boat-crew recruitment emphasizes ability, willingness for hard work, and not socially-ascribed relationships. Many aspects of the Thai villagers' situation are similar to those in Teacapán; there has been a tremendous increase in the incidence of wage labor over the past two decades, paralleling a deterioration of the local fishing and agricultural economy; the former, more integrated traditional social organization has broken down; the quality of interpersonal relations has worsened; technological innovations in fishing have "ended all necessity for crew co-activity ashore."

On the other hand, Blehr (1963) finds that boat-crew recruitment among the rural, bilateral, commercial fishermen of the Faroe Islands does ramify along kinship lines, a pattern opposed to that found in South Thailand and Teacapán. But Faroese society differs in four important ways: first, the Faroese boats require about 28 crewmen, necessitating a much larger, co-active, co-operating group of people. More important, Faroese marriage is conducive to the formation of kin alliances, since they usually involve reciprocal obligations (such as bride service). Further, the Faroese are an isolated, effectively closed island society. But probably most important, the Faroese are not alienated from their region's natural resources: inheritance of land, for example, is an important aspect of local kinship organization. In sum, the Faroese are peasants and not rural proletarians, a crucial difference between them and the Teacapaneños.

The avoidance of nepotism in Teacapán seems motivated by essentially the same criteria which motivate the hirings of employers in large, complex, usually urban societies: cost minimization and avoidance of threats to the employer's individual authority and autonomy. Therefore, even though the Teacapaneños live in a small, rural, personal, kin-articulated society and work close to nature, aspects which at first make their society seem quite unlike an impersonal, industrial or urban environment, the great articulation of their local society and economy with that of the Mexican nation has already produced similar patterns of interpersonal relations. As Harris (1971:322) observes, atomistic, bilateral, rural societies in underdeveloped nations are usually associated with "the pervasive, individualizing, and isolating effects of wage labor, industrial production, and commercial markets." Similarly, Mintz and Wolf (1950:196) observe that in situations of industrial development, "mechanisms of social control based upon biological or ritual kin affiliations give way before more impersonal modes of organization."

Indeed, the foregoing study demonstrates how traditional modes of community organization have been greatly subordinated by national events and individualistic concerns. Although the Teacapaneños still have a personal society, economic welfare amongst them seems less and less an interpersonal matter.

NOTES

1. The fieldwork on which this paper is based was conducted in 1971-72, and is reported in the author's doctoral dissertation (1973). The data appearing in that work have been revised for this study, as a result of new information acquired during subsequent visits in 1973-75.
2. The table portrays average income for actual days worked. Wages in fishing are paid as fractional shares of proceeds from the sale of the catch, and are highly variable. Most fishing and agricultural work is sporadic and seasonal. Shark-fishing work is relatively steady, with a season of nearly nine months. Most town oriented jobs are similarly steady.
3. The Teacapaneño's interpersonal familiarity is demonstrated by their ability to provide personal, detailed anecdotes about practically any adult member of the town appearing in photographs I have shown them.
4. Redfield (1947:30) describes a practically identical fiesta pattern in the coastal villages and towns of Mexico's Yucatán Peninsula.
5. In Teacapán, *tiendas de abarrotes* (small, family-owned grocery stores) replace the traditional central market.
6. A parallel source of economic security for most Teacapaneños are the town's numerous stores and shops, which extend credit on a personal basis. Similar patterns of patron-client relationships are found in small, rural societies the world over (Potter, Diaz, and Foster et al., 1967: 50-57, 135-151, 213-230).
7. The measure of relative affluence was built up as follows: one "affluence point" was awarded for each enterprise owned, such as a boat, store, shop, or other small business; one point was awarded for each small plot of agricultural land or small herd of cattle owned—two points if these are large. For example, a boat owner having only one point owns only a shark-fishing boat, and no other enterprises; the owner appearing at the bottom of the table who has eight points owns three boats (3 points), one large landholding (2 points), one large herd of cattle (2 points), and a restaurant in town (1 point). Of Teacapán's nineteen boat owners, thirteen own one boat each, three own two boats each, while three own three boats each.

BIBLIOGRAPHY

Balán, J. 1970. Clases sociales en un municipio rural no indígena en México. Revista Mexicana Sociología 32: 1227-1250.

Beals, R. L.   1932.   The Comparative Ethnology of Northern Mexico Before 1970. Ibero Americana 2.

Blehr, O.   1963.   Action Groups in a Society with Bilateral Kinship: A Case Study from the Faroe Islands. Ethnology 2: 269-275.

Diaz, M. N.   1964.   Opposition and Alliance in a Mexican Town. Ethnology 3: 179-184.

Foster, G. M.   1967.   Tzintzuntzan: Mexican Peasants in a Changing World. Boston.

Fraser, T. M.   1966.   Fishermen of South Thailand: The Malay Villagers. New York.

Harris, M.   1971.   Culture, Man, and Nature: An Introduction to General Anthropology. New York.

Honigmann, J. J.   1968.   Interpersonal Relations in Atomistic Communities. Human Organization 27: 220-229.

Hunt, E. M., and J. Nash.   1967.   Local and Territorial Units, ed. M. Nash, Handbook of Middle American Indians 6: 253-282. Austin.

Lynch, F.   1959.   Limitations of Kinship in a Small Community. Proceedings of the 35th annual meeting of the Central States Anthropological Society at Madison, Wisconsin.

McGoodwin, J. R.   1973.   Economy and Work on the Northwest Mexican Littoral: An Analysis of Labor Recruitment Among the Shark Fishermen of Teacapán, Sinaloa, Ph.D. dissertation, University of Texas at Austin.

Marino Flores, A.   1967.   Indian Population and its Identification, ed. M. Nash, Handbook of Middle American Indians 6: 12-25. Austin.

Mintz, S. W., and E. R. Wolf.   1950.   An Analysis of Ritual Co-parenthood (*Compadrazgo*). Southwestern Journal of Anthropology 6: 341-368.

Murdock, G. P.   1949.   Social Structure. New York.

———   1960.   Cognatic Forms of Social Organization, Social Structure in Southeast Asia, ed. G. P. Murdock, Viking Fund Publications in Anthropology 29: 1-14.

Piker, S.   1968.   Friendship to the Death in Rural Thai Society. Human Organization 27: 200-204.

Pospisil, L., and W. S. Laughlin.   1963.   Kinship Terminology and Kindred among the Nuniamut Eskimo. Ethnology 3: 180-189.

Potter, J. M., M. N. Diaz, and G. M. Foster. (eds.).   1967.   Peasant Society: A Reader. Boston.

Redfield, R.   1947.   The Folk Society. American Journal of Sociology 52: 292-308.

Reina, R.   1959.   Two Patterns of Friendship in a Guatemalan Community. American Anthropologist 61: 44-50.

———   1966.   The Law of the Saints: A Pokomam Pueblo and its Community Culture. New York.

Rubel, A. J., and H. J. Kupferer *et al.*   1968.   Perspectives on the Atomistic Society. Human Organization 27: 189-235.

Sayres, W. C.   1956.   Ritual Kinship and Negative Affect. American Sociological Review 21: 348-352.

Scott, S.   1967-1971.   Archaeological Reconnaissance and Excavation in the Marismas Nacionales, Sinaloa and Nayarit, Mexico. Department of Anthropology: State University of New York at Buffalo.

Spicer, E. H.   1964.   El mestizaje cultural en el suroeste de Estados Unidos y noroeste de Mexico. Revista de Indias 95/96: 1-26. Madrid.

Spielberg, J.   1968.   Small Village Relations in Guatemala: A Case Study. Human Organization 27: 205-211.

Wagley, C.   1949.   The Social and Religious Life of a Guatemalan Village. American Anthropological Association 51: Memoir 71.

Wolf, E. R.   1957.   Closed Corporate Peasant Communities in Mesoamerica and Central Java. Southwestern Journal of Anthropology 13: 1-18.

Pelagic Shark Fishing in Rural Mexico:
A Context for Cooperative Action[1]

James R. McGoodwin

Numerous studies of peasants report pervasively unco-operative behavior, and many developmentalists assert that this seriously inhibits such societies' potential for social and economic development.

Various reasons for the unco-operativeness and extreme individualism have been proposed. Mintz and Wolf (1950) and Harris (1971), for example, attribute it to the individualizing and isolating effects of wage-labor systems and commercial markets, which break down traditional modes of social integration—those based upon kinship and ritual kinship, for example. Others see such behavior as a rational response to objective conditions; Selby (1975) and others urge that peasants are reluctant to co-operate because they do not perceive that such behavior is capable of reducing risks and uncertainties they associate with important economic activities. Foster (1967: 136) ascribes pervasive unco-operativeness in a peasant community he studied to a world view which he calls The Image of Limited Good. He writes:

Since more Good than already exists cannot be produced, cooperation is a pointless activity . . . The typical Tzintzuntzeño, like most other peasants, sees major cooperative efforts as personal threats . . . Consequently, reluctance to cooperate is, with a Limited Good view of the world, highly rational behavior.

In a different mode, Rubel and Kupferer (1968: 190) think that unco-operativeness in atomistic peasant societies arises from an incongruity in the socialization process, wherein "children are socialized to see the family as the sole group upon which they can rely (but as adults) need to cope successfully with a larger, more complex world."

Among the foregoing, unco-operative behavior in peasant societies seems uniformly taken as a given; the authors only diverge in the causes they ascribe to such behavior. Indeed, Rubel and Kupferer (1968: 189), noting widespread contention, suspicion, and invidiousness in interpersonal relationships in atomistic peasant societies, state: "These attitudes and behavior are normative . . . the quality of interpersonal relations in each society are not in dispute. They are, in fact, a phenomenological reality."

I am concerned that too rigid a view of unco-operative behavior may have emerged from studies of peasant societies. Are peasants so locked into unco-operative behavior patterns by local social and economic structure, dominant societal norms and ideals, and socialization processes, that they cannot behave otherwise, not even in radically different contexts?

I have lived periodically in a peasant and rural-proletarian society since 1971, accumulating about two years total time in residence.[2] The community is extremely atomistic, wage dependent, and manifests the incongruity in its socialization process of the type just described. Moreover, its dominant norms and ideals argue strongly against co-operative endeavors. Nevertheless, I have observed extremely co-operative and even gregarious behavior in one particular economic context: pelagic shark fishing. I feel that the town's shark fishermen, who are as unco-operative as any of their peers while they are in the town, co-operate while shark fishing because such behavior reduces risks and uncertainties which arise from that activity. Their behavior change, as they move from one context to the other, is quite remarkable, suggesting that co-operative versus individualistic action in peasant societies may be highly sensitive to contextual conditions, and not as rigidly determined by societal patterns and norms as heretofore believed. In what follows I will describe the two major economic contexts in which I have observed these fishermen.

THE TOWN: A CONTEXT FOR UNCO-OPERATIVE ACTION

Teacapán, Sinaloa, is a rural town of about 2,600 mestizo inhabitants on Mexico's Pacific coast, about 80 kilometers south of Mazatlán, a large urban port (see Map 1). The people are rural in their basic orientation, but they know enough about the modern world to be embarrassed about their marginal position in it.

The community is a difficult, even desperate place in which to live. It is noisy and crowded. Refuse is scattered everywhere. The climate is hot and muggy and there are onslaughts of biting insects. The local wells are briny, often polluted, and fresh drinking water is usually in short supply. The people suffer from a variety of endemic, chronic diseases: amebiasis, acute infections, severe gastroenteritis, hepatitis, and nutritional diseases. The infant mortality rate is high, and rising, and overall life expectancy is only about 54 years. There are frequent shortages of food, particularly in the late summer when there are no significant agricultural harvests and fishing activity reaches its lowest ebb. Food thefts, which occur frequently during such times, are the subject of a popular local expression, *"en Agosto, mucho león"* (in Au-

MAP 1: The Teacapán Region

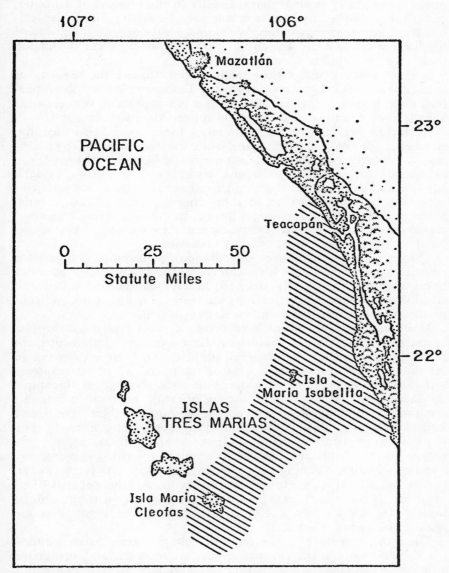

NOTE: Shark fishing occurs in the shaded area.

gust (there are) lots of (hungry) lions). Alcoholism is fairly wide-spread. Family quarrelling and household disintegration are com-monplace. Thievery of all sorts is common and often joked about;

rateros are everywhere. Tragic violence occurs with alarming frequency, especially among males, usually in the context of drinking, and often prompted by insults to one's *machísmo* (manliness) or jealous competition over women. Women are subordinate members of the local society; many are abused, and few enjoy security outside their own households.

A short term, casual visitor might underestimate the severity of living conditions in this town, since the Teacapaneños are obstreperous, great jokers. But their good humor is a superficial veneer; after a while they convince you that they suffer (McGoodwin 1978).

About 44 per cent of the male labor force specialize in fishing, another 42 per cent in agriculture, while the remainder have miscellaneous, mostly town-oriented occupations. About 80 per cent of the male labor force is wage dependent, working either in fishing or agriculture, and nearly all of these must engage in subsistance activities when unemployed in order to supplement household food needs. Some of the agricultural laborers have entitlements to small, marginal *ejido* plots, but like nearly everyone else they must rely upon wage-labor work to supply most of life's necessities.

The community lacks supra-household organizational contexts for collective activities. There is no central marketplace; everyone relies upon a number of poorly stocked, family-run grocery stores and small shops. There is no effective local leadership structure, and religious involvement is insignificant in everyday life.

Many townspeople seem disaffected, cynical and misanthropic. Friendship is brittle and transitory. *Compadrazgo* relationships are generally avoided, and are entered into only with great caution and reluctance.[3] The prevalent norms of interpersonal behavior stress self-reliance, secrecy, and avoidance of encumbering relationships. An incongruity is observed in the socialization process; individuals are taught to distrust nearly everyone outside their immediate households, even close consanguineal kinsmen, but eventually they must seek important new ties—spouses and employers, for example—on the "outside." The ideal person is described as being *muy vivo* (very lively), meaning opportunistic, and *muy listo* (very ready), that is, agile in his defense against threats to personal security. The ideal life is one which can be led *sin compromisos* (without obligations).[4] In essence, the society's dominant norms argue strongly against co-operative action.

The most important local economic strategies are subsistence fishing in the region's labyrinthian estuaries, lagoons, and mangrove swamps; wage-labor work in regional agriculture; and wage-labor work in the local shark-fishing industry.

Subsistence fishing is an undependable, part-time activity, favored by fishermen who have failed to find jobs in local commercial fishing, or who are between voyages. It is usually a solitary and rather secretive activity. Most fishermen attempt to conceal their catches from the prying eyes of hungry neighbors and kinsmen, and give misleading information about their fishing areas, hoping to conceal their favorite spots so that others will not find and quickly deplete them.

The pattern of wage labor in regional agriculture, and its technology, are not conducive to co-operative action. The pool of laborers seeking such work is almost always larger than the number of available jobs, which promotes secretiveness in seeking out prospective employers. Furthermore, most agricultural work is solitary, not requiring co-operative effort: driving a horse-drawn plow or a tractor, for example, or moving a small herd of livestock from one pasture to another. Even those agricultural activities which require large numbers of laborers at one location—weeding and harvesting activities for example—do not promote interdependent efforts. The only coordination required in weeding and harvesting is moving on line across a field. Harvesters customarily are paid according to the weight of the product they individually gather, or the number of crates they pack.

The recruitment of shark-fishing crewmen, which occurs in the town, also reflects the community's extreme atomism. Since all ascriptive social ties—consanguineal, affinal, and ritual kinsmen—are viewed as potentially troublesome, shark-boat owners seeking crewmen from outside their immediate households avoid hiring such ties, preferring instead to hire a "good nobody." The reason is clear; if a "good nobody" does not work hard or becomes intractable, he can be fired without running the risk of endangering ill feelings among one's kinsmen (McGoodwin, 1976).

The town and surrounding region's three most important economic strategies entail risks and uncertainties which can be minimized through individualistic rather than co-coperative action. Specifically, these risks and uncertainties are: not securing food from subsistence fishing, not securing cash because of failure to find wage-labor work, and confounding one's interpersonal situation by hiring laborers who may prove troublesome.

A developmentalist who observed the Teacapaneños only in their town setting would probably conclude that their capacity for co-operative action appears low indeed. But if he were to accompany the town's shark fishermen to the sea, an opposite impression would emerge. In that context even extreme loners become co-operative and gregarious.

PELAGIC SHARK FISHING: A CONTEXT FOR CO-OPERATIVE ACTION

Shark fishing is an important activity for Teacapán, employing about 80 crewmen, an equal number of ancillary workers, and contributing to the economic welfare of nearly half of the town's populace.

The local industry arose in the early 1940s when the Allied Powers began to offer high prices for shark-liver oil. A number of Teacapaneños became specialists in shark fishing, acquiring its basic skills, technology, and capital. The local industry dwindled following the war, but it has now made a total recovery, based upon the marketing of diverse products: shark fins, hides, meat, liver oil, and fishmeal. Along this coast, where nearly all commercial fishing on the high seas is large-scale and government-instituted, Teacapán's shark fishing industry is a rare example of relatively simple, small scale, individual free enterprise.

Each boat owner is a lone entrepeneur in competition with all the other boat owners. The local industry is neither a collective nor a cooperative enterprise, but rather only a number of individuals all engaged in the same activity.

Nineteen men, affluent local household heads, own Teacapán's 28 shark fishing boats. There are a few simple, motorized dugout canoes, but sturdy, seaworthy launches, comprise a majority of the crafts. A typical launch has a wooden hull 30 feet long by 10 feet through the beam, and is equipped with a powerful diesel engine. These vessels represent a considerable investment, about 75,000 *pesos,* or $6,000 U.S. (in 1973). None carry communications equipment, lifesaving gear, or any navigational equipment except simple compasses, even though some voyages extend as far as 80 miles from the mainland coast.[5]

Most shark boats require three crewmen. The essential attributes of a good crewman are that he have a local reputation for being hard working, fearless, and able to get along with others, at least while he is at sea. Many townspeople consider the occupation to be prestigious because it pays well and because it is associated with individual daring and a unique local identity as an *hombre del mar* (man of the sea), or a *tiburonero* (shark fisherman). While most insist that the job is not as hard or monotonous as most work in town, nearly all agree it is considerably more dangerous.

Shark-fishing activities normally occur around *Isla Maria Isabelita,* a small island 20 miles from the mainland coast, and 50 miles by sea south of Teacapán (see Map 1). A primitive work camp on this island is the fishermen's home throughout most of the long fishing season, December through early June. Occasionally fishing activities take them far from their island camp and into the vicinity of the *Islas Tres Marias,* particularly southward of *Isla Maria Cleofas,* near the northern rim of the deep Middle American Trench.

About once a month a fishing crew returns to Teacapán to hand over its catch, but because the boat owners want to keep their craft as productive as possible during the season, the crewmen must soon return to the sea and their island camp. Separation from households, families, lovers, and friends is the most deplored aspect of the profession, and these factors in combination with the occupation's hazards explains the high wages.

Crew membership is predicated upon acceptance into a tight-knit organization; shark fishing is perceived as a way of life. As Kahl

(1968:10) said of life in Latin American peasant communities, "Work is merged into life . . . Work is part of one's status."

Crew organization is explicitly hierarchical, consisting of a *jefe* (boss or captain), a *marinero* (sailor, seaman, or mariner), and a *pavo* (sponger, parasite, an apprentice). The *jefe* and *marinero* spend more time on the water than the *pavo*, who does relatively more processing work at the island camp. One of the crewmen, usually the *pavo*, is always present at the camp to safeguard the boat's gear, the crewmen's shacks, and the catch.

Crewmen are paid out of proceeds from the sale of the catch when they return to Teacapán. Payment is in terms of fractional shares of the proceeds which were agreed to before the start of the voyage. This method of joint payment—an ancient and common practice around the world for compensating seamen, fishermen, and whalers —has no parallel in the payment of labor in any of the work around the town.

In abstract terms, the crew of a shark-fishing boat makes a joint commitment to a venture which may be highly profitable, or which may result in financial loss or physical disaster. Precisely, the risks and uncertainties arising from shark fishing activities are: (1) three or four weeks' absence without producing food or income for one's household, (2) serious physical injury, and (3) loss of life. All of these risks and uncertainties are considerably reduced if the crewmen are co-operative.

Most sharks are caught on longlines in deep water, 10 to 20 miles from the island camp. Every day the crewmen arise before dawn, voyage out to the lines, haul in the sharks, and re-bait and re-set the lines, sometimes also relocating them. Hauling and setting a line requires precision teamwork. Hauling is a particularly dangerous activity; the deck quickly becomes slippery from blood and slime from the sharks which are being brought aboard, and there are usually a number of unhooked sharks swimming in tight circles around the boat. Sometimes these free-swimming sharks become so excited that they viciously bite the craft, even breaking their teeth on the craft's metal rudder or screw. Working as a team, the crewmen methodically haul in the line, and then secure it fast while they lift the large sharks aboard over the stern. Usually the sharks brought aboard are dead, having exhausted themselves and drowned, but sometimes there may be a large, live shark on the line, and if it should suddenly startle and run, it may catch the crewmen by surprise, unleashing coils of line and causing hooks at the end of chain leaders to go flying through the air. Nearly all the fishermen have ugly scars on their bodies from the times when they were snagged by flying hooks. A few have been dragged overboard and drowned in such circumstances.

There is another method of catching sharks that is more productive and not as dangerous for the men, but it is risky for the boat.

Some of the wealthier boat owners equip their craft with large gill nets, which are deployed along the mainland coast during the spring. In this season, schools of spawning sardines concentrate in the surf near the shore bringing with them great numbers of feeding fish and sharks. Placing and hauling the net requires precise teamwork among the crewmen. In the surf close to the shore there is danger of grounding and probably losing the boat. Usually the *jefe* carefully maneuvers the boat through the breaking waves while the *marinero* deploys or hauls the net, a difficult operation because the boat is usually pitching furiously. During hauling the net may become fouled in the boat's rudder or screw, resulting in an immediate loss of power and control. One of the crewmen, usually the *marinero,* must immediately jump into the water to free the net.

The risks and uncertainties of shark fishing not only prompt co-operative action among fellow crewmen, but also inter-crew co-operation, perhaps more significant since it entails co-operation among economic competitors.

It is assumed among all shark fishermen that they will respond to a distress signal from any other vessel at sea, regardless of whether the distressed vessel is another shark-fishing boat from Teacapán, a boat from some other coastal town or village, a shrimp trawler from a distant urban port, or even one of the *gringo* yachts which frequently pass through the area. This behavioral mandate, which has no equivalent in cases of personal misfortune or distress in the fishermen's town society, is an almost universal code among mariners, arising from the dangers of life and work at sea. Any of Teacapán's shark-fishing crews which failed to render aid to a vessel in distress would collectively and individually suffer a great loss of social standing, and could not count on help in any future emergency. The crewmen failing to respond would be labeled as cowardly and undependable and probably would have to leave shark fishing. The men understand this implicitly.

Inter-crew co-operation occurs in other, more ordinary contexts. Crossings between the island and the town, for example, are rarely made alone. They normally take from six to eight hours, depending upon weather conditions and the power, load, and condition of the boat. Generally the *jefes*—either in town or at the island camp—exchange information concerning the timing of their planned departures, usually delaying them until at least one other craft can accompany them. This co-operation sometimes extends to other activities, such as a redistribution of individual loads among the boats that will be making the crossing together. Co-operative action of this sort is not absolute. *Jefes* of craft in seaworthy condition sometimes make the crossings alone, especially in good weather conditions. This form of co-operative action increases as the risks and uncertainties of crossings increase, that is, as weather conditions worsen, as loads get heavier, or as engines begin to run roughly.

Engine breakdowns are a common occurrence; a fire or sinking and abandonment of a vessel happens every year or so. Crossing in company means that a crew can safely transfer from a sinking or burning craft to a companion craft, saving much of their boat's gear and their catch; alone, such a calamity might result in the loss of three human lives, a boat and all its gear, and the catch. Co-ordinating the crossings so that they are made together reduces the risks and uncertainties of such voyages, while the chances of loss of human life is reduced to zero.

Inter-crew co-operative action also appears in other activities arising from shark fishing. Trolling for bait fish, for example, is a co-ordinated, co-operative activity which is usually joined by all the boats on the island. The activity takes place at day's end, around sunset, after the crews have brought their catches back to the island, butchered and salted the sharks, and placed them in the sun to dry. Then the fishermen all board their boats to search for schools of pelagic fish, mackerels and bonitas, which feed near the surface in the waning light. It is an animated, mad melee: boats narrowly miss one another as they criss-cross through the schools of fish, fishermen swing wriggling fish aboard and club them senseless, the men shout, whistle, laugh, and make good-humored and obscene gestures at one another across the water. The scene is one of high camaraderie.

The fishermen believe that the noise causes the fish to feed with greater fervor, and whether or not this is the case, it is true that by trolling together the boats greatly reduce their individual chances of losing contact with the fast-moving schools of fish. Failure to catch fresh fish every day would be serious; without them the longlines cannot be baited, and production would come to an abrupt standstill. And not only is this activity co-operative in that it is undertaken simultaneously, it also prompts other forms of co-operative interaction. Crews catching more fish than they need usually share their catch with other, less fortunate crews, expecting the latter to reciprocate in the future. An excess of fish also prompts enjoyable evenings in the camp. The evening meal, based usually upon dry staples brought from the mainland, is supplemented with fresh fish; optimistic sentiments about future shark production are expressed; and the joking begun in the melee at sunset extends far into the night.

A more complex form of inter-crew co-operative action is co-ordinated tactical planning for hunting shark schools. Every evening in camp there are informal discussions about where sharks were caught that day, how many were caught at various locations, what directions the sharks seem to be moving. This sharing of information, analogous to the simultaneous trolling for fish, reduces each crew's chance of losing contact with the schools of sharks. The nightly discussions often result in a plan for the next day's deployment of the longlines, a plan which involves many boats, occasionally all the boats at the island. Each crew agrees to set their lines along a specified azimuth and at a specified distance from the island. Then, after the results of that co-ordinated effort are compared, a new joint tactic may be formulated. All the crews may not participate in this process. Some *jefes* are partial to certain locations, others play hunches. But generally speaking, this type of co-operative action increases as shark production decreases. When all boats bring back substantial catches, there is very little co-ordination; but after one or two days of small catches, or no catches at all, nearly all the boats at the island participate in a co-ordinated hunt.

This behavior, seen from a vantage point high above the island camp, would appear to be both complex and systematic. When only a few sharks are butchered in the afternoon along the shore of the island camp, that evening a large cluster of fishermen sit about a campfire for some hours, and the next morning the boats deploy away from the island in a sunburst pattern towards all points of the compass. As days pass and larger catches of sharks are butchered in the afternoons, the size of the group around the evening campfire dwindles, the meetings are shorter, and the next morning the boats concentrate in one area at some distance from the island. Should the catches again diminish, the group around the evening campfire would again get larger, and the next day's deployment would again approximate the sunburst pattern.

This complex form of co-operative action is part of an ongoing, adaptive, behavioral process, which responds to changes in the situation. It reduces the risk of uncertainty of not catching sharks, the main goal to which these fishermen are committed.

CONCLUSION

In pelagic shark-fishing activity, any acting out of the pervasive societal norms stressing individualistic action would be unproductive and dangerous, whereas precisely the opposite situation exists in the context of most work occurring around the town. In shark fishing, co-operative action reduces the objective risks and subjectively perceived uncertainties surrounding various calamities which can arise from that activity.

One interpretation of the decision to co-operate in shark fishing, however, might hold that the decision to co-operate was made in port when the crews signed on, so that once they are at sea they really have no alternative but to co-operate. But any such attempt to explain the co-operative behavior cannot explain it away; the men might be begrudging, reluctant co-operators, for example, but that is not the case. Moreover, their behavior in shark fishing remains a radical departure from their usual behavior in the town, with no parallels in their social and economic life there.[6] These men are not rigidly enslaved by their dominant societal norms; instead they can adapt quickly and dramatically to changes in their contextual situation despite the norms.

Co-operative action appears prompted by the desire to reduce the risks and uncertainties of shark fishing, but the work has other facets which are conducive to an improved quality of interpersonal relations. There is less competition among the men over scarce jobs, since once they are away from the town they already have a job. Furthermore, the climate is not as hot at the island camp as it is in town, and there is almost total relief from the mainland's biting insects. There is also usually an abundance of fresh protein-rich food available in the island camp—fish, lobsters, and seabirds' eggs. There is not much drinking of alcohol because the men consider drinking to be appropriate in non-working contexts, and the drinking that does occur is done mostly in secret, since most fishermen feel that drinking while shark fishing is dangerous. In the island camp there is no noise from cars, trucks, or blaring radios, nor from quarreling coresidents, kinsmen, and neighbors. The town's women are not present. Indeed, competition over jobs and women—the major sources of strain in the local society—is almost nonexistent in the context of pelagic shark fishing activities.

But it would be erroneous to attribute the fishermen's greater co-operativeness while shark fishing to a mere improvement of their material circumstances; the sea is a harsh material environment indeed. Through co-operative action, however, many of its dangers may be minimized.

The goals of sustenance and self-preservation seem more powerful determinants of the fishermen's behavior than are the dominant norms of their local society. This suggests that the way in which people go about their work is greatly conditioned by the contexts in which that work occurs.

NOTES

1 The author is an Associate Professor in the Department of Anthropology, University of Colorado, Boulder, Colorado. This paper was written while he was a Research Fellow in the Marine Policy and Ocean Management Program, Woods Hole Oceanographic Institution, Woods Hole, Massachusetts. Early sources of support for this study include the E. D. Farmer International Fellowship Fund, Institute of Latin American Studies, The University of Texas, Austin, and Council for Research and Creative Work, University of Colorado, Boulder. This paper was prepared with funds from the Pew Memorial Trust and Department of Commerce, National Oceanographic and Atmospheric Administration (NOAA), Office of Sea Grant, and the Marine Policy and Ocean Management Program, Woods Hole Oceanographic Institution.

The author especially wishes to remember the crewmen of the "Blanquita," a shark-fishing boat aboard which he served as a "semi-apprentice" during spring, 1972. The fates of these three crewmen, although not typical, underscore the harsh realities surrounding these fishermen's lives both at home and at sea. The *pavo* (apprentice seaman) killed a neighbor with a shark-butchering knife that same spring. The *marinero* (general seaman) eventually found better work aboard the "Haitiano," a shrimp trawler from Mazatlan, then was lost at sea in the fierce *chubasco* (hurricane or typhoon) which struck Pacific Mexico in fall, 1975. The *jefe* (captain) suffered a fatal attack of appendicitis while shark fishing in the vicinity of *Isla Maria Isabelita*, spring, 1976.

2. Definition of what constitutes a "peasant society" or a "rural-proletarian society" varies with different authors. I use these terms interchangeably to mean people living in relatively small rural societies who are among the lowest rural stratum of a larger, stratified, complex state-level society, whose production technology is fairly simple, who must engage in some subsistence and wage-labor activities, who are illiterate to semi-literate, and so forth. For some authors a "peasant" is a person with the above attributes who is basically a farmer, and who owns his own land. Other authors include small-scale "artisanal" fishermen under this term. Furthermore, a "peasant's" neighbor who owns no land and is wage dependent is often termed a "rural proletarian." In my use of the descriptive phrase "peasant and rural-proletarian society," I exclude from consideration the fairly well-integrated plantation communities of the less developed countries, as well as the highly traditional, closed-corporate, rural communities, both of which are minority types in comparison with the number of open, noncorporate, peasant-and-rural-proletarian communities found throughout the less developed countries.

3. Spielberg (1968) observed an almost identical pattern of ritual kinship in a small, rural, Guatemalan community.

4. Foster (1967) stressed the central importance of this life ideal in Tzintzuntzan, a rural Mexican community.

5. A few of the crafts carry innertubes for use as lifesaving gear.

6. Fraser (1966) observed a similar behavioral pattern—extreme individualism ashore, but co-operation while fishing—among rural fishermen in south Thailand.

BIBLIOGRAPHY

Foster, G. M.   1965.   Peasant Society and the Image of Limited Good. American Anthropologist 67: 293-315.

—————   1967.   Tzintzuntzan: Mexican Peasants in a Changing World. Boston.

Fraser, T. M.   1966.   Fishermen of South Thailand: The Malay Villagers. New York.

Harris, M.   1971.   Culture, Man, and Nature: An Introduction to General Anthropology. New York.

Kahl, J.   1968.   The Measurement of Modernism: A Study of Values in Brazil and Mexico. Austin and London.

McGoodwin, J. R.   1976.   Society, Economy, and Shark-Fishing Crews in Rural Northwest Mexico. Ethnology 15: 377-391.

—————   1978.   No Matter How We Asked Them, They Convinced Us That They Suffer. Human Organization 37: 378-383.

Mintz, S. W., and E. R. Wolf.   1950.   An Analysis of Ritual Co-parenthood (Compadrazgo). Southwestern Journal of Anthropology 6: 341-368.

Rubel, A. J., and H. J. Kupferer et al.   1968.   Perspectives on the Atomistic-Type Society. Human Organization 27: 189-235.

Selby, H. A.   1975.   Social Organization: Symbol, Structure, and Setting. Dubuque.

Spielberg, J.   1968.   Small Village Relations in Guatemala: A Case Study. Human Organization 27: 205-211.

Sea Tenure in Southern Sri Lanka

Paul Alexander

The emphasis on the study of land tenure in Sri Lankan ethnography has produced increasingly sophisticated accounts of the organization of agricultural production (Codrington 1938; Pieris 1956; Leach 1961; Obeyesekere 1967). Two of the most important points to emerge from these studies are the complexity of the relationship between the ecology and moral or legal notions relating to land tenure, and the extent to which the basis of the rural social structure has been transformed by colonial legislation and a market economy. Contemporary Sri Lankan social structures cannot be successfully analyzed in terms of a simple opposition between the constraints of economics and the constraints of morality and law, nor can they be understood without an appreciation of their history (cf. Leach 1961).

Obeyeskere's (1967) ideal model of Sri Lankan land tenure contains three elements: the concept of the estate as a common property domain in which the co-owners are also kinsmen, the use of genealogies to allocate floating shares in the estate, and a system of rotation to equalize environmental effects. Such a model seems intuitively well suited to reservoir irrigated rice farming, but similar models are also used to organize other types of agriculture, including rain watered or river irrigated rice (Obeyesekere 1967), shifting cultivation of dry grains (Leach 1961), and village gardens or tree crops. This paper discusses the application of a similar model to a very different ecological niche: coastal fishing using beachseines.

Beachseining is one of the most common fishing techniques used in peasant communities (Bottemanne 1959; Forman 1971; Fraser 1962; Hill 1970). Although Sinhalese fishermen were using small beachseines at least a century earlier, the modern form of large beachseine, *madella* (*mahadella*, lit. "big net") was introduced by migrant fishermen from the Madras coast around 1860 (Wright 1868) and spread throughout the island during the next twenty years. According to local traditions, the first beachseines were brought to Mawelle around 1890 by three brothers who were formerly engaged in agriculture.

Mawelle,[1] the fieldsite for this study, is a Karave (fishing caste) village on Sri Lanka's southern coast, near the end of a belt of continuous settlement which extends 120 miles from Colombo. The 1971 population of Mawelle proper was 1,031, a density of 5,000 per square mile, and many persons from adjoining villages also fish at Mawelle beach. Beachseining is the most important of the three main fisheries producing two-thirds of Mawelle's income and employment for 274 men. Inshore fishing, using traditional craft and small mesh nylon gillnets, is vastly overcrowded and gives only a bare subsistence income (Alexander 1975b), while the government sponsored three-and-a-half ton mechanized craft are not economically viable (Alexander 1975a). The average annual household income is Rs. 1,170, but whereas the 21 households of the capitalist elite have incomes exceeding Rs. 5,000, half the households earn less than Rs. 610.

THE ECONOMICS OF BEACHSEINING

Beachseines consist of a codend (*maduwa*), a large body· (*punchi kata*, lit. small mouth), wings (*maha kata*, lit. big mouth) and hauling ropes. Mawelle nets are approximately 500 yards from the middle of the codend to the end of the wings and weigh about two tons when wet, but larger nets are found near Colombo. The codend has a mesh of 0.4 inches and is made from cotton yarn. Laid flat it is a trapezoid fifteen feet long, five feet wide at the mouth and ten feet wide at the enclosed end. It is attached to the body by lacing ropes which can be drawn tight to prevent fish escaping, and its normal capacity is around a ton of fish.

The body is also made of cotton yarn and consists of eight five-foot sections. Its mesh is 0.6 inches at the point where it joins the codend, increasing to three inches at the wing end. Laid flat, the body is a vertical conical section, 50 feet across at its widest part adjoining the wings. The wings are made of locally produced coconut coir twine forming a coarse gillnet with a mesh that increases gradually from six inches to three feet, and a depth in the water of eight to twelve feet. The headrope along the wings has wooden floats at five foot intervals complemented by stone sinkers along the foot rope. Coir hauling ropes are attached as required and occasionally exceed 500 yards.

In 1971 the cost of materials for the construction of a fully equipped beachseine (including a netlaying craft) was Rs. 3,875 and average annual production costs (excluding labor) were Rs. 665.[2] All nets are named and are linked in a net sequence which corresponds to their numbers in a government registration list.

Beachseining, which still produces about 35 per cent of fish landed in Sri Lanka, requires an area of sandy bottom approximately 6,000 square yards, free from rocks or other obstructions which might rip the net. This restricts operations along the 120 miles of Sri Lanka's southwestern coast to about twenty sites (*padu*), for in most areas with reasonably sheltered beaches the coral reefs lie close to the shore. The site must also be sufficiently sheltered to permit the launching of the one-and-a-half ton netlaying craft through the surf, and most sites can only be used for the six months of the non-monsoon period; September to February for the coastline west of Tangalla, and March to August for the area to the east.

Two aspects of Mawelle beachseining are atypical of the region. First, fishing is possible throughout the year. Mawelle is not affected by the northeast monsoon, and the area of the harbor used for beachseining is protected from the southwest monsoon by a headland. A series of rock shelves, in combination with the action of the surf on the beach, restricts fishing to the southern half mile of the beach which is subdivided into two fishing stations (*patte*): the *varaya* (harbor) and the *galaha* (rock). The second atypical feature of Mawelle beachseining is the type of craft used. At most sites the heavy surf has lead to the development of a specialized, highly buoyant and expensive netlaying craft whereas the more sheltered Mawelle harbor permits the use of secondhand deepsea fishing craft with a consequent saving in production costs.

A detailed analysis of the species taken by the beachseines is beyond my competence, but the bulk of the catches were identified by informants as *hal messa* (anchovies), *sudaya* (sardines), *udassa* (silver biddy), or *katuvalla* (herrings). Anchovies account for more than half the catch and the fishermen expect a series of large catches once a year, around September. Two other species, *saleya* (ribbon fish) and *atavalla* (mackerel tuna), also provide occasional large catches. The most valuable single catch any of my informants could remember was in late 1963, when 3,500 mackerel tuna were sold and many were simply given away. The entire catch is used except for poisonous varieties such as blowfish, and occasional turtles.

There is no question of beachseining depleting fish stocks. This is an important point and one which should be stressed. The anchovies that comprise the bulk of the beachseine catch are migratory fish and research by the Sri Lanka Fisheries Department suggests that only a small proportion of shoals venture sufficiently close to the shore to be taken by beachseines or other peasant fishing techniques (Canagaratnam and Medcoff 1956). Using current methods the present yields could be sustained indefinitely, although the use of large industrial craft could radically alter the ecology.

As far as labor requirements are concerned the essential feature of beachseining is that the fish are enclosed by the net and chased towards the beach, not dragged in by the mesh. The codend is not opened until the net has been hauled to within twenty yards of the beach, and as soon as the fish have entered the codend is laced closed to prevent their escaping. Consequently, except for the last few yards of the haul, a heavy catch requires no more labor than for an empty net. A net is normally launched and hauled by a permanent crew of nine, though in the last stages of a big catch as many as 50 men participate. With a minimum size crew beachseining is a very efficient technique; the 1970-71 catch divided by the minimum labor requirement gives a figure of 12.2 lbs. per man hour, which compares very favorably with the 14.5 lbs. per man hour from the mechanized craft.

The average net takes three hours to launch, set and haul, although during periods of good fishing the period between the landing of successive nets is seldom more than two hours. As only nine daily hauls are possible in each of the two fishing stations, and as the need to dry nets precludes the use of an individual net more than once a day, the optimum number of nets for Mawelle beach is eighteen. Assuming that an individual could participate in the hauling of three nets per day, the optimum number of nets could be worked by a labor force of 54. In 1970-71 there were 99 nets in use on Mawelle beach and 274 men were engaged in beachseining, 180 of them fulltime.

Beachseine Output

Fish landings by the 99 Mawelle beachseines over three complete netcycles are summarized in Table I.[3] The three cycles occupied 317 days. Beachseining during the remainder of the year lifted the total catch by only Rs. 8,732 and did not increase the earnings of any individual net by more than Rs. 300.

The annual cash receipts were nearly Rs. 160,000. There was a marked fall in

TABLE I
Beachseine Landings June 1970-April 1971

	CYCLE ONE (June-Sept.)	CYCLE TWO (Sept.-Dec.)	CYCLE THREE (Jan.-April)	ALL CYCLES (June 1970-April 1971)
VALUE OF CATCH	Rs.	Rs.	Rs.	Rs.
Total Catch	11,627	79,021	67,081	157,729
Average Per Haul	124	352	176	225
Average Per Net	113	798	678	1,589
Highest Net	2,064	5,244	5,647	7,762
Lowest Net	NIL	NIL	NIL	38
HAULS				
Total No. of Hauls	94	225	382	701
Average Per Net	0.9	2.3	3.9	7.1
Highest Net	3	9	8	14
Lowest Net	NIL	NIL	NIL	4
CATCH PER MAN-HOUR	Rs. 1.3	Rs. 5.7	Rs. 3.3	Rs. 3.7

the catches during the June-September cycle, but although this coincides with the last months of the southwest monsoon, the reason for the fall in the catch was scarcity of fish, not difficulties in launching the net. Returns from inshore fishing were so low in June and July that only 37 beachseine hauls were attempted, of which only seven had a catch worth more than Rs. 25.

By contrast, October was a month of very high catches. Eighteen days fishing, between October 5th and 25th, produced nearly one-third of the annual catch, with the daily catches averaging Rs. 3,500 and two days producing more than Rs. 6,500. The other two-thirds of the catch were spread throughout the remaining eight months of the year. During these eight months few days produced less than Rs. 500, but the catch exceeded Rs. 2,500 on only three days. The contrast between the flush period and the rest of the year is normally more marked than Table I suggests, for the ban on night fishing following an insurrection in April 1971 lifted fish prices by more than 150 per cent. If this price rise had not occurred more than 40 per cent of the annual yield would have been taken during the flush period.

It is not possible to provide quantitative data on annual catch fluctuations, although all informants, both fishermen and members of the Fisheries Department, stress that yearly fluctuations are considerable. Mawelle fishermen claim that the 1970-71 catch was better than the preceding year, but argue that it was still slightly below the average annual catch of around Rs. 200,000.

The average haul during 1970-71 gave a cash sale of Rs. 225 which is approximately one-third of a ton of fish. Even during cycle one the average haul was Rs. 120. Prospective returns are calculated in cash, rather than numbers of fish. The net is not set if the prospective return is less than Rs. 25 because a smaller catch would be distributed among the shore crew rather than sold, and owners who did not work the net would receive nothing. Further, when fishing is poor the return per man is higher in handlining or rock fishing than beachseining.

During 1970-71, less than eight per cent of the hauls were under Rs. 25 and most of these small catches were in the first haul of the morning. The first catch on the harbor side is normally the best of the day, and unless fishing has been poor for a long period the net due in this position is always used (see below). The result of this haul sets the pattern for the remainder of the day. If the catch is a good one, around Rs. 250, and especially if the catch is mainly anchovies, following nets will be used as soon as their turns fall due. If the catch is smaller, around Rs. 50, the nets will only be used if a shoal is spotted entering the harbor.

Seven hundred hauls were completed during the year, averaging little more than two per day. The average number of turns per net per cycle was less than three, although some nets were used as many as nine times in a single cycle. The fact that the average net was used only seven times during the year, and that the most heavily utilized net was hauled on only eighteen occasions, demonstrates the excessive number of nets.

Table I also indicates considerable fluctuations in the results of individual nets. In both cycles two and three, some nets were not used at all while the top ten nets received more than Rs. 5,000. Over the three cycles the top net received Rs. 7,762, while the least successful net received only Rs. 38. This marked maldistribution of the catch is shown more clearly in Table 2.

Less than a third of the nets receive two-thirds of the catch, while the least successful third of the nets receive only nine per cent of the annual proceeds.

While there are differences in the skill of individual netcrews, these have very little influence on the annual operating results. Whether a particular net has a successful season is almost solely a function of its position in the net cycle. In 1970-71 the ten most successful nets occupied positions eighteen to 27 in the net sequence and sixteen of the top twenty nets occupied positions eleven to 28.

Annual Operating Results

One of the reasons for the excessive number of nets is shown in Table 3, which gives the annual operating results of the average individual net.

Even at the present excessive levels of capital investment, the average net still gives a profit (excluding labor costs) of Rs. 803. If the net is operated by its owners, this returns 21 per cent on the investment, and even if the owners have to pay hired labor it is a return of eight per cent. As other avenues of investment open to village entrepreneurs are being rapidly closed by the government's policy of nationalization, the beachseines are a very attractive investment.

In view of the fluctuations in the returns to individual nets, a comparison between the returns of each net and its operating expenses is the most satisfactory basis for an evaluation of annual operating results. Nearly 40 of the owner operated nets did not cover their operating costs and a further 30 made profits of less than Rs. 1,000, while the ten most successful nets had profits greater than Rs. 4,000. Only half the hire operated nets made a profit, but the ten most successful had average profits of Rs. 2,500, which is more than double the average annual household income.

Individual nets show tremendous differences in operating results. Whereas the least successful net had a catch worth less than Rs. 50, the most successful net had a catch of more than Rs. 7,000. Moreover, the success of a net is not a function of capital or labor inputs and is only slightly affected by the skill of the crew; it is almost solely a matter of chance.

Fishing is regarded everywhere as an industry of great risk and uncertainty (Beverton and Holt 1957; Turvey and Wiseman 1957). Mawelle beachseining bears out the point to a marked—almost grotesque—degree. Not only do

TABLE 2
Distribution of Beachseine Catches Among Participating Nets

NUMBER OF NETS	TOTAL CATCH Rs.	PERCENTAGE OF CATCH	CUMULATIVE PERCENTAGE
Top 10	48,900	31	31
11-20	25,100	16	47
21-30	20,400	13	60
31-40	16,700	11	71
41-50	13,700	9	80
51-60	9,900	6	86
61-70	7,700	5	91
71-80	6,200	4	95
81-90	4,700	3	98
Bottom 9	3,000	2	100

annual yields fluctuate, but 40 per cent of the catch is taken during a non-predictable flush period of less than a month. The level of investment in the nets is five times optimum, with the result that the average net is used only seven times a year. The community could take exactly the same catch with only

TABLE 3
Annual Operating Results, Average Individual Net

	OWNER OPERATED* Rs.	HIRE OPERATED Rs.
Capital Cost	3,875	3,875
Cash Sales	1,589	1,589
Less: Wages⁑		508
Running Costs	670	670
Interest+(3%)	116	116
Total Expenses	786	1,294
	=====	=====
Return on Capital		
Total	Rs. 803	Rs. 295
	21%	8%

* The distinction between owner and hireoperated nets is discussed below.
⁑ One-third of the cash sales less minor expenses.
‡ The larger owners include interest on invested capital when calculating operating results, small owners do not. Three per cent may appear to be a low figure for the opportunity costs, but given the nonmonetary benefits large owners derive from the ownership of beachseines it is a realistic figure.

eighteen nets, which would lift the community's annual profit from Rs. 80,000 to Rs. 143,000.

THE ORGANIZATION OF BEACHSEINING

One consequence of the introduction of large beachseines was a new system of ownership. Whereas the earlier gear, made from local materials, was owned by individual fishermen, the new beachseines were beyond the reach of even the wealthiest fishermen, and a system of shareownership developed in southern Sri Lanka. Initially the share system operated on an *ad hoc* basis; individuals gave varying sums towards the purchase of nets, and disputes over revenue and responsibility for repairs were common (Wright 1868). But by 1920, in Mawelle at least, the nets were being operated within a complex share system with a series of norms governing the rights and obligations of the owners, the relative shares of the revenue due to capital and labor, and the rights of access to the water. Nowadays the interpretation of these norms is changing, and the basic structure of the share system may itself be radically altered in the near future (Alexander 1973); nevertheless, the organization of beachseining in Mawelle in 1970 was essentially unchanged from the situation 50 years earlier.

The Share System

Each net is divided into eight shares called *kottas* or *pangu*. The latter is the usual term for shares in a wet rice field and, in conjunction with other features described later, support the view that the beachseine share system was derived from agriculture (Obeyesekere 1967; Leach 1961). An essential feature of *kottas* is that like stockmarket shares they refer to the enterprise as a whole, not to particular portions of the net. Although when new nets are constructed or old nets are repaired it is usual for shareholders to contribute readymade sections of netting, once the net is in operation individuals have no particular rights to the sections they contributed.

The fishermen claim that the reason for the eight-fold division is that eight is the minimum sized crew, and the division stems from an earlier period when all members of a netcrew were also shareholders. Observation suggests that the first part of the claim at least is correct, although under present conditions of abundant labor most nets now have a permanent crew of nine. Since 1933 a government appointed official, the *patabendi arrachi*, has been responsible for compiling an annual list of shareholders.[4]

An individual may hold more than one share in a net and a share is often held by more than one person. For example, two siblings who inherit two shares from their parents will often register each share jointly; each thus retaining a one-sixteenth share in two nets rather than a one-eighth share in one net. The motive is both to share the risk of not participating in the flush period and a moral notion that inherited property should be jointly shared by all siblings, not divided among them. In 1971, five per cent of the shares were jointly owned, mostly by pairs of siblings.

Women are eligible to register shares and indeed owned seventeen per cent of them in 1971. They are not, however, permitted to participate in the operation of the net nor in the division of its proceeds, and therefore have to surrender *de facto* control to a male nominee. In some areas in Sri Lanka many of the small fish traders are women, but Mawelle women play no overt part in fishing and seldom visit the beach (Stirrart 1974).

Shares may be freely bought, sold, and used as security for various forms of mortgage. In former years they were often the most valuable item inherited, and, less frequently, were included in dowry payments. Although shares are freely transferable, in the sense that the other shareholders in the net do not have a legal veto over a prospective sale, the other shareholders do have a strong practical veto. Shareholders must work closely together and few men would buy a share in a net where the other shareholders strongly objected to the sale.

In the past the shareholders in each net (*kottas karriyo*) were probably also close kinsmen, but it is now unusual for close kin to own shares in the same net and in most cases the *kottas karriyo* has no functions outside the economic context. The exceptions are the 42 nets controlled by one of the three political factions which today dominate village life, but as these factions are a post-1966 development they are outside the scope of this article.

The Net Crew

Most nets have a permanent crew of nine men (one for each shareholder plus an extra man paid by the crew as a whole) who under the supervision of the *marrakalai* are responsible for all operations of the net. The term *marrakalai* has two connotations. First, it refers to the role of fishing expert (Firth 1966) who remains in the netlaying craft when the beachseine is hauled, directs the shore crew with hand signals and decides when the codend should be opened. It also refers to the man who organizes the net crew, supervises the sale of the catch, and collects money from the buyers.

In the 42 nets controlled by one of the three political factions, the two roles are separated. The fishing expert is normally the oldest man in the crew, for this is the least physically demanding task and the fishermen place little emphasis on differences in skill. The marketing and organization role is the preserve of the faction leader or his nominee, who alone makes such decisions as when the net will be launched, whether extra men will be taken on, the price at which the catch is sold, and what repairs are needed. Other shareholders, whether members of the faction or not, have little control over the net's operation, and this is one of the reasons why men do not like to buy shares in a faction controlled net (Alexander 1973: 277-282). While the two roles are usually performed by one man in the nonfaction nets, all significant decisions are reached by consensus among the shareholders.

Apart from these two roles there is no permanent division of labor within the net crew; a man may row on one occasion and remain ashore or serve as netlayer on the next. The only exception is that a crew that anticipates chasing a shoal will place its youngest and fittest men at the four oars.

When discussing the selection and organization of the permanent netcrew, the fishermen draw a distinction between men who own shares (*kottas karriyo*) and men who work on a hired basis for the owners (*kuli karriyo*). Although ownership of a share carries the obligation to work the net when required, owners can deputize other men to work on their behalf. In 1971, 64 per cent of owners worked all their own shares, but many of these men were only small owners, and half the total shares were worked by *kuli karriyo*. The owners who employ hired labor are a disparate group with disparate motives: women who must employ men to work on their behalf; men living outside the village; men who derive most of their income from nonfishing activities; and village faction leaders who use the shares to provide employment for their clients.

For analytical purposes it is useful to divide the *kuli karriyo* into two categories. First, there are the men who work for close relatives; mainly sons working shares owned by a parent, and men working their brother's, sister's, or brother-in-law's shares. In this case there is not a clear distinction between share-owner and hired worker for most own some shares and work others on a hire basis (Leach 1961:80). The other situation is where the relationship between the *kuli karriyo* and *kottas karriyo* has strong patron-client connotations and is much closer to a class relationship.

Of the fourteen largest shareholders in the village, who together control 22 per cent of the total shares, only five shareholders work all their own shares. Six of the remaining nine receive the bulk of their income from the ownership of shares, but employ others to work on their behalf, and the remaining three shareholders receive the bulk of their income from activities other than fishing. For the nine men who do not work their own shares, ownership of the shares has two advantages; it is an investment which gives a safe and reasonably good return, and it gives them a mechanism for recruiting and maintaining a political following. For the three men who receive only a small part of their income from the ownership of *madell* shares, the primary motive for the acquisition and retention of these shares is the maintenance of their political following. Although some of the hired workers are relatives of the owners, the basis of their recruitment is political allegiance, not the kinship tie.

By 1971 slightly more than half the shares were regularly worked by people other than the owners. If the shares worked by close relatives (brothers, brothers-in-law, and sons) are excluded, 136 shares (eighteen per cent of the total) were worked by men of the *kuli karriyo*.

About three months after the catch was landed, when payment is received from the middlemen,[5] the proceeds from the sale of the catch are distributed at a formal meeting. There are some differences of opinion about the principles that should govern this distribution. All informants are agreed that the catch minus the "expenses" (the cost of small running repairs, wage payments for drying and stacking the net, and a payment to the man who records the sales and collects the proceeds from the fish traders) should be equally divided among all eight shareholders. If the net has a "ninth man," a payment of about half a regular share will also be deducted at this time. There are no special payments or extra shares for specific roles in the net crew. When the share is being worked on a hire basis, most informants also agreed that two-thirds should go to the owner and one-third to the hired man. But others argued that the hired workers should receive the whole proceeds if these were less than a certain amount, in most cases Rs. 250. The divergence in informants' statement reflects both differences in the current distribution practices among various nets and differences in the status and composition of the *kuli karriyo*.

When the hired man is a close relative, often a member of the same household as the owner, the division between capital and labor is based on mutual arrangements rather than normative rules. While the son is young and unmarried, the owner takes all the catch; clothing and feeding the son in return. As the father grows older the positions are reversed. When the owner and hired laborer are siblings or brothers-in-law, my impression is that the person who is nominally the hired man usually takes over the running of the share, including the responsibility of meeting the repair costs, and pays the owner a small amount once a year. Similar arrangements apply to shares owned by a woman.

The relationship between *kottas karriyo* and *kuli karriyo* is gradually altering from a relationship between kinsmen, broadly governed by kinship norms and without status differentials other than those based on kinship status or relative age, to a patron-client relationship founded on political allegiance and characterized by marked asymmetry. In the latter case the two-thirds to one-third division is the generally accepted norm, but the practices vary greatly according to the economic standing, source of income, and political ambitions of the patron, and the client's economic position and the strength of his ties to the patron. In some cases the client takes complete control of the net, retains all proceeds, and gives small formal gifts to the owner on festive occasions. In other cases the client receives only one-third of the proceeds irrespective of the amount.

Normally only the permanent crew work the net, but during the flush period large numbers of casual bystanders join in and later loudly demand some fish for their efforts. The netcrew have a very ambivalent attitude toward these helpers; for while the last stage of a heavy catch requires extra labor, far more men than are necessary participate, and most make only a nominal contribution. The efforts of these helpers to secure a few fish before the catch is sold is a constant source of disputes.

Access to the Water

With a total of 99 nets, only eighteen of which can be used in a day, the rules governing access to the water are obviously of great significance. The following are the principles by which net owners decide when their turn is due. All nets are named and each owner is aware of the names of the nets immediately preceding and following his in the sequence. The fishing area is divided into two fishing stations: the *varaya patte* (harbor side) and the *galaha patte* (rock side). The net cycle begins on the harbor side. A net can be used on the harbor side at any time during the day after the net immediately preceding it in the cycle has been used. After a net has had the dawn turn on the harbor side, it is entitled to the dawn turn on the rock side on the succeeding day. Subsequently, it may be used on the rock side at any time of the day once the net immediately following it in the sequence has been used. In addition the net with the dawn turn in either fishing station must be used before midday or forego its rights.

The sequence of net use over a period of five days, in each of which there were four nets used on both fishing stations, is shown in Table 4. It will be appreciated that the situation is considerably more complex in practice, because the number of nets used varies from day to day, and on some days more nets are used at one fishing station than at the other.

The moral principle underlying this system, as stated to me by informants, is one of equal opportunity (Obeyesekere 1967). As opposed to a more simple system, for example the single use of each net in strict rotation, it meets four

TABLE 4
Sequence of Net Use

DAY	FISHING STATION							
	HARBOR				ROCK			
	MORN. ⟶			NIGHT	MORN. ⟶			NIGHT
One	9	10	11	12	8	7	6	5
Two	10	11	12	13	9	8	7	6
Three	11	12	13	14	10	9	8	7
Four	12	13	14	15	11	10	9	8
Five	13	14	15	16	12	11	10	9

conditions. (1) The two fishing stations are not equally desirable; most of the big catches come from the harbor side, although the average catch on the rock side during a period of poor fishing is usually larger. (2) All turns of the day are not of equal value; the biggest catch of the day is usually the first turn on the harbor side, and fish caught in the morning bring higher prices. (3) The number of hauls during the day is not constant; during periods of poor fishing no nets at all may be used, in good periods, as many as eighteen. Nor is the speed of the haul constant; nets with big catches are hauled more quickly, in part because more people participate, in part to give the fish less chance to escape. Thus a system allocating access at a set time of the day would be inefficient. (4) A disproportionate amount of the total labor input is concerned with preparing the net for the haul and restacking it afterwards; a system in which each net was only used once would be an inefficient use of labor.

Although this system gives equal opportunities to all nets it does not result in equal returns, especially over the short term. During the flush season, which lasts only a month, the nets whose turns are due not only get bigger catches, they are also hauled on more occasions. For much of the year, only three nets are used each day and thus a net is unlikely to be used on more than two occasions in each net cycle. But in the flush season, between ten and eighteen daily hauls are made on up to eighteen successive days, and individual nets may receive up to nine turns in each net cycle. In 1970-71 only 25 of the 99 nets received turns during the flush period. It is clear therefore that the annual returns of any net are governed, almost solely, by its position in the net cycle. If its turn is due during the flush period it will make heavy profits; if it is not, it will be lucky to recover its production costs.

The disparity between the moral notion of equal opportunity and the great differences in individual returns is due solely to the large number of nets. As long as the total number of nets was less than twenty, all nets received relatively equal returns and the system was an efficient and equitable means of regulating access to the water. But as the number of nets increased, the distribution of the catch became more and more unequal.

Although this system does not give equal returns over a single year, returns should even out over a longer period. Because there is no fishing on the quarter-moon holiday (*poya*), a net sequence takes about 105 days to complete. This means that a particular net's turn is not tied to any point in the year, and over a four year period each net will be used in every month. As the fishermen are unable to predict the flush period with any great accuracy, each net has an equal chance of good catches in any one year, and theoretically every net should make a good catch once in every five years.

THE EVOLUTION OF THE SHARE SYSTEM

The Mawelle fishermen are aware that many of the community's problems are due to the excessive number of beachseines. If there were twenty nets, the catch would remain constant while profits would increase by two-thirds and would be more equally distributed among the participants. As this is clearly apparent to the fishermen two important questions must be answered: what are the historical circumstances that gave rise to such a large number of nets, and why is the number of nets not reduced?

The Semisubsistence Economy: 1840-1940.

Mawelle fishermen hold that the sole rights to beachseining belong to the descendants of the three brothers who introduced the nets to Mawelle around 1890. While they do not argue for a single founding ancestor (and many are unaware that the three men were brothers) informants are adamant that the founders of the Paranamanage, Abraham Gallipattige and Wijetunga Liyana Pattibendige families brought the nets to Mawelle and that fishing rights descend from these three men.[6] As fishing rights, along with other property, are subject to bilateral inheritance, men marrying into the village could acquire rights through their wives. Oral history and genealogies indicate that all of the households engaged in beachseining prior to 1939—about three-quarters of the total Mawelle households—held access rights either by descent or by marriage. Informants often described the beachseiners of this period as *eka pavul kattiya* (lit., a family group); a kingroup comprising the descendants of the three founders and their affines, who married endogamously and settled disputes on a kinship basis.[7]

There is consensus that shares were rarely sold at this time and that the price of the few shares that were sold was always lower than the cost of construction. Share inheritance was also relatively unimportant, for the maintenance costs of a share over five years was equivalent to the cost of a new net. In any case sons gradually took over the operation of the net as their fathers grew older, and the legal transfer following the death of both parents was a purely formal acknowledgment of existing arrangements. As dowry, the importance of the share transfer between father-in-law and son-in-law lay not in the economic value of the share, but in its confirmation of the son-in-law's rights to fish at Mawelle beach.

Although there was no limit on the number of nets, and anyone holding access rights was entitled to construct a net and use it at Mawelle beach, several economic considerations inhibited construction of new nets. Before 1939 beachseining was semisubsistence activity. As much as 40 per cent of the catch was consumed in the village and (although perhaps half the catch was dried, much of it for later sale in the interior villages) the prices for dried fish were very low.

There was little surplus finance available in the village and no incentive to invest in gear other than the minimum required to provide employment. Further, it must have been clear that once the number of nets exceeded those that could be used in a day, additional nets would not increase the total catch and profits would decrease even further. As the fishermen were essentially a single kinship group, it is reasonable to suppose that informal agreements were partially effective in restricting the number of nets. Nevertheless, the nets did gradually increase from around twenty in 1920, to 36 in 1938 (see Table 5).

Apparently the main impetus for the increases in nets was demographic pressure. The Mawelle population grew by 70 per cent between 1901 and 1931 and a greatly disproportionate increase occurred among beachseining families (Alexander 1973: 49-59). Before 1910, the beachseiners, handicapped by a severe labor shortage, had encouraged their sons-in-law to live in Mawelle, and by 1931 many of these mens' children were themselves marrying. Because exploitation of the fishery resource was tied to the eight share system, sons from large families had to construct additional nets if they wished to continue beachseining. A hypothetical example will make this clear. If there are twenty nets, a man with one net will receive 1/20th of the annual catch. But if after his death his two sons take joint ownership of his net, they each receive only 1/40th

TABLE 5
Increases in Number of Nets

YEAR	NO. OF NETS	SOURCE OF INFORMATION
1970–71	108	Registration List.
	99	Personal Observation.
1967	108	Informants.
1964	83	Registration List.
1957	77	Informants.
1946	77	*Patabendi Arrachi's* Notebook.
1945	71	*Patabendi Arrachi's* Notebook.
1938	36	*Patabendi Arrachi's* Notebook.
1933	32	*Patabendi Arrachi's* Notebook.
1920	20 (?)	Informants.

of the catch, whereas if one constructs a new net they each receive 1/21st. Thus, although the construction of new nets was clearly uneconomic from the viewpoint of the community as a whole, there were good reasons why individual fishermen, especially those from large families, should construct new nets. The optimum number of nets was reached before 1920 and the consequent increase involved additional investment of which the marginal product was zero.

The tendency towards an increase in the number of nets as a result of population growth was partially offset by other factors. The most important is that many sons could not afford to finance new shares and were forced into other less desirable fisheries such as deep sea fishing or handlining. Further, as the number of nets increased, the probability of any particular net participating in the flush period decreased, and men unable to meet the maintenance costs of their share following a poor year dropped out in favor of newcomers. As the returns from other fisheries were very low it was very difficult for men in either category to amass sufficient finance to return to beachseining.

Taken together, these factors support the inference that although finance that would otherwise have been used for the construction of additional nets was redirected into the acquisition of relinquished shares, the rate of population growth was too high to permit the system to reach an equilibrium. As increasing nets did not produce larger catches, a point was reached where ownership of a single share was insufficient to sustain life and large numbers of men were forced to find other occupations. The function of the rights of access concept was not to limit the number of nets but to ensure that outsiders did not construct nets for use on Mawelle beach and thus accelerate the fragmentation process.

In 1933 the government introduced legislation to register beachseines throughout Sri Lanka and only men with a license were permitted to fish off a particular beach. Although the government accepted that in some areas fishing rights were not individually owned but belonged to the community as a whole, it was uncertain as to how joint ownership could be translated into legislation (Anon, 1922). In most sites beachseines were by this time owned by one or two men. In these cases the government simply issued licenses to the owners and crystallized the *status quo*. In the few sites on the west coast where each net had several owners, fishing cooperatives were established which quickly became either bankrupt or mere facades for the activities of a capitalist elite. But in areas along the southern coast (including Mawelle) where share ownership was widely distributed throughout the community, the fishermen refused to form cooperatives. As a compromise the government limited the number of nets at any site to those in use in 1933 and codified the criteria for allocating access to the water.[8]

This legislation effectively destroyed the notion of rights of access. Whereas previously all people in the community had the right to build nets and participate in the fishery, now men could participate only by buying a share in an existing net. The legislation also permitted sales of shares to men without hereditary rights to the fishery and many of the share sales following 1940 were to such people. The legislation would have had the positive effect of limiting the number of nets but this proviso was not enforced and nets had increased to 36 by 1938.

The 1938-39 season was the last in which the beachseines operated within a semisubsistence economy. In 1935, according to the *patabendi arrachi's* note-books, one man in Mawelle had three shares and six men had two shares each. If it is true that the remaining participants owned only a single share each, then 208 households derived part (in most cases the major part) of their income from beachseining.

The living standards of the beachseiners had dropped steadily between 1920 and 1938. The number of men and nets engaged doubled, as did the production costs, while the volume of the catch remained constant. Nor did the value of the catch increase substantially; dried fish prices rose by only 25 per cent (Government Agents Reports 1920-38) and wet fish prices remained static. By 1939 the beachseine share system was near to collapse.

The Commercial Economy 1940-1960

The parameters of the Mawelle *madella* economy changed radically between 1940 and 1942 when improved communications, availability of ice, and increased demand led to a five-fold increase in the price of fish (Fish Sales Union 1942-6; MacDonald 1954; Director of Fisheries 1940- 66). Previously most of the catch had been distributed to shareholders and was dried for resale by members of their families but now, with increased prices and demand, all fish could be sold in fresh form and the net owners retained only sufficient fish for their own consumption. Beachseining changed within two or three years to a fully commercial enterprise.

A less desirable consequence of the increase in fish prices was an immediate increase in the number of nets. In the seven years following 1938 the nets nearly doubled, from 36 to 71. There were three main reasons for this spectacular increase. First the increased prices made beachseine shares a very profitable investment. If it was possible for a man to scratch a subsistence living from the proceeds of a single share in 1938, by 1940 the same share would have given a very large return. Although the marginal product of additional capital remained at zero, the amount of profit had substantially increased. Thus the return on capital was very high. The beachseines were converted from a technology used by peasant fishermen for a subsistence living, to a channel for very profitable investments by entrepreneurs. Second, the availability of money increased. While the benefits of the increased fish prices were not equally distributed, there were now several people who had large amounts of capital and few avenues for investment. Third, as the number of nets began to increase, individual shareholders were forced to join in the construction of new nets, for otherwise their equity in the total catch would diminish. At the same time, the profits from the shares they already held were sufficiently large to leave a surplus for investment. Thus once the process of net construction began, it took on increasing momentum as each individual attempted to maintain, or if possible increase, his equity in the catch.

The structure of the share system was consequently radically altered. The owner-operator with only a single share was replaced by entrepreneurs with up to twelve shares, many of them operated on a hire basis. In 1945, there were six men with ten or more shares and a further eight men with five or more shares, but the true holding of the entrepreneurs was closer to 30 per cent, for many registered shares in relative's names.

As the entrepreneurs began to dominate the shareholdings, smaller owners found it increasingly difficult to retain their shares. With more nets, the time any individual net spent in the water was shorter and its chances of participating in the high catch period was reduced. Consequently net sales became more frequent, and as many of these sales were to men who were not descendants of the original owners, the final nails were hammered into the coffin of the rights of access, and the kinship basis of the shareholder's group was destroyed.

By 1945 the beachseine economy had taken on most of its present features: the shares were a profitable investment, even when the owner had to pay labor to work the net; the number of nets was considerably larger than could be worked in any one day; the system of allocating turns, in conjunction with the very short period of high catches, led to a very unequal distribution of the catch among individual nets; and the peasant operator was being forced out by the capitalist entrepreneur.

The changes in the economy also led to changes in the relationship between share owners and hired men. Prior to 1940 most shares were worked by their owners or by the potential heir of the owner, and while some of the entrepreneurs who introduced new nets between 1940 and 1946 were not themselves fishermen, they normally gave their shares to close relatives among the fishermen to operate. Thus the commercial economy did not result in immediate changes; most hired men were relatives of the shareowners and many were, or would become, shareowners in their own right. The development of the shareowner-shareworker relationship into a markedly asymmetrical relationship was a gradual response to three factors. First, the one-third share of the hired man amounted to a considerable sum when the net was successful. Second, small owners displaced by the entrepreneurs were forced to seek alternative employment and employment prospects in other fisheries and other industries were increasingly bleak. Third, village level political leaders began to use the beachseines to recruit and maintain a political following.

Between 1946 and 1955 there were also several attempts to reduce the number of nets either by increasing the number of shares in each net or by introducing a cooperative. None of these attempts was successful, mainly because the small shareholders felt that both alternatives would eventually result in the loss of their rights. In the case of the cooperatives this was a realistic view for most fishery cooperatives eventually became fronts for large net owners (MacDonald 1954). The proposal to reduce the number of nets to twenty, but increase the number of shares in each net to 24, also failed. It failed partly because small shareholders felt that their shares would be embezzled, partly because agreement could not be reached on the procedure for amalgamation, but mainly because by this time the right to work a net had a high value in itself for small shareowners and a crew of 24 was regarded as too large to be efficient.

Despite the government ordinance, six further nets were added between 1956 and 1964, and in 1964-66 a further 25 nets were constructed, giving 108 in 1971. The circumstances behind the rapid increase in 1964-66, and the principles governing investment in the post-1966 share market, are beyond the scope of the present paper and will be discussed elsewhere (Alexander 1973: 257-84). Here it is sufficient to note that the domination of the market for the beachseine catch by a small coterie of traders, increasingly severe unemployment, and the emergence of powerful political factions restructured the share system after 1966.

In most of the *padu* in Sri Lanka where beachseining is carried out today, the fishing is controlled by one or two licensees, who own the nets, take all the proceeds of the catch, and pay the crew on a wage basis. If the system used in Mawelle was once common to all beachseine *padu* in Southern Sri Lanka, why is the system found only in Mawelle today?

The main reason is that before the introduction of the commercial economy in 1940, Mawelle, unlike the other beachseining centers, did not give opportunities for high profits. In the more profitable *padu* which were linked to the main communications networks, rapid expansion in the number of nets (a post-1939 development in Mawelle) had occurred much earlier. Because of the lack of any limit on the number of nets the share system had collapsed and the elite had gained control well before 1930. Thus, the licensing system introduced in 1933 merely confirmed the elite's control. But in Mawelle there was no economic incentive for share accumulation before 1940, for the few men with ready capital could more profitably invest in trading enterprises. By the time the accumulation of shares became profitable, several competing factions were attempting to acquire shares and it was impossible for a small elite to gain control, over the short term at least. In other sites, the number of nets has been held to an optimun level, but only by limiting ownership to a small elite. In Mawelle the system of widespread individual shareholdings has been partially preserved, but only by increasing the number of nets far beyond an economic level.[9]

FISHING AND AGRICULTURAL PRODUCTION SYSTEMS

The structure underlying the organization of Mawelle beachseining bears several close resemblances to the structure of Sri Lankan wet rice production systems as described by Leach (1961) and Obeyesekere (1967) among others. The view of the resource as a common property domain in which the co-owners are also kinsmen, the concept of the floating share, the system of rotation to equalize environmental effects, and the moral notion of equal opportunity are common to both. In view of these similarities it is not surprising that an implicit comparison of the two systems underlies much of the preceding analysis, but the similarities should not obscure the equally important differences (see Firth 1966).

The most obvious difference is that agricultural systems have strict spatial boundaries. With wet rice, for example, cultivation is limited to the areas with adequate water supplies. In a sense the area of a fishery is also bounded—the use of a particular technology applies relatively strict constraints on the area that may be fished economically—but the fish are not bounded by these limits. This point may appear rather trivial but it has the important consequence of giving the fisherman much less control over his annual yield. Unlike wet rice economies where in the absence of disasters such as drought or blight the yield remains relatively constant from year to year, annual fishing yields fluctuate considerably. This makes production planning very difficult. The natural fluctuations make it hard to assess the effects of technological innovations; over-fishing may increase to a point well beyond the maximum sustainable yield, and the results of overfishing may be felt several years later in an area several hundred miles away (Cf. Christy and Scott 1956; Beverton and Holt 1957; Bottemanne 1959).

A second important feature of fisheries is that they are natural common property resources; no single user has exclusive rights to the resource nor can be prevent others sharing in its exploitation.[10] As the yield is strictly limited, this has the consequence that an increase in the number of participants affects each user's enjoyment of the resource. The individual user is in competition with all others in an attempt to secure a larger share of the resource for himself and if he restrains his own efforts, he merely increases the share available to others. Further, there are often vast differences among individuals in their share of the community yield. In many cases these differences are not a function of relative effort, capital invested, or skill, and are completely outside the control of individual fishermen.

There are considerable differences in the consequences of additional labor inputs. Yields in peasant wet rice agriculture can often be lifted substantially by higher labor inputs, but this is seldom possible in fishing; higher gear utilization rates seldom result in greatly increased yields over the long term. Further, some additional labor inputs in agriculture, for activities such as weeding or trans-planting, may lift yields without requiring additional finance. But if greater yields are to be achieved in fishing, the investment in gear must also be increased, usually by mechanization. Finally, because fishing does not require sustained participation, there is more opportunity for the entrance of marginal workers, and this reduces the incomes of those depending upon fishing alone for their livelihood.

Capital investment also has different features in the two economies. In agriculture, the main capital investment is the land itself and investment in other forms of capital such as workstock and gear are usually small (Mellor 1966). Thus there is little risk involved in the investment, and the land apart from its productive function may serve as an avenue of saving. In fishing the entire investment is in the gear. Fishing equipment has a short operating life, high maintenance costs, rapid depreciation, and is subject to high risks of loss or damage. Add to this the problems of predicting output and it is evident that investments in fisheries involve very high levels of both risk and uncertainty. It should also be noted that mortgage or leasehold arrangements are easier to control in an agricultural community, for it is easier for the lender to estimate the potential yield and to supervise the annual or semiannual harvest.

Firth (1966: 2-3) has pointed to several other significant features of peasant fisheries which bear upon production costs. Fishermen produce fluctuating quantities of a highly perishable product which is not the major item in their diet and thus there is more scope for the development of specialized middlemen. In addition, fishermen's capital requirements are difficult to predict and may amount to a sizeable sum over a very short period. Taken together these factors account, in part, for the close relationships between fishermen and middlemen which often have a patron-client and an exploitative character.

These factors impose differing constraints on the way in which the two production systems adapt to population increases. In an agricultural community the interests of the basic economic unit (the household) and the interests of the community as a whole are similar. The effects of an overall drop in output per head are felt most strongly in the households directly responsible for the fall, those with the most children. An increase in household size does not directly lead to an increase in the household's share of the community's resources, and thus large households must either increase production on their share of the land by developing new techniques or find alternative employment for some of their members. In fishing, an increase in household size often does lead to a larger share of the community's resources and it may well be in the best interests of the household to encourage as many of its members as possible to continue fishing, even though the output per head throughout the community is falling (cf. Hardin 1968). Further, as both men and women usually participate in agriculture, each addition to the family is also an addition to the labor force. This is not true of fishing and households with a high percentage of daughters are in a very vulnerable position, especially if daughters must be dowried.

A secondary, but nevertheless important, point is that in a situation where output per head is falling increased capital investment in fishing may continue. There are several reasons for this: (a) because of the catch fluctuations, the point where profit is maximized is difficult to establish; (b) even when no overall profit remains, the great fluctuations in individual catches may give high profits to individual participants; (c) speculators may invest increasing amounts, sustaining short term losses, in the expectation that small operators will eventually be unable to meet the maintenance cost of their gear and will be forced out.

This brief discussion suggests the hypothesis that the two economies will react in very different ways to population increases. In an agricultural community, population increases can be absorbed over a long period by increasing labor inputs and raising yields. Households with particularly high rates of growth will be gradually forced out, but the transition towards ownership of the means of production by an elite will be slow, several generations at least. In a fishing community the process is much more swift. Once the output per head falls, the disintegration process accelerates and the transition from ownership by independent peasant producers to ownership by a small elite, will be very rapid.

NOTES

1. Fieldwork in Sri Lanka from February, 1970 to August, 1971, and July, 1973 to February, 1974 was funded by the Australian National University and the Myer Foundation. For a more detailed account of Mawelle social structure see Alexander (1975a; 1976) and Yalman (1967: 271-281)

2. The average annual production costs of a Mawelle beachseine include: replacement of worn sections, Rs. 535; repairs to netlaying craft, Rs. 65; dyeing and restacking net, Rs. 65.

3. The bulk of the beachseine catch is sold in units of a "box." These hold 90 to 120 lbs. (with an average of 100 lbs) depending on the species of fish and how high the box is heaped. As the fishermen seldom receive payment from the middlemen in less than three months, they are very careful to record the price and buyer for each box and it is these records that provided the data for Table 1. Apart from the fish sold to middlemen, about a tenth of the catch is distributed to crew members and bystanders without payment, or is sold in subsidiary sales. This fish is not included in the table.

A net cycle was defined as the period between the use of net number one in the first position on the harbor side.

4. Although there are 108 nets listed in the shareholders' list compiled by the *patabendi arrachi* in 1971, only 99 nets actually exist. The other nets have been burnt during faction fights over the past three years and the owners have yet to replace them. When one of these "phantom" nets is due to be used, its turn is taken by the following net. Registration lists are deposited in a local government office and I was able to copy complete lists and the changes in registration from 1964 to 1971. The earlier shareholders lists from Mawelle are no longer extant, but I had access to notebooks kept by the *patabendi arrachi* between 1933 and 1957 in which are recorded the number of nets for some years as well as valuable, if unsystematic, data on the numbers of shares owned by individuals at various points in the past. As these data were usually gathered in the context of disputes over shareownership, I have not placed much weight on their veracity and have mainly used them to cross-check data gathered from informants.

5. More than 80 per cent of the Mawelle catch is bought by a coalition of three brothers who have driven out other competitiors by a combination of violence and superior business ability. Thus the auctions pit the faction ridden fishermen against a monopsony. The fishermen can in theory retail the catch themselves if they are dissatisfied with the price, but in practice they are seldom able to arrange transport. The middlemen buy on credit and delay payment as long as possible so as to increase their bargaining power. Fish auctions are always very tense situations and fights between fishermen and middlemen are common.

6. Although the three families have different names it is clear from the marriage and land records that they are all descendents of a single marriage (cf. Obeyeskere 1967: 225).

7. This kinship group is structurally equivalent to the *vasagama* found in agricultural villages. "Literally *vasagama* means *vasa* (residence) and gama (estate), that is, those who reside in, enjoy rights in, a common estate" (Obeyesekere 1967: 14). See also Tambiah's (1965) account of the Kandyan *gedera*. In my view many of the apparent anomalies in accounts of Sinhalese social structure stem from the fact that many of the terms used for kinship groups are polysemous. Functionally and structurally equivalent groups may be referred to by a variety of terms within a single conversation. Thus the group referred to in the text may be called a *vasagama* or a *pelantiya*, as well as the usual term, *pelapata*.

8. The account of the legislation given here is that which was accepted by the community at the time. In fact, although the legislation limited the number of nets, it did not limit the nets to those in use in 1933. If an excessive number of nets were presented for registration a ballot was to be held and the nets eliminated were to be the first registered in the succeeding year. This loophole was used to introduce an additional 25 nets in 1964-66 after which the legislation was amended.

9. Further support for this argument can be derived from an examination of the registration lists from other beachseine *padu* which were as isolated as Mawelle prior to 1940. Suriyagahawelle, a small beach which could only be used during the six months of the north-east monsoon, had seventeen nets when it was abandoned in 1965. Nilwelle, a village equal in size and isolation to Mawelle, had 47 nets when the harbor was taken over as a mechanized boat anchorage in 1968. Both these *padu* were only large enough for one net at a time to be used. Tangalla, a much less isolated site, but one which was still cut off from the heavily populated southwest coast market before the Matara ice factory was built in 1940, had 139 *madell* operating in three *padu* when a cooperative was formed in 1937. By 1968, the cooperative had collapsed and the 22 nets were owned by sixteen men.

10. This point is more true of some fisheries than others. Where fish are attracted by a lure, for example, the owner of the lure may have full rights to fish beneath it. But normally he cannot prevent other fishermen setting up their own lures nearby.

BIBLIOGRAPHY

Alexander, R. P.   1973.   Risks, Rewards and Uncertainty: Fishermen of Southern Sri Lanka. Unpublished Ph.D. dissertation. The Australian National University.

———— 1975a. Innovation in a Cultural Vacuum: The Mechanisation of Sri Lankan Fisheries. Human Organization 34: 333-344.

———— 1975b. Do Fisheries Experts Aid Fisheries Development? The Case of Sri Lanka. Maritime Studies and Management 3: 5-11.

———— 1976. The Modernisation of Peasant Fisheries in Sri Lanka. Marine Policy and the Coastal Community, ed. D. Johnston, pp. 279-296. London.

Anonymous.   1922. · Report of the Industries Commission. Colombo.

Beverton, R. J. H., and S. J. Holt. 1957. On the Dynamics of Exploited Fish Populations. London.

Bottemanne, C. J.   1959.   Principles of Fisheries Development. Amsterdam.

Canagararatnam, P., and J. C. Medcoff.   1956.   Ceylon's Beachseine Fishery. Fisheries Research Station, Ceylon, Bulletin No. 4. Colombo.

Christy, F. T., and A. Scott.   1956.   The Commonwealth in Ocean Fisheries. Baltimore.

Codrington, H. W.   1938.   Ancient Land Tenure and Revenue in Ceylon. Colombo.

Director of Fisheries.   1940-66.   Administration Reports. Colombo.

Government Agents.   1920-38.   Administration Reports, Government Agent Hambantota. Colombo.

Firth, R.   1966.   Malay Fishermen (2nd ed.). London.

Fish Sales Union. 1942-46. Annual Reports. Colombo.

Forman, S.   1971.   The Raft Fishermen. Indiana.

Fraser, T. M.   1962. Rusembilan, A Malay Fishing Village in South Thailand. Ithaca.

Hardin, G.   1968.   The Tragedy of the Commons. Science 162: 1243-1248.

Hill, P.   1970.   Rural Capitalism in West Africa. London.

Leach, E.   1961.   Pul Eliya: A Village in Ceylon. London.

MacDonald, A. H.   1954.   A Survey of Ceylon Fisheries with Special Emphasis on Cooperatives and Co-Op Development. Unpublished Report to Dept. of Fisheries, Colombo.

Mellor, J. W.   1966.   The Economics of Agricultural Development. Ithaca.

Obeyesekere, G.   1967.   Land Tenure in Village Ceylon. London.

Pieris, R.   1956.   Sinhalese Social Organization. Colombo.

Stirrart, R. L.   1974.   Fish to Market: Traders in Rural Sri Lanka. South Asia Review 7: 189-208.

Tambiah, S. J.   1965.   Kinship Fact and Fiction in Relation to the Kandyan Sinhalese. Journal of the Royal Anthropological Institute 95: 131-173.

Turvey, R., and W. Wiseman (eds).   1957.   The Economics of Fisheries. Rome.

Wright, W. D.   1868.   Report of the Commissioners Appointed to Inquire into the Sea Fisheries of Ceylon. Colombo.

Yalman, N.   1967.   Under the Bo Tree: Studies in Caste, Kinship and Marriage in the Interior of Ceylon. Berkeley.

The Organization
of Coastal Fishing in Tamilnadu[1]

Kathleen Fordham Norr

This paper provides an account of the work organization and economic structure of a South Indian fishing hamlet, and includes previously unrecorded techniques and activities. The critical need for high quality protein foods throughout India makes an understanding of customary fishing organization important for social scientists and planners alike. In addition, fishing is an example of an important traditional work organization outside agriculture, and thus provides a perspective for comparative analysis. An awareness of how ocean fishing differs from agriculture increases understanding of the impact of environmental demands and of the caste and *jajmani* systems in nonindustrial work organization in India.

THE VILLAGE OF MINAKUPPAM

Minakuppam is a small hamlet of ocean going fishermen, located just outside the city of Madras in Tamilnadu state. The village's 150 homes, mostly thatch-roofed huts, are clustered together between a dense palm grove behind the village and a broad sandy beach and the blue waters of the Bay of Bengal in front. The surrounding area is barren, treeless sand, making the village look very isolated and desolate. There are two other fishing hamlets half a mile distant along the beach in opposite directions, and a multi-caste community of farmers and city workers is located a mile inland. Just a few hundred yards from the village is a paved road, used by city residents who come to the beach to swim and by villagers who walk three miles to a bustling suburb with many shops and with buses running into the city of Madras. Despite its isolated appearance, Minakuppam residents rely upon the city to market their fish, to buy supplies, and to provide entertainment. In addition, the city and visitors to the beach provide full and part-time job opportunities for some villagers, and the life style of these visitors has become increasingly differentiated from that of the fishing majority.

The coastal fishermen around Madras city and indeed along most of the Tamilnadu coast are all members of the same low caste of *Pattanachettiars,* so Minakuppam, unlike most agricultural villages, contains only members of a single caste. Fishing is considered a dirty, polluting occupation, and other castes look down upon the fishermen. Although the fishermen do not regard themselves as Untouchable, they are on the government list of Scheduled Castes. The village is similar to an Untouchable hamlet in an agricultural village in that its members are all relatively poor and are bound together by common caste sentiment and customs, kinship bonds, and a community temple and festival. However, it is very different from an Untouchable hamlet in its economic independence and general lack of informal contacts and formal ties with higher caste persons.

Minakuppam is fairly representative of the fishing villages around Madras city, which accounts for approximately 20 per cent of the ocean fishermen in Tamilnadu (Chacko *et al.* 1957). There are ocean fishing hamlets all along the coastline of the state, but they are most heavily concentrated in the north, where the city of Madras provides a ready market for fresh fish, and near the Cape, where fish are most abundant. The Fisheries Department survey indicates that fishing technology is roughly similar throughout the state (Chacko *et. al.* 1957). In the south, most of the catch is dried and the marketing system differs from that of the northern villages like Minakuppam where almost all the catch is sold fresh. Until there are more studies of fishing in other areas of India, it is impossible to say how similar work organization in Minakuppam is to that of other fishermen.

The Organization of Fishing

Nearly every household in Minakuppam depends on fishing. Of 190 male workers in the village, about three-quarters are totally dependent on fishing, and only 29 men do not fish at all. In addition, fishing-related activities provide part-time employment for many women and older men. The returns from fishing are highly variable and uncertain from day to day and from season to season, and during the monsoon storms no fishing is possible. The unpredictibility and excitement of these day to day economic activities have a pervasive effect on the village.

Fishing Techniques

The men of Minakuppam use very simple equipment and techniques for fishing, but these are well adapted to their needs. There are no sheltered coves or backwaters, and boats must be brought through the surf and beached each day. These boats are especially simple and even crude looking.

The major type of boat is a simple log raft that the fishermen call a catamaran, although it does not have outriggers. The logs are unlashed and dried on the beach after each day's fishing; they are lashed together again in the morning. Rafts vary in length from eight to fifteen feet, and their cost varies by size from Rs.125 to Rs.1,200. The fishermen carefully guide the raft through the rough surf with long poles. On rough days, if they misjudge the waves the raft and its occupants are overturned. Beyond the surf, a paddle thrust through the logs serves as a crude rudder. The men either hoist a sail, or tie on blocks of wood that serve as fulcrums and then row from one side with only one oar each.

Only one other type of boat is used in the village, the *peria badaga* (big boat). It is a double-ended row boat, fifteen to twenty feet long, of rib and plank construction, and with an unusually deep draft for its length. The big boat costs Rs.2,000 to make. It is very awkward to manage and is used only for beach seine fishing when the sea is very calm, a total of about six months spread throughout the year. This boat too is poled through the surf, and the men row and steer it with long oars.

Four major types of fishing are carried on in the village: beach seine, purse seine, gill net, and line fishing. The seasonal variations in types of fishing and other details of each technique are presented in Table 1. The fishermen also use small hand nets for catching crabs and shrimp in the backwaters during the monsoon when they cannot go out on the ocean.

TABLE 1

Fishing Techniques Used in Minakuppam

Type of Net	Tamil Name	Crew Required	Cost	Size	Season	Type of Fish
Beach Seine	Peria Valle	15 men Large boat	Rs. 1500	Inner Bag— 50' across 20' deep Total Length 200 yds.	Jan., Feb. May, June Sept., Oct.	Nethali (whitebait) plus many others
Purse Seine	Thuri Valle	2 rafts 4-6 men	Rs. 500	75 yds. long Inner Bag 15 ft. deep 10 ft. across	All year, esp. good in Nov.,Dec. Jan., May, June	Mixed fish and prawns
Gill Net	Kavale Valle	1 raft 2-3 men	Rs. 250— 600 by	50 ft. to 100 yds.	Jan., Feb., May, June Sept., Oct. All year (less profitably)	Kavale (perch) Mixed fish and prawns
Gill Net	Patnool(nylon) Valle	Same	Rs. 500— 1200 by size	Same-tend to be longer	All year	Mixed fish and prawns

Beach Seines: In terms of both the numbers of persons involved and the initial investment required, the beach seine (*peria valle* or "big net") is the most complicated type of fishing undertaken in the village. There are only three of these nets in the village. A net costs about Rs.1,500, and an additional Rs.500 must be loaned to prospective employees. It is used with the big boat during calm periods. The beach seine is a fine mesh bag with long wings of gradually increasing mesh size on each side, all made of jute coir. The inner bag alone is about 50 feet across and 20 feet deep, and the wings extend about 75 yards on each side.

When used, the rope attached to one end of the net is left on shore, and the boat is rowed out beyond the surf for a quarter to a half mile. Then the net is laid in the water parallel to the shore, the rope attached to the other end is brought back to shore, and the fishermen begin the arduous task of pulling the net through the surf onto the beach. At least fifteen men are needed to take the boat out, and many more people join in pulling the net, including old men, young boys, and women. By the time the net is landed, 30 or more people are involved. This net traps large schools of whitebait (*nethali*), tiny fish prized for their taste and ease of drying. In addition, a variety of other fish are caught in the net. Catches are often spectacular at the height of the season, when all three nets are in use, and as many as half of the villagers are involved in this type of fishing.

Purse Seines: Complicated fishing techniques are also needed for purse seines, but they require far fewer laborers and are much less costly than the beach seine. All the purse seines and gill nets are used on the same mud-bottomed fishing grounds, most with depths of eight fathoms or less. The bottom supports the plant life on which the fish feed. These fishing grounds are limited in number and size, and arguments sometimes develop when two boats arrive simultaneously or nets become entangled as a result of fishing too close to each other.

There are several different types of purse seines known and used by Tamilnadu fishermen. The only one commonly used in this village is the *thuri valle* (bag net). It is about 75 yards in total length, shaped like the beach seine only smaller and of finer mesh, partly jute and partly cotton cord. There are over thirty of these nets in the village, and each costs about Rs.500.

The *thuri* net requires two rafts and at least four men. The net, the lower edge weighted and the upper with floats attached, is lowered into the water. Each raft takes the line from one end of the net and the men row in opposite directions, stretching the net out fully. Then they row toward one another, forming a circle. The catamarans are tied together and anchored, and the men slowly draw the net toward them, trapping the fish. The *thuri* net is very popular despite the hard work its use entails, because the net can be used throughout the year and is at its best in relatively rough weather. The *thuri* catches all kinds of prawns and fish, and no one species predominates. Most of the fish are small, but occasionally there are a few larger fish up to two feet in length.

Gill Nets: The simplest nets used in the village are gill nets, requiring the fewest workers and the least skill. The fishermen know many different types of gill nets, but all are simple lengths of netting weighted on one edge. They differ mainly in the size of the mesh and therefore the size of the fish caught. There are more than 25 of each of the two gill net types that are most common in the village, the *kavale* net made of cotton and the *patnool* (nylon) net. The nylon nets have been used in the village for only three years. Nylon is more efficient in trapping fish and less easily torn, and has become very popular. However, nylon thread doubles both the initial cost and the cost of repairs for the net. Both nets vary a great deal in length, from 50 feet to 100 yards, and cost from Rs.250 to Rs.600 in cotton and twice as much in nylon.

Gill nets are all used in the same way, and require only one raft and two or three workers. The net is lowered into the water perpendicular to the prevailing current. One edge is weighted and rests on the bottom of the sea. After waiting for up to an hour, the men lift the net out of the water and remove the fish. Gill nets can be used throughout the year. Like the *thuri* net, they catch a variety of small fish and prawns, with no one species predominating. During the same months that the beach seine is used, the *kavale* catch contains many *kavale,* small silvery perch-like fish.

Hand Line Fishing: Of all the techniques used in the village, line fishing requires the least capital, the fewest workers, and the smallest amount of planning. Setting the hook and landing large fish without poles requires a skill quite different from net fishing. Some of the village men feel that they are especially lucky at line fishing, and use this technique frequently. Almost everyone does line fishing at least occasionally, either for the whole day or in the afternoon when the nets need little repair. The cost of equipment is less than Rs.25 and includes just a nylon line and some hooks. No poles or reels are ever used, even for large fish.

Several spots that are breeding grounds are very good for line fishing at certain times of the year. The most popular area is the site of an old airplain wreck only about a mile from shore. Although the number of fish caught is smaller than with nets, they are usually larger and of the more expensive varieties, such as seerfish, red mullet, perch, and small stingrays.

Lines are often put out for large fish while waiting to pull in nets. At certain times of the year, some men also go out with heavy lines just to catch large fish, including seerfish, salmon, red mullet, pomfret, and sharks. Thirty-pound fish are the largest that can be landed, because larger fish either break the line or drag the boat.

Procuring Equipment

All types of boats and nets are made in the village with materials purchased outside. The long logs used for the raft come from Kerala. One fisherman in the village specializes in shaping the catamarans, and most people hire him to make their rafts. Labor is a relatively small part of the cost of a raft, only Rs.200 for a raft costing Rs.1,200. Making a new big boat is a relatively rare event. Professional carpenters come to the village to build it with the help of the prospective owners and crewmen.

Everyone in the village over eight years of age knows how to weave nets and does so at least occasionally. Most men hire three to ten people to work on sections of a new net that are later joined together. Each person is given the jute, cotton, or nylon thread and receives a payment equal to the cost of the thread he or she is given to weave. Net-making is a small but important supplement to the incomes of retired fishermen, widows, and poorer families. A new net can be completed in this manner in a month, and labor represents one half of the net's cost. Most men who need a new net want it urgently because it will greatly increase their earning power. A man with more time than money can make his own net gradually for about half the cost, but it would take about a year. Most net owners try to keep large sections of netting made up so that they can repair large tears rapidly, and if a net is hopelessly damaged these large sections form part of a new net.

In addition to the construction of new boats and nets, there is a lively market in secondhand equipment, especially nets. More prosperous owners try to replace their old equipment every few years as it begins to need more repairs. Enterprising men without equipment get their start with cheaper used equipment they repair in their spare time.

Work Relationships

The technology and the local ecology of Minakuppam together provide a set of constraints on the economic life of the village. Fishing activities must be physically and therefore socially separate from other activities. The type of fishing, degree of success, and size of work groups shift with the seasons, so the labor system must be flexible.

A second set of constraints arise from the uneven distribution of fishing equipment in Minakuppam. Only 40 per cent of the households in the village—about half of all the households that depend on fishing—own equipment. They organize fishing expeditions, and other villagers depend upon them for employment. The amount of equipment owned determines the number of workers needed. Over one half of the owners have equipment worth Rs.1,000 or less, usually one raft and a gill net. Most of these men need only one or two additional workers. About 45 per cent of the owners have equipment worth Rs.1,000 to Rs.2,000. Most of these men have one or two rafts and several nets. Unlike owners with only one net, they can use the type of net that is best suited for each season. Most owners require at least two workers, and up to four if they regularly use a *thuri* net. The three men in the village with equipment worth more than Rs.2,000 all own beach seines and big boats, and have a raft and other nets as well. Each has two or three year-round employees and an additional ten to fifteen workers during the beach seine season.

There are three types of work relationship in Minakuppam, family workers, regular employees, and casual workers. When an owner has a son over twelve living in his house, the son nearly always fishes with his father. This arrangement is highly profitable for the family, because the son's help usually allows the family to eliminate a hired worker. The fishermen follow a stem family pattern, so most sons establish separate households at or soon after marriage. At any given point in time, only about a quarter of the owners are able to fish with a work team entirely from their own household.

The employer-employee relationship in Minakuppam entails definite obligations for both the employer and the employee. The employer binds men to work for him by giving them an interest-free loan. The loan need not be repaid unless the man wants to work for someone else or to become independent. Often the money lent by the new employer will be used to repay the former one. The owner is also expected to give his employees additional small loans for domestic needs and events such as funerals and marriages. The employee is obligated only not to work for others; he cannot be compelled to work on any given day. Often a man is employed for only one type of fishing, usually the beach seine, and he is obligated to work for that employer only during that season.

There are also a number of workers in the village who are not regular employees. They are free to choose the fishing arrangement they prefer each day, and the employer has no obligation to ask them to accompany him regularly. While fishing, casual workers have the same duties and receive the same rewards as regular employees. These unattached fishermen provide the flexibility necessary for the labor system as a whole. If regular employees cannot work on a certain day, they are replaced by independent workers. When an owner decides to use a purse seine rather than a gill net, he adds a few unattached laborers; when he goes back to the gill net, they can be dropped without disturbing the core of his work group.

A work group may consist of any combination of owner, workers from within the household, regular employees, and temporary workers. None of these distinctions cause differences in the way fishing is conducted.

The villagers disagree a great deal about the role kinship should play in fishing. Sons whose fathers own equipment fish with them until the sons set up separate households, but conflicts often arise as sons get older. Boys whose fathers do not own equipment seldom fish regularly until they are sixteen to eighteen years of age. Because they receive only token payments, it is unprofitable, and only a few years of experience are needed. When they do fish, it is more often with nonrelatives than with their fathers or equipment-owning relatives. Many owners prefer to hire kinsmen because they like to help their relatives and because a relative should be more diligent about net repairs. Other owners avoid relatives as employees because they find kinsmen lazy and difficult to control. Workers also have differing views. Some prefer to work for relatives because the kinship bond makes the relationship more stable, while others resent working for their more prosperous kin. Younger men often prefer to fish with nonrelatives as they do not have to defer to them or refrain from smoking in their presence. It is important that men who fish together for long hours on a small raft like and respect one another. If relatives get along well, they are likely to fish together; if they get along poorly, neither economic factors nor village sentiments require them to fish together.

Organization of Fishing Work Groups

Work relationships during fishing are quite egalitarian. The owner decides what type of equipment to use, gathers the men together in the morning, and finds substitute workers if necessary; but decisions about matters such as where and how long to fish are usually discussed by the crew as a whole. Tasks are relatively undifferentiated and are shared equally. The owner does not direct the work, but participates in it as an equal. Some workers are recognized as more skilled or experienced than others and their judgments are often deferred to, but they do not receive any special compensation or privileges. Only young boys still learning to fish are treated differently from other workers and expected to defer to the decisions of their elders. Owners supply the materials necessary for repairing nets; the owner and all the workers repair the net together after they return.

The fishermen depend upon one another's skill for survival in any crisis at sea. Their tasks are fairly simple, but require close co-ordination. They spend long hours together in a very restricted space. Catches are far more affected by seasonal and daily fluctuations than by differences in skill and knowledge of crew members. In addition, workers belong to the same caste and social group as do employers, and they often have kinship ties. All these factors emphasize the equality and interdependence of a work group.

In Minakuppam, economic relationships are rather clearly separated from non-economic ones. While employers expect support from their workers in any local quarrels or in politics and expect to help the worker with loans in times of trouble, employers cannot ask their workers to do any tasks outside of fishing, and they must work beside them in fishing activities. Work relationships are more amiable among friends, but friendship does not alter the duties of worker and owner. Kinship bonds are seldom allowed to interfere with economic relationships.

Selling the Fish

For most types of fishing, men set out very early in the morning and return home about midday. The afternoon is spent repairing the net. While the men are away, the beach is deserted, and the village is quiet as women go about their household tasks and children play in small groups or go to school. When the boats return, everyone gathers on the beach. Wives come to care for their husband's catch; the widows of the village and other women who want to earn a little money come to buy small amounts of fish they can sell in the market; men from outside the village come to buy fish on a larger scale. In addition, many other villagers, including children, old men, and those who did not go fishing, are drawn to the beach to see who was lucky and perhaps to get a few fish from a friend or relative.

The owner's wife helps to unload the boat and selling the fish is now her responsibility, although the husband often stands by and gives advice. The fish auction occurs on the beach as soon as a boat is unloaded. Everyone crowds around to watch the drama; in the end the highest bidder pays cash to the fisherman's wife and takes off his fish. Then the noisy process starts all over again, ending only when the last boat has returned to shore.

Most of the fish caught in the village are bought by men who come from the city or nearby suburbs. They do not represent any single caste group, although many are Muslim traders. They purchase as much fish as they can afford, and then take them to market. There they sell the fish directly to customers or to a person with a market stall. They are relatively small operators and most make under Rs.5 per day. Their relations with the fishermen are strictly impersonal. There are no customary arrangements to sell fish to a specific buyer, and no credit is ever extended to the buyers by the fishermen.

The price of a catch varies greatly. One important factor is the time of day at which the fish are brought in. The buyers come to the beach by 10:00 a.m. and want to leave with their fish by noon or 1:00 p.m. When the first boats return, 20 or 30 people are bidding for fish, and the competition drives up prices. By one o'clock prices are much lower, and on some days all the traders are gone. Then the wife must either sell the fish at a low price to one of the village women who sell fish or take them to town herself. A few traders and some of the village women buy more fish in the late afternoon to sell in the evening markets, but prices are lower because any fish not sold by the end of the day have to be dried and sold for much less than fresh fish.

The relative scarcity of fish also affects fish prices, both from day to day and from season to season. During the monsoon, fish prices more than double. The variety caught is somewhat less important. Large fish that can be cut into steaks command slightly higher prices, as do certain species thought to be more tasty, including seerfish, ocean salmon, sharks, red mullet, and the tiny whitebait. The premium given for size and variety is higher during periods when fish are abundant and declines when they are scarce. However, the demand for fresh fish of any kind in the city markets is always high.

Division of Proceeds

In Minakuppam, workers receive a share of the proceeds rather than a daily wage. Before the auction, each man takes a few fish from the catch for his family's evening meal. After the fish are sold, a fixed percentage is set aside for the net owner as an extra share. The percentage varies by tradition according to the type of net used, from a high of 50 per cent for all gill nets to a low of one extra share for the *thuri* net, usually about 20 per cent (see Table 1 for details). The size of the owner's share seems to be inversely related to the degree of skill and co-operation among workers needed for success with a particular net, not its costliness. The proportional return to owners may seem excessive, but it must be remembered that this is his gross income. Out of it he must pay the cost of upkeep, repairs, and eventual replacement of his equipment. In addition, he must lend money to his crew and distribute a generous bonus on lucky days if he hopes to keep them as regular workers.

After the owner's share has been set aside, the remaining cash is divided equally among the workers. Young boys learning to fish get only a token payment. The owner nearly always goes fishing and he receives an equal share of the money as a workman in addition to the percentage of the catch he receives as owner of the equipment.

The distribution of money among the workers for the beach seine net follows a somewhat different procedure. When the catch brings Rs.100 or more, the owner receives half the catch; otherwise, he gets a third. The casual helpers who pull on the nets but do not go out with the boat are given a small sum. Then the regular workers receive unequal shares of the remaining money. Those who have been with the owner the longest receive the largest shares. If the catch was large, the owner gives his workers more money, until the owner's original half share is reduced to about a third share. This money can be distributed as the owner sees fit. In addition to rewarding loyalty, he often gives extra money to the old men, widows, and other particularly needy people who helped to pull in the net. In this way the owner enhances his reputation for generosity and makes it easier for him to gather together his crew for the next day's fishing.

OTHER ECONOMIC ACTIVITIES

Although fishing activities predominate, fishing is not the only source of income for the men of the village. Each day 29 men go into the city of Madras to work where they perform a wide variety of tasks, mostly as unskilled laborers. Because of their regular work in the city, the full-time workers are less involved in the ongoing life of the village. They are more aware of what goes on outside the village and have frequent, regular, and somewhat more personalized relationships with urban residents than do the other villagers. Although some fishing owners make more money, most urban jobs pay quite well relative to fishing.

About 25 men regularly supplement their earnings from fishing by working for people who come to the beach. Usually they look after a hut which a family has built to change clothes and store chairs. These men make a little money by carrying things down to the beach for people, selling them shells, and doing other small services. Unlike the Madras workers, the beach workers remain integrated into the fishing economy, but their regular income from outside sources gives them some independence and greater security during the monsoon. The contacts beach workers have with urban dwellers are perhaps more intense though less frequent than those of the Madras workers, and they have contacts with people from a higher social stratum. Since bathing is a relatively new phenomenon in Indian society, the people who come to this beach regularly are all middle or upper class, wealthy, and relatively westernized.

Many women in the village work outside the household to augment their family's cash earnings. There are eleven houses in the village where the main earner is a woman, usually a widow. Many other women also work some of the time to supplement their family's income. The most common economic activity of women is selling fish. Others make and sell illicit liquor. A few women run small stores selling candy, betel leaf, and other miscellaneous items. Some women with extra money lend it to others at high interest rates, thus earning small sums.

ECONOMIC CLASSES AND SOCIAL MOBILITY

None of the villagers is wealthy by urban standards, but the differences in wealth among the villagers are quite important in daily life. During the monsoon when no one can fish, tension exists between the poor and the well-to-do. About twelve households in the village contain no active men and depend entirely upon the earnings of an old man or widow. These households are very poor, and often require the aid of kinsmen and neighbors. The majority of families make enough to live from day-to-day but seldom enough to accumulate any savings. The men of these households are usually fishing laborers who own no fishing equipment and have no other capital.

The families of equipment owners are usually much more prosperous than the laborers, although they differ widely in their wealth and the amount of equipment they control. Although they do not live much differently from the average fishermen, their greater economic security and their control of the economic activities of others make equipment owners an important group of men for the village.

The twenty-two men who work at the beach are also more prosperous than fishing laborers, and some of them earn more than equipment owners. Some of the men who have regular jobs in the city are the wealthiest in the village. They do not have the economic control that equipment owners do, but villagers admire them because they no longer fish—an occupation that is risky, has uncertain rewards, and is looked down upon as "dirty" in Hindu society. Fishermen also envy both the Madras workers and beach workers for their secure income that comes regardless of season or weather. The wider horizon and urban contacts of the city and beach workers also give them prestige.

These economic groupings are the most important cleavages in the village, but the boundaries are far from rigid. Upward and downward economic mobility seems to be quite frequent in Minakuppam. Future and past mobility is a favorite topic of conversation among fishermen, and they clearly regard mobility as part of the normal lot of many fishermen.

Men who begin as fishing laborers can accumulate equipment in a variety of ways. A man can put aside money when he has an especially lucky season, or he may inherit some equipment or money. A wife can help by selling fish or by lending small sums of money to other women at high interest rates. A laborer can build up his holdings gradually with second-hand equipment and his own labor, or he can borrow from relatives and repay them from his increased earnings. Loss of equipment in rough weather or from normal wear and tear, a system of equal inheritance among sons, and pressures to consume rather than invest cause some equipment-owning families to suffer a decline.

FISHING AND AGRICULTURE IN SOUTH INDIA

Ethnographies of 20 Indian agricultural villages, including all those available for the southern region, provide a basis for a comparison of fishing and agriculture (see Norr 1972 for details on villages selected and coding). Fishing, in comparison with agriculture in South India, involves greater variation of work and income, greater separation of home and workplace, greater physical risks and need for skill and teamwork, and lower costs and faster depreciation of capital equipment. Ownership of the means of production is more widely distributed in the fishing village. Work in ocean fishing is organized with less hierarchy and more clearly defined duties, and workers receive a greater share of the proceeds. Work relationships are more egalitarian and more separated from other social relationships in fishing. Mobility among economic classes seems to be more frequent in the fishing village.

In the fishing village there are three basic work relationships: unpaid work for a common family enterprise, a long-term employment, and temporary day labor. Each of these relationships also exists in Indian agricultural villages. In addition, there is tenant farming, which is most common in the villages located in the south. Widespread use of tenant farming makes the labor system more complex by adding a layer of non-cultivating owners at the top of the system. Unpaid family labor plays a much larger role in farming than it does in the fishing village. Women and children are not involved directly in fishing operations, while in agricultural villages women and children perform many tasks with the men.

Regardless of whether workers are day laborers or permanent employees, the actual work of farming is organized differently from fishing. Owner and laborers perform the same tasks co-operatively in fishing, whereas jobs in farming often are allotted by status. Untouchables usually do the dirtiest tasks. If he can afford to do so, the agricultural employer will supervise his workers but do no manual labor himself. Even those employers who work in the fields generally supervise their employees, allot tasks, and determine each day's goals without consulation. The employer has very wide authority over his workers within the economic sphere. In southern rice growing areas, there is a major exception to this hierarchical work organization. Transplanting of paddy is usually done by teams of women, generally of the same caste grouping, who have a leader and organize their own labor. Tasks like plowing are sometimes done by special teams of men who organize their own work. In comparison with the fishing laborer, the agricultural laborer has much broader obligations to his employer, frequently including non-farming work, political support, and ritual duties. The extent of the laborer's obligations varies considerably, and is greatest in those villages where contract labor is an outgrowth of previous hereditary serfdom or where tenant farming is common.

In both agriculture and fishing, the division of proceeds favor the owner of capital rather than the laborer. Depending upon the type of equipment, the fishing owner receives from about one-fifth to one-half of the total catch in addition to his share as a worker. Returns to the owners are more difficult to determine in agricultural villages because pay schedules for different types of working arrangements differ. Both day laborers and long term employees are paid a fixed sum. Most ethnographers imply that wages are as low as possible and often inadequate to sustain a family which does not have several workers.

Tenant farmers receive a fixed share of the harvest (or, less often, pay a fixed sum for use of the land), and their share can be compared to the shares of fishing laborers. In many states the government has fixed the owner's share of the harvest—in Tamilnadu, at one-third of the yield. In no village examined, however, does the owner actually take less than half the produce. In two Tanjore villages, owners receive four-fifths to two-thirds of the harvest (Gough 1955; Beteille 1965). On balance, it seems that owners of capital are rewarded even more highly in agricultural villages than among fishermen.

In the fishing village, workers receive equal shares, reinforcing the equality and mutual interdependence of the work team. In agricultural communities, different types of working arrangements have different terms of payment. At harvest times the tenant-farmer pays the owner rent out of his proceeds and permanent employees are paid in grain. The ceremony of payment emphasizes the unequal status of the land owner and his workers. Day laborers are paid a fixed sum at the end of each day's work, and unlike tenant farmers and permanent employees, are not regarded as partners in a common enterprise.

The absence of data, especially time series, makes it difficult to evaluate patterns of mobility within fishing and farming. However, there seems to be more mobility in Minakuppam than in Indian agricultural villages. Certainly, the fishermen themselves believe mobility in fishing to be unusually high. A great deal of the difference in mobility can be attributed to the greater ease with which productive capital can be accumulated or lost in fishing.

ACCOUNTING FOR DIFFERENCES IN WORK ORGANIZATION

Three differences in the social and ecological context of fishing and farming in South India appear to be important in accounting for differences in work organizations. First, ocean fishing, unlike farming, is not organized in a network of *jajmani* relations. Second, it is performed by a single caste, low in status. Third, the environmental and technical constraints of fishing differ in significant ways from those of agriculture.

The *jajmani* system of hereditary, economic and ritual ties between land owners and other castes has long provided the general model of employer-employee relations in rural India. The *jajmani* network of work relationships between the same individuals and families persists over time and tend to become generalized to non-economic areas. Caste ideology and ritual observances reinforce the hierarchical and unequal character of the relationship. Even in those areas where the *jajmani* networks have broken down, this view of work relations tend to persist. The fact that ocean fishing has never been in a *jajmani* network facilitates a more egalitarian model of employer-employee relations.

Almost everywhere in India farming is a multicaste activity. Ocean fishing in Tamilnadu is the occupation of a single low caste group. This encourages the fishermen to emphasize their common bonds and to minimize differences among them. Generally, low castes seem to place more emphasis upon caste solidarity and equality while higher castes give greater emphasis to internal status differences (cf. Gough 1956).

There are major differences between the technical and environmental demands of ocean fishing and of agriculture. Fishing requires flexibility, while farming requires continuity. In agriculture, work is organized in a seasonal cycle of plowing, planting, and harvesting; the meaningful unit of planning and activity is not the day but the planting season. The fisherman has to take his irregular daily profits and use them to satisfy his daily needs, to finance the next day's fishing, and to provide for an undefined period of unemployment when the weather prevents fishing.

Differences in timing lead to a greater need for teamwork and co-operation in fishing than in farming. There are many regular tasks in fishing, such as pulling in a net or maneuvering a boat through heavy surf, where all the crew members must work together smoothly and quickly. While a number of agricultural tasks are performed by groups, most of the time workers individually do the same task simultaneously and have little effect on the activities of their fellow workers.

Fishing in the ocean makes a number of physical demands upon the worker. A combination of physical risks and long separation from shore makes it difficult for fishing to include less than fully active workers, women, or children. The physical separation of work makes it more difficult for work organization to be integrated with other social relationships, and thus work roles tend to be specific and limited to work related activities. The less diffuse relationships in fishing curtail the scope of authority of owners. In addition, greater physical risks increase the importance of workers and the need for interdependence.

The somewhat more equal distribution of the means of production in fishing as compared with agricultural villages appears to be partially related to techniques of production. Fishing entails higher risk of equipment loss, and fishing equipment depreciates quickly. The value of capital needed for peasant level fishing tends to be less than the value of land and equipment needed for farming. These factors make it easier to accumulate and lose fishing equipment and thus lead to greater upward and downward mobility.

The over-all impact of the lower level of capital investment and technical constraints is to make the authority and rewards of owners in fishing rather limited and the social and economic distance between owners and laborers in fishing relatively small. In agriculture, at least under favorable environmental conditions, there seem to be fewer technical restrictions on the power and rewards of land owners.

A comparison of Minakuppam with other peasant level ocean fishing villages in six other culture areas suggests that peasant level ocean fishing requires equality and close co-ordination in work relationships (Norr and Norr 1974). Where the prevailing work relationships in agriculture are hierarchical and inegalitarian, as they are in south India, ocean fishing must either be organized relatively inefficiently or work relationships must be very different from those of the more prevalent agricultural model. In South India, this problem seems to be solved by organizing fishing as an occupation of a single caste, relatively isolated from farmers, with a very low status. This solution provides an ideological and social organizational basis for co-operation and relative equality among fishermen. Because ocean fishermen are physically isolated and are held in low esteem, these deviant and perhaps threatening egalitarian relationships are insulated from the predominately agricultural society.

NOTE

1. Fieldwork in Minakuppam took place from June, 1965 to May, 1966. All references to prices and seasonal fluctuations in weather and fishing are for this period. During 1965, there was no June monsoon, and the fall one came very late, in November and December. The official exchange rate then was nearly Rs.5 to US$1, but the local purchasing power of the rupee was much higher than the official rate indicated. My deepest thanks go to my co-worker and translator, A. Golpala Krishna, then an

anthropology student at the University of Madras, whose many contributions to the success of the fieldwork cannot be enumerated.

BIBLIOGRAPHY

Chacko, P. I., S. George, and P. P. Krishnaswamy. 1957. Census of the Sea Fisher-folk and Fishing Crafts and Gear in Madras State. Madras Fisheries Statistics Report No. 53.

Gough, K. 1956. Brahmin Kinship in a Tamil Village. American Anthropologist 63: 826-853.

Norr, K. L. 1972. A South Indian Fishing Village in Comparative Perspective. Un-published Ph.D. dissertation, University of Michigan.

Norr, K. L., and J. L. Norr. 1974. Environmental and Technical Factors Influenc-ing Power in Work Organizations: Ocean Fishing in Peasant Societies. Sociology of Work and Occupations 1: 219-251.

A Comparative Study of Work Groups in an Eastern Canadian Peasant Fishing Community: Bilateral Kinship and Adaptive Processes[1]

Yvan Breton

With regard to patterns of work organization, fishing communities are often characterized as relatively "fluid social units." Anthropologists such as Firth, Barnes, and Barth have analyzed social and economic activities in such communities to demonstrate the validity of this assertion. In Malay villages, fishing groups scarcely form permanent units of co-operation and have little corporateness given the predominance of individual proprietorship and the greater importance of contractual rather than familial relations in the recruitment of personnel. This situation leads Firth (1966) to apply economic concepts to his analysis and to insist upon the numerous choices which fishermen face. Barnes (1954:41-43) develops the network concept in a Norwegian community, distinguishing between a stationary field related to land cultivation and a fluid field dependent upon fishing. In a similar way, Barth (1966:6-10) illustrates the relations between skippers, net-boss, and sharemen in another Norwegian fishing village in order to operationalize his generative model.[2]

Besides their common participation in fishing, these societies share another characteristic: they all have bilateral kinship systems. Recent studies also show that the dominant feature of these systems lies in their "extreme flexibility" and the amplitude of the field opened to individual initiative for the manipulation of economic and political alliances (Godelier 1970: 115).

Since St. Paul River in Quebec is a "peasant fishing community" with a bilateral kinship system,[3] the present article contributes to the existing body of literature discussed above. However, rather than verifying the applicability of particular theories or resolving terminological problems,[4] my aim is to show, by examination of work groups in four activities, how the socio-economic organization represents an adaptive response to a specific geographical and social environment and how a bilateral kinship system offers great flexibility for adaptive strategies.

GENERAL FRAMEWORK: ECONOMIC HISTORY OF THE VILLAGE

During the seventeenth and eighteenth centuries only a few entrepreneurs

129

inhabited the coastal region of St. Paul River, making a living on seal fishing and commerce with the native Indian population.[5] Around 1820, outside companies specializing in cod fishing also obtained rights of exploitation in the area.[6] Every summer they hired large groups of fishermen, mostly English and Irish, on a wage basis. After a few decades, some of these fishermen settled down permanently and engaged in secondary activities such as sealing, fur animal trapping, and caribou hunting during the off-fishing season. Cod fishing was controlled by external agents who monopolized the equipment, especially the cod-trap,[7] and provided local inhabitants with products not available in the community.

By the end of the last century, decreasing productivity forced the companies to sell their equipment to the highest bidder, generally at a very low price. This promoted the emergence of an essentially local enterprise for fishing and stimulated new patterns of work organization in which kinship gained importance. Also from 1920 to 1950, fishermen increased their participation in fur animal trapping, benefitting from relatively good prices for their products.

During the period since World War II, the opening of mining centers in the north of the Province of Quebec[8] brought significant changes in the traditional economic organization, producing a temporary emigration of many family heads and young adults. At the same time, prices for fish and fur lowered considerably.[9] Only recently has cod fishing recovered some importance. Meanwhile, the traditional secondary activities have been abandoned. Contemporary occupational statistics reveal that some 85 per cent of the active male labor force subsist as cod fishermen supplemented in the winter by communal labor projects financed by the government.[10]

Table 1 shows that since its beginning the economic organization of St. Paul River has undergone several modifications. The synchronic examination of any given economic phase reveals the constant plurality of the sources of income. Fishermen successively worked for outside and local employers, in large and small groups, and successively adopted and abandoned several activities. In other words, they continuously adapted themselves to an unstable economic situation. Our task is to define more precisely the nature of their flexibility and to explain its modalities.

STRUCTURE AND FUNCTIONING OF WORK GROUPS

One can presuppose that the exploitation of codfish, seals, and terrestrial mammals implies the utilization of different technologies which give rise to socio-economic formations of a particular nature. On the other hand, these activities have been conducted by people of the same community, with relatively homogeneous cultural models and economic possibilities. It is thus logical to assume that characteristics of a given work group in one activity may also be operative in another group in a different activity. The first part of the analysis is devoted to the determination of these characteristics. Three comparative axes (recruitment, division of labor, and division of product) will be successively applied to each production unit and will serve to define their structural and operational nature. Crew

TABLE 1
Economic History of St. Paul River

Period of Sedentarization	Demographic Characteristics	Local Sources of Income	Economic Relations with the Exterior	Factors of Change	Results
I. 1820–1900	Seasonal immigration. Local population reached 120 persons at end of period.	Cod fishing, sealing, trapping, hunting.	Companies controlled fish production and provided local people with outside goods.	Abolition of the system of concessions and good market for cod.	Cod fishing replaced sealing as the major activity. Familiarization with the interior zone.
II. 1900–1950	By natural increase population was 260 persons at end of period.	Cod fishing, sealing, trapping, hunting.	Itinerant merchants perpetuated the peonage system of the companies.	Departure of the companies. Increased price for fur.	Fishing becomes a local enterprise. Full exploitation of the natural resources.
III. 1950–1968	Village included 438 persons at time of the study.	Cod fishing, government assistance.	Itinerant merchants with less control. Local people go outside more often.	Decreased price for fur. Opening of mining centers in the north.	Temporary emigration. Abandonment of secondary activities. Specialization in cod fishing.

size and kinship relations among its members provide a statistical model
that indicates the ideal form of grouping for the exploitation of a specific
resource. The division of labor, during acquisitive and transformation
processes, shows the groups in action and explains their structure of
authority. Finally, the division of the product indicates the extent to which
the sharing of responsibilities entails differential rewards and how the
continuity of the productive system is maintained.

Cod Fishing

Since the beginning of sedentarization, cod fishing has been a central
activity in St. Paul River. For this reason, contrary to other activities
discussed below, the analysis of its production units will be done dia-
chronically, emphasizing transformations that have taken place at different
periods. The structure and functioning of the present cod-fishing crews
cannot be understood without reference to their predecessors.

At the time cod fishing was carried on by outside skippers, precise statistics about group formation and qualitative information concerning the nature of the relations between members are not available.
Oral tradition reveals that membership was based on contractual relations
(generally for one year) and that each skipper recruited his personnel
in his own region. There was a tendency for the local inhabitants to stay
with the same skipper during several fishing seasons. The peonage system,
in which outside goods were exchanged for local labor, reduced mobility
among fishermen and minimized competition between skippers. As a
result, although kinship was not a determinant factor in the overall
composition of the crews, members of local families often worked for the
same skipper.

By correlating technical requirements and partial statistical data, we
can deduce that the size of the fishing groups varied between ten and
fifteen men, with the exception of the large firm of Whitely and Sons,
who hired between 100 and 150 men during several years. The skippers
came into the region of St. Paul River at the end of each spring with
one or several schooners. Each schooner carried a certain number of dories
which could accomodate two or three fishermen.[11] These boats were adapted
to hand-line and trawl fishing, conducted on the open sea, mainly on
the banks which lie a few miles off the coast. The report of the Commissioner of Crown Lands of Canada between 1859 and 1868 gives some
idea about the importance and the nature of fishing at that time. For
instance, in Bonne-Esperance, a fishing station at the souhtwest end of
the archipelago, there were 42 schooners, 142 dories, and 482 men in the
summer of 1861. In 1865, there were 16 schooners, 51 dories and 138 men.
In 1866, the same station had 31 schooners, 119 dories and 340 fishermen.[12]
Examples could be multiplied, but these are sufficient to indicate that each
schooner had an average crew of ten men working three dories.

The first part of the day was spent in the capture of pelagic species,
either herring, capelin, or squid[13] that were later used as bait for cod
fishing. At the end of the day, the whole group returned aboard the

schooner and processed the fish. Processing necessitated a division of labor according to specific tasks, such as cutters, throaters, and splitters. In the case of those working for Whitely and Sons, the organization of labor required greater specialization. The use of a wider range of techniques (cod seines and cod-traps besides hand-line and trawl) entailed work groups of different size. Those fishing with the cod seines went to sea in groups of nine; those with a cod-trap in groups of six. Finally, handliners and trawlers worked in groups of ten (three dories), under the direction of a skipper. About one-third of the employees constantly remained ashore to process the fish.

The independent skippers paid their men according to the share system (see below), whereas Whitely paid fixed wages for the whole season. Fishing in the second half of the last century thus depended upon the presence of outside employers with differential amounts of capital. This promoted the emergence and maintenance of heterogeneous work groups whose structure and functioning varied considerably.

With the departure of these entrepeneurs, cod-fishing groups became progressively more homogeneous. This was a two-fold process explained by technical and socio-demographic factors. In the previous decades, the cod-trap had proved its superiority and had been purchased by all skippers who could afford it. At the beginning of the present century, another technological innovation, inboard motors replacing sail boats, increased productivity. As a result, although some fishermen continued to fish in small teams with hand-line and trawl, the majority preferred to work with local skippers who owned the best equipment. At this time there were few local skippers (only four in 1910), and as local population reached only 120 individuals, kinship strongly influenced the recruiting of personnel in cod fishing. This activity became essentially a familial enterprise after the departure of outside employers.[14]

The tabulation of kinship ties between the skipper and the sharemen in three crews is given in Table 2 and points out their strong agnatic basis. Eighty eight per cent of the sharemen were agnatic consanguineals of the skipper, among which 32 per cent were sons and 24 per cent were brothers. Recruitment was based on residence at the fishing stations, itself depending upon agnatic groupings given the predominance of virilocal residence. The average size of the crews was relatively high.

TABLE 2

Kinship Relations Between Skippers and Sharemen in Cod Fishing (1910–20)

No. of Crew	Sons	Br.	BrSo.	FaBrSo.	WiBr.	Strangers	Total Sharemen	Crew Size
1	3	1	2	1	1	—	8	9
2	3	3	1	1	—	1	9	10
3	2	2	2	1	—	1	8	9
Total:	8	6	5	3	1	2	25	28

A partial explanation may be that two of the skippers owned two cod-traps. Also, several young adults and sometimes boys participated in fishing, thus somewhat exaggerating the numerical size of the crews. On the other hand, two of these skippers (no. 1 and 3) were the local representatives of outside merchants, and at the end of the fishing season served as middlemen between local fishermen and outside buyers. It was advantageous for them to hire as many people as they could in order to negotiate the production of independent handliners or trawlers. This was best achieved by giving a job, whenever possible, to members of their families.

The division of labor did not differ significantly from that of the earlier period. One can assume that with the introduction of inboard motors, more time was allocated to the capture of fish. Oral tradition reveals that cod-traps were hauled as many as four times a day when fish were plentiful. The crew processed the fish ashore after each catch, repairing nets and other parts of the equipment between each trip.

However, the sharing of income followed more uniform rules. No local skipper paid fixed wages. Fishermen were given a receipt at the end of the season with which they could purchase goods at local stores.[15] In the division of product the skipper took one-half of the total catch, after deducting operating costs. The remaining half was allocated to all members participating in fishing (including the skipper if he worked at sea) according to a share system very similar to that prevailing today. In addition to the income based on production, sharemen were housed and fed by the skipper during the entire fishing period.

By the summer of 1968, the number of owners probably reached its maximum size, with 35 skippers exploiting cod-trap sites in the vicinity of the archipelago (see Map 1 for the location of sites).

Table 3 again conclusively illustrates the agnatic basis of the present cod-fishing groups, 85 per cent of the sharemen being patrilaterally related to the skipper. Only three are uterine kin. Compared with those of the beginning of the century, contemporary crews show a marked reduction in size, averaging three people instead of nine. Even nine crews include only two fishermen, a number below the minimum required to operate a cod-trap regularly.[16] The fractionating of the means of production, due to an increase in individual capitalization, has produced a relative scarcity of personnel. By the same token, the agnatic extended family has lost much of its relevance as a basis for recruitment and is replaced by the nuclear family. Sons now form 70 per cent of the total number of sharemen instead of 30 per cent as previously. This does not imply changes in the kinship system itself. Crew size acts as a dependent variable in this structural "narrowing" and explains why fishing groups do not now include as many collateral kinsmen. Nonetheless, the agnatic extended family is still of some importance in more informal types of co-operation. Skippers of the same fishing posts, often linked by strong kinship ties, collaborate in ancillary activities, such as the repair of boats and nets, temporary loans of equipment, and mutual aid in selling fish.

Map 1: Location of Cod-Trap Sites in St. Paul River

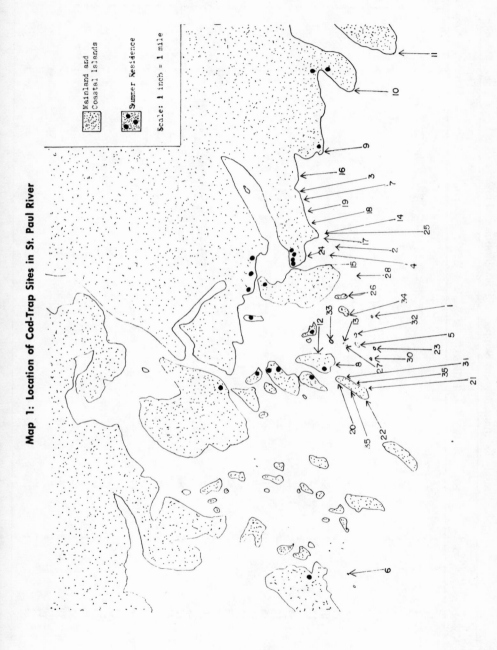

TABLE 3

Kinship Relations Between Skippers and Sharemen in Cod Fishing (1968)

No. of Crew	Sons	Br.	BrSo.	FaBrSo.	SiSo.	WiBr.	DaHus.	Others	Total sharemen	Crew size
1	1	1	—	—	—	—	—	—	2	3
2	2	—	—	—	—	—	—	—	2	3
3	1	—	—	—	—	—	1	—	2	3
4	1	1	—	—	—	—	—	—	2	3
5	1	—	1	—	—	—	—	—	2	3
6	1	1	—	—	—	—	—	—	2	3
7	3	—	—	—	—	—	—	—	3	4
8	1	1	—	—	—	—	—	—	2	3
9	1	—	—	—	—	—	—	—	1	2
10	2	—	—	—	—	—	—	—	2	3
11	1	1	—	—	—	—	—	—	2	3
12	1	—	—	—	—	—	—	—	1	2
13	2	—	—	—	—	—	—	—	2	3
14	2	—	—	—	—	—	—	—	2	3
15	2	1	—	—	—	—	—	—	3	4
16	—	—	—	1	1	—	—	1	3	4
17	1	1	—	—	—	—	—	—	2	3
18	2	—	—	—	—	—	—	—	2	3
19	1	—	—	—	—	—	—	—	1	2
20	1	—	—	—	—	—	—	—	1	2
21	2	—	—	—	—	—	—	—	2	3
22	1	—	—	—	1	—	—	—	2	3
23	1	1	—	—	—	—	—	—	2	3
24	1	—	1	—	—	—	—	—	2	3
25	2	—	—	—	—	1	—	—	2	3
26	1	—	—	—	—	—	—	—	1	2
27	1	—	—	—	—	—	—	—	1	2
28	2	—	—	—	—	—	—	—	2	3
29	2	—	—	—	1	—	—	—	3	4
30	1	—	—	—	—	—	—	2	3	4
31	1	—	—	—	—	—	—	—	1	2
32	2	—	—	—	—	—	—	—	2	3
33	—	—	—	—	1	—	1	—	1	2
34	2	—	—	—	—	—	—	—	2	3
35	3	—	—	—	—	—	—	—	3	4
Total	48	7	2	1	3	1	2	3	67	102

Task performance, to which some reference has been made for historic periods, deserves further attention. Two major types of status within the crew (skipper and sharemen), plus secondary types between fishermen themselves (cutter, throater, and splitter), entail various rights and responsibilities. The skipper makes decisions and commands in every operation. He tells the hands when and how to set the nets. He stands at the stern of the boat using the compass in foggy weather. He decides when a net should be taken ashore for repairing. During the fish-drying process, he determines when the fish are to be spread out or put in the stages. He negotiates with outside buyers at the end of the fishing season, and, once payment is received, he divides the returns among the members of the crew.

On the other hand, fishermen provide labor for the skipper and have no contractual stipulations concerning the hours of work or the type of task to which they are assigned, although the division of labor is well institutionalized. Since most of the processes, either in the acquisition or transformation activities, have to be done with celerity, the fishermen's alertness is a condition essential to the success of a crew. Among the sharemen, the splitter is commonly the oldest man. His relation to the skipper is complementary in that he sometimes controls the fish processing or takes over the direction of the group when the skipper is absent.[17]

Kinship ties presently existing among the cod-fishing crews facilitate the existence of a "comprehensive subordination and command" between the skipper and the sharemen.[18] But even without such kin relationships, the authority of the skipper can never be imperative. He rather influences the actions of his men in accordance with given rules. The cod-fishing season is relatively short, and fishermen often work from fifteen to twenty hours per day when fish are plentiful. The skipper must convert his contractual agreement with the sharemen into a voluntary and spontaneous activity by exercising authority only to the extent that his requests are approved and acceped by his sharemen, and the labor expenditures demanded of them are proportionate to their rewards.

The unequal distribution of authority and responsibility among members of the fishing units entails differential division of the catch. Theoretically, the whole catch is divided into two equal parts after deduction of expenses for fuel, twine, etc. If the skipper owns all the equipment, he receives the first half. If not, this part is shared according to the amount of each individual's investment in equipment. The second half is divided among all members of the crew who worked at sea. Age and experience (not kinship) are the most important factors determining crew shares. Thus an individual may receive a full share, half a share, or even a quarter of a share according to his contribution. For instance, Table 4 shows that in a crew of three sharemen hired on a full-share basis, and with the skipper owning all the equipment and participating in the fishing operations, each shareman receives one-fourth of one-half of the catch, while the skipper receives one-half plus one-eighth of the catch.

Since the system greatly benefits the skipper, one easily understands why so many people have tried to become the owner of a cod-trap and

TABLE 4
Division of Income in Cod Fishing

Members	Total Catch		
	Part for equipment	Part for labor	Individual income
Skipper	1	1/4	5/8
Shareman no. 1	—	1/4	1/8
Shareman no. 2	—	1/4	1/8
Shareman no. 3	—	1/4	1/8
Total	1/2 of total	1/2 of total	1

to have a crew of their own.[19] Given the large number of owners and the low productivity of some sites, this model of division is presently undergoing transformations to the advantage of the sharemen. The half share and the quarter share have almost completely disappeared, and most of the sharemen now get a full share even if they are relatively young. Given the scarcity of personnel, illustrated by the minimal number of fishermen in the majority of the crews, the skippers must distribute a greater part of the income to their sharemen. In some cases, the skipper, although working at sea, even gives his full share to his crew, taking only his part for the equipment. This has followed a new technological innovation in recent years, i.e., the introduction of gill nets.[20] If this technique proves to be superior to the cod-trap, the work organization in cod fishing will undergo several modifications and the sharing of income will be done on a more egalitarian basis.

Sealing

Sealing, a reliable activity when conducted by a few outside entrepreneurs, could never have supported a large population in St. Paul River. Seals had already declined in number at the end of the last century, and productive sites were very scarce (only seven according to informants). Other factors explain why sealing never became a generalized practice for local inhabitants. Formerly it took place in December and January, a time at which the majority of the families had returned to the winter settlement and were engaged in festivities. Compared to sites in neighboring communities, those of St. Paul River had an inferior productivity and the fishermen were reluctant to invest in them.[21] Finally, the high cost of the equipment left few individuals able to afford its purchase and maintenance.[22] The community thus never contained more than two or three sealing groups at any given time, and the equipment was always shared by co-owners.

In the seven crews for which I possess information, eight co-owners were brothers, four were agnatic cousins, and two were brothers-in-law (see Table 5). In order to study the kinship relations between members of the crew, I arbitrarily chose the eldest of the co-owners as the skipper.

TABLE 5

Kinship Relations Between Skipper and Sharemen in Sealing (1920–1950)

No. of Crew	Sons	Br.	FaBrSo.	FaFaBrSo.	MoBrSo.	SiHus.	Total of sharemen	Crew size
1	2	1	1	1	—	1	6	7
2	1	2	1	—	1	—	5	6
3	2	2	—	—	—	1	5	6
4	—	3	—	1	—	—	4	5
5	3	1	1	—	—	—	5	6
6	2	2	—	1	1	—	6	7
7	1	—	3	—	—	—	4	5
Total	11	11	6	3	2	2	35	42

Since in four cases the co-owners were brothers, and since in six additional cases, the co-owners were agnatic kinsmen, the overall tabulation would not be substantially modified if another method of skipper selection were used. Table 5 once again emphasizes the agnatic orientation of recruiting. Sons and brothers represent 62 per cent of the total number of sharemen, while agnatic cousins comprise 25 per cent. Sealing groups often formed through the amalgamation of two cod-fishing groups, the two skippers being the only individuals to own the costly equipment required for the capture of seals. Generally, the crew lived in the skipper's summer residence on outlying islands. Recruitment was influenced by summer residence patterns, and sealing groups present strong affinities with cod-fishing crews.

As in the case of cod fishing, the work organization in sealing reflected a dichotomy between skippers and sharemen. The most experienced of the co-owners, usually the eldest, assumed direction of the crew, taking advice from his partner in crucial moments. Each crew member in turn spent hours watching the sea. At the approach of a school, they notified the skippers, who then decided when to launch the boats and which parts of the nets were to be hauled first. Once the seals were caught, they were brought ashore either with boats or dog teams and left frozen in the stage during the whole winter. In the spring, the skippers again assembled their men for the processing of the seals (the removal of the skin and melting of the fat).

The sharing of the income was similar to that followed in cod fishing. The sharemen's effort was considered equivalent to the owner's risk and depreciation of his invested equipment. After deduction of the expenses, half the catch went to the owners. With the co-owners system, this first half was split in two. But as the owners also fully engaged in fishing, each was entitled to a full share on the remaining half. For instance, in a crew of four sharemen with two co-owners, each co-owner received one-third and the sharemen one-twelfth of the total income. Since the price for seals varied according to the species and their size, the animals were first classified into different categories and the division was made for each category.[23]

Trapping

The exploitation of the interior zone depended upon a specific technology that favored the emergence of socio-economic groups very different from those operating in the maritime region. Fur animal trapping and caribou hunting, no longer important, were associated with production units whose characteristics illustrate significantly the diversity of groupings in the traditional economic system.

Trapping took place in the months of October, November, December, and sometimes in the spring, by groups of two men.

The examination of the kinship ties among the members of 31 teams at the time trapping was general shows a predominance of agnatic ties (68 per cent). Among these, co-operation between two brothers was most frequent, followed by brothers-in-law. Although the lack of uterine kin in the sample may be accidental, such a factor cannot explain the relative importance of brothers-in-law. It indicates rather that consanguine relations were not strictly determinant in the group formaion. This is corroborated when one takes into account the age of the participants. The majority of the trappers were between 20 and 40 years of age, and in most of the teams formed by brothers, agnatic cousins, and brothers-in-law, age differences were small. Only certain individuals could stand an expedition that required great effort and endurance, and co-operation was best achieved between partners of similar age. These factors resulted in a strong tendency to generational grouping in recruitment.

The various operations of trapping, such as repairing of camps, the repair and regular inspection of traps, and the processing of the fur,[24] were performed equally by the partners. At the beginning of the day, they often set out in opposite directions, covering different sections of the territory and returning to a stipulated meeting point at night. The partners decided together the nature and amount of work to be done, and during the fur-selling period they consulted each other before undertaking transactions. Trapping groups were not characterized by a significant structure of authority.

The teams included in the sample all operated between 1920 and 1950. They made an almost clear profit, given the fact that trapping started with the beginning of sedentarization and that the first exploitants spent

TABLE 6
Kinship Relations in Trapping Groups (1920–50)

Type of relation	No. of cases
Father-son	2
Brother-brother	12
Sons of two brothers	4
Paternal uncle-nephew	3
Brothers-in-law	10
Total	31

a substantial amount of capital for the purchase of initial equipment.[25] Both partners equally assumed the replacement cost of damaged traps, generally at minimal expense. As in the case of cod-fishing and seal-fishing, an equal amount of labor gave right to an identical share of the product.

Caribou Hunting

Conducted in the months of February and March, a period of the year during which snow accumulation greatly facilitated traveling, the hunting of caribou was of vital importance in the traditional economic cycle. Since hunting was done in the remote sections of the mainland, dog teams were needed to transport the men and their equipment (guns, tents, food) and to bring back the caribou into the winter settlement. Several features distinguish caribou-hunting groups from the others described above. First, compared to the technology used in other activities, caribou hunting involved a smaller capital outlay. The only expensive items were the guns, which lasted several years and could be easily borrowed. Second, the groups were of variable size. Although six to seven men were considered to be the minimum required for a fruitful trip, some groups included as many as fifteen. Third, examination of the kinship relations among group members reveals that recruiting rules were very flexible.

In the nine crews included in the sample, agnatic ties still predominated in the groups' formation. But their importance was greatly reduced (only 54 per cent), while uterine ties became more significant (30 per cent). Moreover, the number of parallel and cross-cousins indicates a tendency to generational grouping, as in the case of trapping groups. The criteria of physical capacity once again imposed limits upon recruiting and promoted co-operation between people of the same age group.[26] Hunting groups had no continuity and dissolved once the groups returned to the village. They can be considered as "occasional" groups, an individual manifesting his intention to "take part" and available men joining him. Recruiting was largely informal. Nevertheless, the recruiter always sought individuals who could guide the group safely in any part of the region. Since there was a direct correlation between the people's familiarity with a given zone and its distance from the village, the inclusion of individuals exploiting the trapping territories most remote from the community was of great importance if the caribou were to be hunted deep in the interior. Such a situation also influenced the size of the group.[27] Since traveling was done with dog teams, and a hunter rarely had more than one team, the farther the group planned to go, the more individuals he needed, the teams taking turns in carrying the loads.

No permanent authority structure prevailed during traveling. Occasionally, a member crossing his trapping territory would indicate the best direction to follow. Otherwise, the group would rely upon the man best acquainted with the particular terrain. Groups often split in two, rejoining each other at the end of the day. Once the group had located the herd, the most experienced man took the lead, and he held temporary leadership until the hunt had

TABLE 7

Kinship Relations Between Members and the Temporary Leader of Caribou Hunting Groups (1940–1950)

No. of group	So	Br	BrSo	FaBrSo	FaSiSo	MoBrSo	MoSiSo	MoFaBrSo	SiHu	Others	Total members	Group size
1	1	1	2	1	—	—	2	—	—	—	7	8
2	—	3	1	2	—	—	—	1	—	1	8	9
3	2	—	1	1	—	3	—	—	—	—	7	8
4	1	1	2	—	—	2	—	—	1	—	7	8
5	3	—	—	1	3	—	—	3	—	3	13	14
6	—	2	1	1	1	2	1	—	2	1	11	12
7	—	1	—	1	1	1	1	1	—	1	7	8
8	1	—	—	2	1	1	1	1	—	—	7	8
9	—	2	—	1	—	—	1	1	2	1	8	9
Total	8	10	7	10	6	9	6	7	5	7	75	84

completely ceased. As the caribou often spent the day on elevated ground (where snow is less abundant and lichen more easily found), the first maneuver consisted in encircling the herd. Taking into account patterns of footprints and wind direction, the leader assigned a position to each hunter. At his signal, two or three individuals caused the animals to run. In nearly all cases, a single hunter had the chance to shoot and to kill all the caribou.

The sharing of the product was done on a basis of equality but in a manner somewhat different from the procedure followed in trapping. Division did not depend upon the amount of work provided by the hunters but upon their familial responsibilities. Those having the largest families received the largest animals. If, after a first distribution, there remained an odd number of caribou, they were cut into pieces and distributed in an identical manner. The temporary leader did not receive a supplementary allowance for his role.

WORK GROUPS AS ADAPTIVE STRATEGIES

The foregoing description demonstrates the variability and the diversity of the work groups that characterize, in both historic and contemporary periods, the economic organization of an eastern Canadian community. Although restricted in number and utilizing an essentially pre-industrial technology, its members have shown great flexibility in the pursuit of their economic goals. They have been able to associate themselves in socio-economic groups best suited to the exploitation of diverse resources. Each group, although sharing one or several characteristics with the others, presents unique features that illustrate the dynamics of the system. In other words, each work group differed from the others because its existence depended upon the performance of a specialized task. Even the sharing of a tendency toward agnatic grouping does not imply a strict uniformity. Although agnatic kinsmen are in the majority in each of the above groups, their relationship varies quantitatively and qualitatively (lateral and lineal range) and some groups include a significant proportion of uterine kinsmen or affinal relatives.

We have so far specified the factors influencing the formation of groups and have shown how patrilineality varied from one type of group to another. We now have to explain why such a variation exists and the reasons underlying the selection of particular forms of grouping. The answer will be obtained through the establishment of a continuum in which the corporate character and the lineality of the groups will be correlated. We will demon-

TABLE 8

Tabulation of Kinship Ties in the Several Work Groups[28]

Type of relations	Cod Fishing		Sealing	Trapping	Hunting
	Period A	Period B			
Agnatic	88%	85%	87.0%	68%	54%
Uterine	—	6%	6.5%	—	30%
Affinal	4%	3%	6.5%	32%	6%
Strangers	8%	6%	—	—	10%

strate that the more corporate a group is, the stronger is its lineality, both characteristics depending upon adaptation to a particular economic context.

Corporate Groups

If we define a corporate group as an entity having a continuity' and a structure of authority, cod fishing and sealing groups can be said to be corporate. Their members engage in the pursuit of a common goal, they have precise rules of membership giving rights to an estate kept within the group, and they perform tasks through a status-role differentiation entailing an unequal sharing of income. We then ask why these groups are corporate and what are the factors explaining their emergence. The answer lies first in the access to and control of the resources exploited. Cod-traps and sealing equipment are set near the shore, but only where water is relatively deep and currents minimal. The scarcity of sites promoted, at the very beginning, mechanisms of appropriation and control in order to regulate access rights among exploiters. The first occupant of a site became its owner and acquired exclusive rights of exploitation. Specific ecological factors such as the differential productivity of sites (those located near sandy coves permitted the capture of salmon that represented a substantial increase in the fishermen's income) and their proximity to the fishing stations (a nearby site reduced the time and effort required for the acquisition and processing of the product) reinforced the general trend. The owner then tried, whenever it was possible, to confine his privilege to his own family or at least to his closest relatives.

Figure 1 gives several examples of this situation. It represents the transmission of cod-trap sites within one of the families of the community.[29] At generation C, four individuals (C_1, C_2, C_3, C_4) acquired sites, either by buying them from Whitely and Sons or taking unoccupied sites. Their transmission to the following generation involved three exchanges between fathers and sons (D_2, D_3, D_4), one with an adopted brother (D_1), and one with a brother's son (D_3). At generation E, three exchanges took place between fathers and sons (E_1, E_7, E_8) and two with a brother's son (E_5). So among the eight sites presently owned by this family, six were inherited from agnatic kinsmen. Similarly, among the 35 present cod-trap owners, 22 received their sites from their fathers, eight from other agnatic kinsmen, and only five purchased them from nonrelatives. Patrilineal inheritance assures, the continuity of a group and facilitates the transmission of technical knowledge, permitting the future exploitant to become familiar with the site at a relatively early age.

The corporate character of the fishing groups is enhanced by the substantial value of its estate. To own a fishing station with a residence, a wharf, a shed to store fish, one or two boats with motors, and all the necessary gear (trawl, handline, gill nets, cod-trap, or sealing equipment) represents a substantial sum of money. The accumulation of such capital can be achieved only at an advanced age. A young fisherman has no choice but to work with his father or closest agnatic kinsmen (cf. the virilocal residence patterns of the fishing stations). This is well illustrated in the relatively large size of the cod-fishing and sealing groups at the beginning of the century. This gives

Figure 1: Transmission of Fishing Sites in St. Paul River

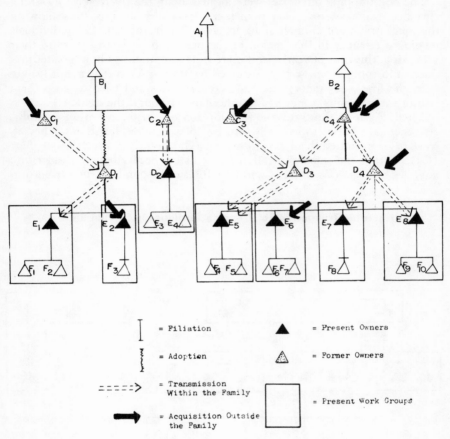

I	= Filiation	▲ = Present Owners
{	= Adoption	△ = Former Owners
- - - ->	= Transmission Within the Family	▢ = Present Work Groups
➡	= Acquisition Outside the Family	

rise to a significant division of labor based on a structure of authority between the sharemen and the skipper. Consequently, agnatic ties in fishing groups, while paralleling a form of grouping already present in the residence sphere, have been an adaptive response to the relative scarcity of certain economic resources (fishing sites and capital) and appear very functional for the transmission of technical knowledge, the success of a crew often being related to its acquaintance with specific grounds.[30]

Semi-Corporate Groups

Trapping groups do not possess all the structural characteristics of the fishing groups. Although trapping grounds were transmitted in the agnatic line, the membership of trapping groups was somewhat more fluid (32 per cent of affinal relatives). More important, they were not characterized by a permanent structure of authority. Their corporateness also derived from the relative scarcity, differential productivity, and proximity of the sites exploited.

The best trapping territories were located along the river. With its strong currents, it always froze later than lakes or smaller streams, thus allowing the concentration of animals along its shore late in the fall. The individuals owning a territory in this section of the mainland could easily get to their grounds at this time of year, spend more time trapping, and have greater production in comparison with less situated territories. As in the case of fishing sites, the first exploitants chose the best territories and tried to keep them within their families. Once again, inheritance through the agnatic line was adopted. Figure 2 illustrates the transmission of territories within a famliy. At generation B, two individuals (B_1, B_3) first acquired territories. They afterwards transmitted them, one to his son (C_1) and the other to his nephew (C_5). Within the same generation C, exchange occurs between older and younger brothers (C_1 to C_4; C_5 to C_7). This corresponds to the period dur-

Figure 2: Transmission of Trapping Territories in St. Paul River

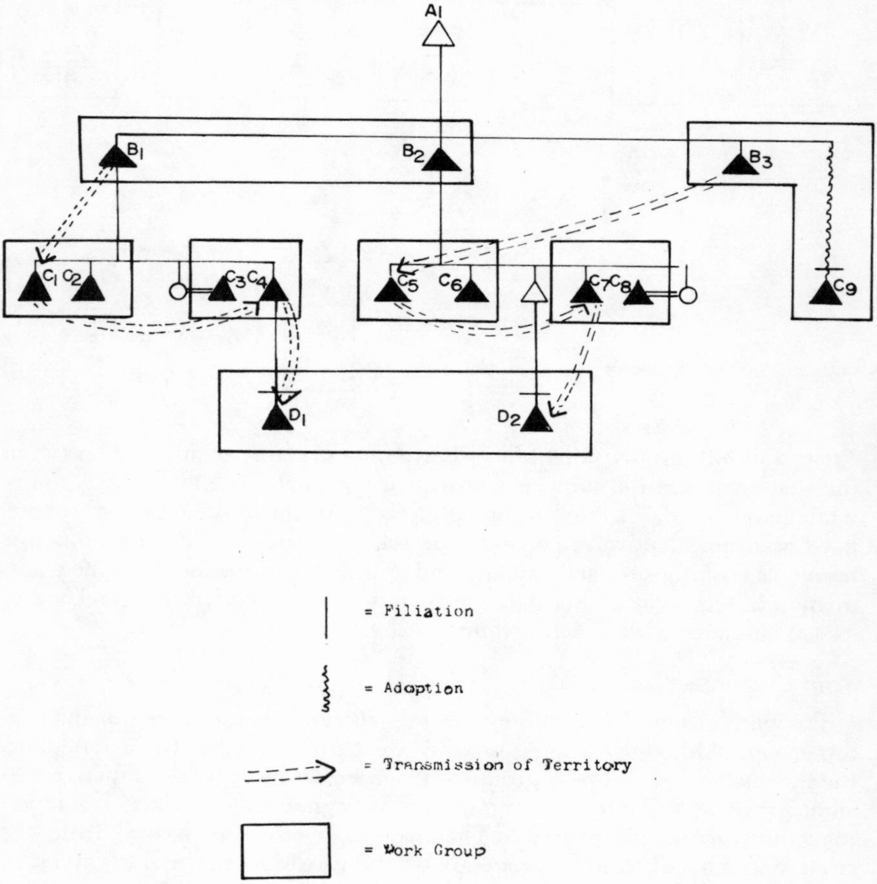

| = Filiation

{ = Adoption

- - - -> = Transmission of Territory

▢ = Work Group

ing which trapping was generalized and the territories fully exploited. The transmission to generation D implies processes similar to the initial exchanges—to a son (D1) and to a nephew (D2). Here the merging of original territories is explained by the fact that the transmission occurred during the post-war period, at a time when trapping had lost most of its adepts. At the community level, transmission of sites followed similar patterns. In the 25 cases for which I possess information, ten exchanges occurred between father and sons, nine between brothers, and six between other relatives.

The fact that the trapping groups contained a significant proportion of affinal relatives illustrates the flexibility of the system. It indicates that if at least one of the exploitants must be patrilineally related to the former owner, his partner need not be a close consanguineal relative. We have seen that age was a determining factor in the composition of the teams. The generational emphasis in recruiting thus explains the transmission of sites between older and younger siblings.

The adoption of inheritance through the agnatic line was also relevant for task performance. Trappers had not only to possess a good ethnozoological knowledge but also to have a detailed acquaintance with the territory, since each trap had to be set in a determined place. Such familiarity was best achieved between members of the same family, either informally by conversation, or directly by making occasional trips with the uninitiates.

Trapping groups are defined as "semi-corporate" groups because they lack a status-role differentiation and a real structure of authority. This is coincident with the low amount of capital required for the maintenance of the equipment. Once acquired, it could be utilized over a long period at a very low cost to both members. The differential cost of equipment and its maintenance thus remains the most useful element to distinguish trapping groups from fishing groups and explains their lesser corporateness.

Occasional Groups

Caribou-hunting groups were clearly distinct from the others on the basis of their recruiting. They constituted the only socio-economic formation to include a significant proportion of matrilateral kinsmen, and they showed a marked bilaterality. They represented temporary groups which rarely included the same individuals and dissolved once their goals were achieved. In terms of adaptive processes, they cannot be explained by the factors discussed previously. Hunting was done on communal land, the sites exploited varied continuously, and, as in the case of trapping groups, equipment could be maintained at a relatively low cost. The variety of the kinship ties between the hunters indicates that to work with a kinsmen was not an essential condition. The fact that hunting groups were formed by relatives was due simply to the small size of the community. Their adaptive characteristics are better explained by the generational emphasis of the recruiting, hunting expeditions being reserved for individuals with a certain physical capacity. But another characteristic seems to be their most significant adaptive feature: contrary to the fur-bearing animals exploited by trapping, caribou occur in large concentrated herds that migrate constantly and are best hunted in fairly sizable groups.[31] These groups were purely occasional and temporary, and they required a certain number of individuals to assure the productivity of the hunt.

The differential aspects of the work groups point out a strong correaltion between their degree of corporateness and the number of factors influencing their formation, their structure and functioning being more rigid and more complex in relation to the number of adaptive requirements. The flexibility of the productive system of St. Paul River lies in a progressive "structural loosening" between the work groups exploiting the maritime and terrestrial zones. Table 9 gives a better insight into this process by comparing the work groups in terms of the factors and social forms of production. An overall tabulation first shows that each group shares one or several characteristics with all the others. At the level of the social forms of production, there appears a clear dichotomy between groups of the maritime and terrestrial zones, the one lineal, the other generational. But it is at the level of the factors of production (which influence the basis of recruiting) that each type of group achieves greater specificity. Although their formation is influenced by socio-demographic factors, such as residence patterns and community size, they depend primarily upon particular ecological and technical requirements. Work groups must consequently be seen basically as "adaptive strategies" for the exploitation of a given resource and only secondarily as a "social formation" whose characteristics may be found in other fields of activity. This has several methodological implications that will be discussed in the conclusion.

Figure 3, an ideal model, shows that co-operation between only twelve patrilineal kinsmen (the inclusion of uterine or affinal relatives would not have modified the size of the groups) can be actualized in four work groups of different nature: large and lineal, large and generational, restricted and lineal, restricted and generational. The dynamic aspects of the kinship system lies in its capacity to combine operationally a small number of elements into related but nevertheless specific structural arrangements.

Conclusion

With some exceptions, anthropological studies of bilateral kinship have been conducted mainly through a synchronic-structural analysis of marriage, residence, and inheritance rules. The present paper points out that, although this methodological orientation is generally valid and useful, it sometimes underestimates the adaptive possibilities of such systems and can lead to unsatisfactory explanations of their dynamic qualities. The combining of structural and diachronic analysis shows how the relations between empirical processes and structural forms are generated, maintained, and transformed. Its use demonstrates how a system, although undergoing modifications through internal and external pressure, maintains a certain continuity. The structure and functioning of contemporary cod-fishing crews, for instance, cannot be understood fully without some reference to the production units at the beginning of the century. They are the results of a twofold process: an initial mode of exploitation that promoted the emergence of large corporate

TABLE 9

A Comparison of Structural Features of the Work Groups[32]

Comparative Axes	Maritime Zone			Terrestrial Zone	
	Cod Fishing		Sealing	Trapping	Hunting
	Period A	Period B			
Factors of Production:					
Capital required for technology	Important	Important	Important	Initially important	Initially important
Technological knowledge	Complex	Complex	Complex	Complex	Simple
Type of co-operation	Large	Restricted	Large	Restricted	Large
Production units:					
Recruiting basis	Agnatic ext. fam.	Nuclear family	Agnatic ext. fam.	Nuclear family age group	Kindred
Social Forms of Production:					
Ownership	Individual	Individual	Dual	Individual	Individual
Distribution of product	Differential	Differential	Differential	Equal	Equal
Structure of authority	Skipper-sharemen	Skipper-sharemen	Skipper-sharemen	Partners	Partners

Figure 3: Models of Cooperation Between Agnatic Kinsmen

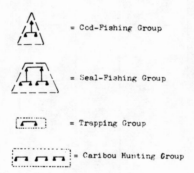

  = Cod-Fishing Group

  = Seal-Fishing Group

= Trapping Group

= Caribou Hunting Group

groups, which were subsequently modified numerically by the adoption of marine motors.

This emphasis upon ecological-economic factors significantly supplements the information revealed by the analysis of social factors. For instance, the examination of the kinship system of St. Paul River would have underscored its tendency to patrilineality.[33] No marriages occur between persons of the same patronymic, and virilocality predominates (77 percent) as the marital residence rule. However, an analysis simply of social frameworks never would have indicated the type of flexibility characteristic of the system. Its bilateral character would have been emphasized only by the rule of third degree bilateral exogamy which, given the lack of women in the community, cannot be fully actualized.

The methodology adopted here also explains how the increase of patrilineality has been a dynamic process, permitting in the case of trapping groups the association of agnatic inheritance with relatively fluid rules of membership. And taking into account the past and present characteristics of the economic organization, it is logical to assume that the importance of patrilineality will be reduced in the near future. An increasing dependence upon fishing cannot be achieved without profound technological transformations that will lead to the relinquishment of cod-trap sites and to the utilization of more industrialized methods. Once again, recruitment will depend upon contractual relationships, and fishing groups will lose their corporate character, the system recovering its original aspects.

NOTES

1. The data were collected during eleven months of field work in St. Paul River in 1967 and 1968. The research was made possible by a grant from the Canada Council and was carried out under the direction of Dr. Marc Adélard Tremblay of Laval University. This paper was drafted for presentation in the course on Economic Anthropology conducted in the winter term of 1969 by Dr. Scott Cook of Michigan State University, to whom I express my appreciation for helpful comments and criticisms. I am also grateful to Dr. James C. Faris of the University of Connecticut and to John C. Kennedy of Michigan State University for valuable suggestions. However, I take full responsibility for the analysis presented.
2. Norwegian fishing is highly industrialized, and this characteristic largely explains the dynamic aspects of its work organization. Nevertheless, fishing groups in St. Paul River, though using a relatively simple technology, share many features with the Norwegians.
3. I find the term "peasant" useful to describe the present socio-economic conditions of the St. Paul River fishermen. Though there now exists much disagreement among anthropologists with regard to the meaning and the applicability of this term to an occupational group other than agriculturalists, I believe that the following characteristics give the term "peasant" a certain operationality. St. Paul River is one of fourteen villages of a region in Eastern Canada called the "Lower North Coast of the St. Lawrence." The size of communities varies between 100 and 900 people. All are geographically isolated from urban centers; and given the dominant feature of their economic organization, i.e., exploitation of marine resources, they have always maintained relations with the exterior for the acquisition of consumer goods not produced locally. Such dependence is also found at the juridical and political levels.
4. For instance, Pehrson (1954); Goodenough (1955); Davenport (1959); Murdock (1960); Freeman (1961); Chowning (1962); Blehr (1963); Firth (1966, 1967).
5. Principally Montagnais and Naskapi who during the fall, winter, and spring, engaged in fur-animal trapping and caribou hunting on the mainland and returned into the coastal area in the summer.
6. These companies came principally from Jersey, Newfoundland, Nova Scotia, and New England. Most of the fishermen were English and Irish. For more information, see Charest (1970: 60-78).
7. The cod-trap is a net box set on the ocean floor. Fish are driven into it by an adjacent net, called the "leader." Though the dimensions of the instrument depend upon specific ecological conditions, most of the traps reach a 400 foot perimeter, with an average depth of 6 fathoms. The length of the leaders varies between 200 and 300 feet. Besides the capital required for its purchase ($400 at the beginning of this century and $2,000 now), the owner must spend a substantial amount of money in annual repairs. Around 100 pounds of new twine is needed each year to replace damaged parts.
8. Sept-Iles, Wabush, and Labrador City. For more information about the nature of work done by fishermen in those centers, see Lamarre and Baril (1970: 167-175).
9. While the decline in the price for cod was related to temporary fluctuations in the

international market, the lowering of the price for fur was definitive. The products of local trappers could not compete in price and in quality with those of industrial ranchers who began to monopolize the market. Incidently, many of the ranchers, a few years before, had bought living animals from trappers of St. Paul River and neighboring communities in order to found their enterprises.

10. In the summer of 1968 six people were carpenters, while the remaining sixteen worked in the tertiary or service sector as wharf keeper, fishery officer, game warden, postmaster, telegrapher, lighthouse keeper, and teacher.

11. A dory is a small boat, about ten feet long, with a flat bottom. Dories could be easily piled up on the bridge.

12. Reports of the Commissioner Pierre Fortin generally cover all the fishing stations of the archipelago. Besides including data about the history of the fishing posts, they indicate, for a period of ten years, the port of departure of each schooner, the type and size of gear used in cod fishing, sealing, and salmon fishing, as well as information about the production of the crews. Unfortunately, such data are not found for the remaining years.

13. Herring *(Clupea harengus)*; capelin *(Mallotus villosus)*; squid *(Loligo ommastrephes)*, cod *(Gadus morhua)*.

14. If we apply the actual percentage of the active male labor force to the total of people in 1910, we can deduce that around 40 people were engaged in fishing at that time.

15. Since the family head always ran into debt with the outside merchant or his local representative, he was not really able to negotiate his production and to obtain good prices. The two local merchants, also owners of cod-traps, took advantage of the situation and grew rich at the expense of other members of the community. Such situations still influence the present socio-economic stratification, the sons and close relatives of these merchants being the most affluent owners.

16. In these cases, the skippers own marginal cod-fishing sites and have to rely on other techniques such as trawl and gill nets in order to maintain a reasonable production. They work with cod-traps only when they know that fish are plentiful in neighboring sites. We nevertheless include them in the sample in order to reach a certain homogeneity in the comparison of the overall groups. The remaining crews also fish with trawl and gill nets, but only at the end of the fishing season. Most of their production comes from the cod-trap. It was thus significant to choose the crews attached to a cod-trap in order to define the types of relations that prevail in the organization of cod fishing.

17. Since cod-fishing crews now average three people, the skipper in most cases also participates in the processing of the fish either as cutter, throater, or splitter. Thus the reduction in the size of fishing groups, besides modifying the characteristics of recruiting, brought some transformation in the division of labor itself. When crews were larger, the division of labor was somewhat more rigid and a greater prestige was attached to the role of splitter. For more details about fish processing, see Junek (1937: 27-35), and Tremblay, Charest, and Breton (1969: 52-72).

18. Barth (1966: 7). The division of labor in cod fishing at St. Paul River has several aspects in common with that of the herring fisheries in Norwegian communities.

19. This system of distribution of earnings is not peculiar to St. Paul River. Its general characteristics are found not only in Eastern Canada but in geographical areas as diverse as Asia, Northern Europe, the Caribbean, and South America. Cf. Faris (1966: 138-147); Beaucage (1970: 105); Firth (1966: 235-257); Barth (1966: 6), Davenport (1956: 184, 230); Kottack (1966: 142).

20. Gill nets are rectangular nets (100 × 20 feet) fixed on the ocean floor. They cost around $50. They were introduced in the 1960s by Newfoundlanders visiting neighboring communities in the summer, and they are becoming very popular in the whole area. Besides their relatively low cost, they sometimes prove to be very efficient in the months of July and August when cod move into deeper grounds. Like the hand-line and the trawl, they are set on the banks and permit the crew to go from site to site according to their productivity. Their great advantage lies in the

fact that no bait is required in their utilization. Interestingly enough, they were first acquired in St. Paul River by skippers who owned the less productive trap sites. Since their introduction only one young skipper has purchased a cod-trap, the others preferring gill nets. For a detailed description see Tremblay, Charest, and Breton (1969: 61).

21. On the Lower North Coast of the St. Lawrence, villages like Blanc-Sablon, Old Fort, St. Augustine, La Tabatière, and Baie Rouge were known as the best sealing stations. One village, that of La Tabatière, always had the highest production and was used by all as a reference point to measure the numerical importance of seals from year to year. In this community, cod-fishing was a secondary activity and sealing gave rise to the formation of large agnatic groups with a complex division of labor and repartition rules (cf. Beaucage 1968 and 1970).

22. Sealing gear resembles the cod-trap with the difference that there is no bottom net and that two or more leaders are used to drive the animals into it. In 1940, its cost varied between $800 and $1,000. For a description of the diverse types of sealing equipment, see Beaucage (1968) and Breton (1969: 60-68).

23. The harp seal *(Phoca Groenlandica)* is the most common species. Fishermen used the terms "bedlamer," "smoddy harp," and "yellow flippers" to differentiate harp seals according to their age and size. Another species, the "square flippers" *(Erignatus barbatus)*, is sometimes also caught.

24. This operation required a great deal of skill, and techniques varied according to the species. Very often, the price received depended upon the quality of the processing. The most common species caught in St. Paul River were: mink *(Mustela vison lowii)*, marten *(Marten Americanus brunalis)*, otter *(Lutra canadensis chimo)*, beaver *(Castor canadensis)*, lynx *(Lynx canadensis)*, muskrat *(Ondatra zibethica aquilonis)*, and fox *(Vulpes fulva bangsi)*.

25. The original exploitants had to purchase iron traps, in some cases as many as 300, in order to ensure production. Though some techniques involved sole utilization of natural elements (e.g., the deadfall), iron traps permitted the capture of more animals, and the fur obtained was of better quality since the animal remained alive until the visit of the trapper. Traps were of different size, depending upon the strength of the animals. They generally lasted for several decades.

26. Although caribou hunting trips lasted rarely more than two weeks (compared to two months in the case of trapping expeditions), they required great physical effort. Traveling was often complicated by snow storms and snow drifting, very frequent at this period of the year. Several hunters developed pneumonia after falling through the ice while crossing brooks and rivers with heavy loads. In addition, since the hunt was done in the most remote section of the mainland, help was hardly available in case of accident and several days were needed to get back to the village. Finally, the chances of getting lost were enhanced by the fact that the people were less familiar with this part of the country.

27. The "expected rentability" of the trip also influenced the number of hunters. People always knew approximately the location and the size of the herd. They communicated by radio from one village to another, and the pilots in charge of mail and transportation service in the area often provided useful information.

28. In Tables 8 and 9, period A corresponds to the beginning of this century and period B to the summer of 1968.

29. In order to simplify Figures 1 and 2, I have included only the individuals involved in the transmission of sites or who were necessary to indicate genealogical ties between the participants. In St. Paul River, there are fifteen patronymics, two of which (those utilized above) represent 33 percent of the total number of inhabitants. For more detailed information, see Breton (1970: 125-128).

30. Comparing Lowie's and Fortes' definition of lineages, Beaucage (1970: 115) explains the formation of such groupings in the sealing organization of La Tabatière by the initial mode of transmission of sites and associates their emergence with partible inheritance.

31. This adaptive feature has been noted by Steward (1955: 120-150).

32. The comparative axes have been borrowed from Terray (1969: 133).
33. Cf. Breton (1970: 120-150).

BIBLIOGRAPHY

Barnes, J. A. 1954. Class and Committee in a Norwegian Island. Human Relations 7: 33-59.

Barth, F. 1966. Models of Social Organization. Royal Anthropological Institute, Occasional Paper 23.

Beaucage, P. 1968. Technologie de le pêche au loup-marin sur la Côte-Nord du St-Laurent. L'Homme 8: 98-125.

—— 1970. Organisation économique et parenté à La Tabatière. Recherches Sociographiques 11: 91-116.

Blehr, O. 1963. Action Groups in a Society with Bilateral Kinship: A Case Study from the Faroe Islands. Ethnology 2: 269-276.

Breton, Y. 1968. La culture matérielle des Blanc-Sablonnais. Université Laval, Centre d'Etudes Nordiques, Collection des Travaux Divers 19.

—— 1970. Morphologie sociale et mariage à Saint-Paul River. Recherches Sociographiques 11: 117-151.

Charest, P. 1970. Le peuplement permanent de las Basse-Côte-Nord du Saint-Laurent. Recherches Sociographiques 11: 59-91.

Chowning, A. 1962. Cognatic Kin Groups Among the Molima of Fergusson Island. Ethnology 1: 92-101.

Davenport, W. 1956. A Comparative Study of Two Jamaican Fishing Communities. Unpublished Ph.D. dissertation, Yale University.

—— 1959. Nonunilinear Descent and Descent Groups. American Anthropologist 61: 557-572.

Faris, J. C. 1967. Cat Harbour: A Newfoundland Fishing Settlement. Newfoundland Social and Economic Studies 3. St. John's.

Firth, R. 1966. Malay Fishermen: Their Peasant Economy. Rev. edit. Hampden.

—— 1967. Bilateral Descent Groups: An Operational Viewpoint. Royal Anthropological Institute, Occasional Paper 16.

Fortin, P. 1859-68. Annual Report of Pierre Fortin, Esquire, Stipendary Magistrate, Commander of the Expedition for the Protection of the Fisheries in the Gulf of St. Lawrence. Quebec.

Freeman, J. D. 1961. On the Concept of Kindred. Journal of the Royal Anthropological Institute 91: 192-220.

Godelier, M. 1970. Préface. Sur les sociétés précapitalistes: textes choisis de Marx, Engels, Lénine, pp. 13-142. Paris.

Goodenough, W. H. 1955. A Problem in Malayo-Polynesian Social Organization. American Anthropologist 57: 71-83.

Juneck, O. 1937. Isolated Communities: A Study of a Labrador Fishing Village. New York.

Kottack, C. 1966. The Structure of Equality in a Brazilian Fishing Community. Unpublished Ph.D. dissertation, Columbia University.

Lamarre, N., and L. Baril. 1970. L'adaptation des Nord-Côtiers à Labrador City. Recherches Sociographiques 11: 167-175.

Murdock, G. P. 1960. Cognatic Forms of Social Organization. Social Structure in South East Asia, ed. G. P. Murdock, pp. 1-14. Viking Fund Publications in Anthropology 29.

Pehrson, R. N. 1954. Bilateral Kin Grouping as a Structural Type: A Preliminary Statement. Journal of East Asiatic Studies 3: 199-202.

Steward, J. 1955. Theory of Culture Change. Urbana.

Terray, E. 1969. Le marxisme devant les sociétés primitives. Paris.

Tremblay, M. A., P. Charest, and Y. Breton. 1969. Les changements socio-culturels à Saint-Augustin. Travaux et Documents du Centre d'Etudes Nordiques, Université Laval.

Action Groups in a Society
with Bilateral Kinship:
A Case Study from the Faroe Islands[1]
Otto Blehr

The role of bilateral kinship in social organizations has been the subject of much recent attention and debate. Attempts at analyzing its relevance (e.g., Pehrson 1954, 1957; Freeman 1961; Goodenough 1961, 1962) have largely revolved around the concept of the kindred and the relationship between the kindred as a category and the empirical action groups based on kinship that emerge in bilateral societies. I shall here explore the composition of kinship-based action groups in one bilaterally organized society, the Faroese. I shall attempt to show that a description of these action groups as kindred based is inadequate and, in the analysis of the material, shall introduce an alternative concept of seemingly greater structural utility.

The Faroe Islands are situated in the North Atlantic roughly 160 nautical miles north of the Shetlands and a little more than twice as far west of Norway. The present population of about 35,000 lives in hamlets and villages on seventeen of the eighteen islands which make up the archipelago (cf. Williamson 1948).

The islands were settled by Norwegian Vikings in the ninth century, and since its inception the society has been based on a bilateral organization. Its economy has mainly depended on the utilization of land, but during the last century commercial marine fishing has grown more important and is now the primary economic pursuit.

The privately owned land (*odalsjord*)[2] consists of permanent fields and is inherited equally by the owners' children. Spouses share their estate as co-proprietors, and it is not divided until both are dead. Owing to their expectation of inheritance the children share a common interest in their parents' estate, but until the death of the parents they depend on them for access to it.

Children establish independent households on marriage and therefore need land for a house plot, for agriculture, and for peat cutting, and, since they have not inherited from their parents, they must rely on them for land. Some of the land which is given to the children in usufruct is held by them in individual plots, while some is held jointly by them and their parents and only the products are divided among them.

Each child depends upon his siblings and his parents to help him work the plots to which he has the sole usufruct, and this help is reciprocal. On land where only the products are divided the whole natal family works together; as the parents grow old and feeble, their children become increasingly responsible for the manual labor on the land and take a greater fraction of the products for consumption in their own growing households.

Children do not, however, have identical work roles. There is a division of labor between the sexes, and it is the men who are responsible for agricultural work. Furthermore, although spouses are co-owners of their estates, the rights and responsibilities of the women are exercised by their husbands. The equality of siblings, which is a predominant aspect of Faroese society, is extended to brothers-in-law. Thus, on marriage, a man becomes engaged to work on two different estates, those of his parents and of his wife's parents. This is diagrammed in Figure 1, where the solid triangles numbered

Figure 1: Action Groups Working Estates In Land

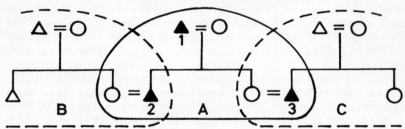

2, 1, and 3, designating respectively Ego, his father, and his brother-in-law, represent the males who make up the action group working estate A. Similarly, 2 and 3 are also members of the action groups working estates B and C respectively.

Since the core of the action group working an estate is regularly composed of the male owner with his sons and/or sons-in-law, it is not surprising to find that the term for brother-in-law, used reciprocally between WiBr and SiHu, is also extended to WiSiHu.

The composition of the action group working an estate is not essentially altered by the death of both parents and the subsequent division of the land among the children. The father will be missing, to be sure, but this situation may also precede the division of the estate if he dies before his wife or becomes too feeble to participate in the work. The action group in such cases is composed of the former owner's sons and/or sons-in-law, helped by other members of their households, until each of them has sons and/or sons-in-law who can help them.

The core of action groups engaged in agricultural work is thus regularly composed of men who are lineally, collaterally, and/or affinally related to each other, i.e., of persons both within and outside the kindred. We lack a technical term for such a category of persons, and this leads to a frequent misapplication of the term "kindred" to groups of such a composition.

I suggest adoption of the term "kith" for the category of persons —consanguines and affines—from which such a group is drawn. The Oxford English Dictionary gives this term the following definition:

The persons who are known or familiar, taken collectively; one's friends, fellow-countrymen, or neighbours; acquaintance; in later use sometimes confused with kin.

This connotation of kinship is also seen in the definition of the phrase "kith and kin":

Orig. country and kinsfolk, one's friends and relatives; in mod. use often taken merely as a pleonastic phrase for kinsfolk, relatives, family connexions.

The contemporary usages give sufficient justification for using "kith" in a technical sense analogous to "kindred." Hereinafter, therefore, I shall employ "kith" to mean persons related by consanguineal and/or affinal ties involving mutual obligations.

Before discussing kith ties with reference to the mutual obligations they involve, let us examine the composition of the action groups formed to man fishing boats. The boats in question are of many different types, of which the most common are modern steel vessels with crews of about 25 men, old wooden smacks with crews of fifteen to twenty, and open motor boats with crews of four to six. The first two types are used in ocean fisheries, while those of the third type fish off the west coast of Greenland or locally off the Faroes.

Figure 2: Composition of a Particular Boat Crew

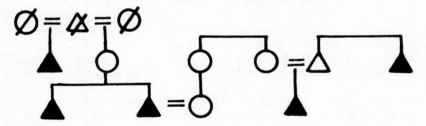

Figure 2 shows the composition of the crew of a boat from the village of Sandur in the autumn of 1960, when the local cod fisheries were exceptionally good. This crew is quite typical in that all its members are linked to each other through consanguineal and affinal ties. Furthermore, it is clearly not drawn from the kindred of any single Ego, nor would it seem to be reasonable to describe all its members as the kith of any one centrally located person. This is confirmed by my ethnographic material on the mobilization of such groups. The process is one involving dyadic relationships between persons who recognize mutual obligations through kinship or marriage ties, i.e., who are kith to each other.

The initiative whereby a man becomes incorporated into a crew may be taken either by someone who is already a member of such a common-interest action group or by an outsider who wants to become a member. Who will activate the kith ties in each case depends upon a number of factors. On a steel vessel with a skipper who is considered good, for example, men outside the crew will activate kith ties with men who are already members of the crew in order to join the ship. On the other hand, if the skipper is inexperienced, he and the men he eventually manages to mobilize will try to activate their kith ties in order to assemble a full crew. Once a man has been drawn into the action group, he thus becomes a new point for the attachment of further crew members.

Figure 3: Recruitment of a Boat Crew

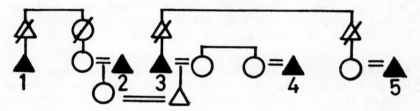

Figure 3 illustrates the mode of recruitment. It shows a crew made up of old men, averaging 69 years of age, from the village of Sandur who were engaged in the local fisheries in the autumn of 1960. The open boat used was owned by three of the sons of 1 who, at that time, were fishing with another open boat off Greenland. They had left the boat at the disposal of 1, who became the point of innovation for the crew by recruiting 2, his FaSiDaHu. The membership of 3 in the crew, since he was not kith to 1, can only be understood by reference to 2; he was the DaHuFa of 2, and it was through this kith tie that he was mobilized. In like manner, the recruitment of 4 and 5 was based on their kith ties to 3. Had more men been needed, as on the larger boats, other kith ties would have been activated. Since each new member of the action group adds the able-bodied men of his kith to the total number of potential members, the action group can expand indefinitely through this unfolding mobilization. I shall call such action groups kith-based since they are based on the unfolding of dyadic kith ties between individuals.

What is the boundary of the kith category in Faroese society? In order to answer this question I have counted the different types of consanguineal or affinal ties[3] which directly link the individuals composing the boat crews of the village of Sandur in the summer of 1961 (see Table 1). For the crew represented in Figure 3, for example,

TABLE 1

Kith Ties in Faroese Boat Crews

Type of Boat	Ties Represented in Crew Members
1 A steel vessel of c.250 tons that fished with long lines and hand lines off the west coast of Greenland.	3 Br-Br, 2 Fa-So, 1 FaBr-BrSo, 1 MoBr-SiSo, 4 FaBrSo-FaBrSo, 1 MoSiSo-MoSiSo, 1 FaSiSo-MoBr-So, 1 MoMoBrSo-FaSiDaSo, 2 FaFaBrSo-So-FaFaBrSoSo, 5 WiBr-SiHu, 1 FaSiHu-WiBrSo, 1 MoSiHu-WiSiSo, 1 PaSbDaHu-WiPaSbSo, 1 MoBrSo-WiBr-SiHuFaSiSo, 1 FaFaBrSo-DaHu-WiFaFaBrSoSo
2 Similar to 1.	2 Br-Br, 2 Fa-So, 2 MoBr-SiSo, 1 MoSiSo-MoSiSo, 2 PaSbChSo-PaPa-SbSo, 1FaFaSiDaSo-MoMoBrSoSo, 3 WiBrSiHu, 1 WiFaBr-BrDaHu
3 A wooden vessel of c.80 tons that fished with long lines of the Faroes and with herring nets in the Norwegian Sea.	2 Br-Br, 1 MoSiHu-WiSiSo, 1 BrWiSiHu-WiSiHuBr
4 A wooden smack of c.95 tons that fished with long lines off Iceland and with herring nets in the Norwegian Sea.	1 Br-Br, 1 FaBr-BrSo, 1 MoBr-SiSo, 1 WiBr-SiHu
5 An open boat of c.3.5 tons that fished with hand lines off the west coast of Greenland.	1 Br-Br, 1 MoSiSo-MoSiSo, 1 WiMoMoBrSo-FaSiDaDaHu
6 Similar to 5.	1 WiBrWiSiHu-WiSiHuSiHu
7 Similar to 5.	1 Br-Br, 1 Fa-So, 1 WiFaBrDaHu-WiFaBrDaHu
8 Similar to 5.	2 Br-Br, 1 WiMoBrSo-FaSiDaHu
9 Similar to 5.	1 Fa-So
10 Similar to 5.	1 Fa-So, 1 WiBr-SiHu
11 An open boat of c.2.8 tons that fished with hand lines locally.	1 Br-Br, 1 Fa-So, 1 WiBr-SiHu, 1 FaBrWiBrSo-FaSiHuBrSo

the ties are the following: FaSiDaHu-WiMoBrSo (linking 1 and 2), DaHuFa-SoWiFa (linking 2 and 3), WiSiHu-WiSiHu (linking 3 and 4), and FaBrDaHu-WiFaBrSo (linking 3 and 5). The basis of this counting is the assumption that the relative strength of different ties will be shown by the number of times the ties in each of the different categories are activated, as compared to the number of individuals we ideally might expect an Ego to have available in each category. We should be able to determine in this manner who are within and who outside the range of kith obligations, as well as to register how the strength of these obligations falls off from a central core of near kith to a weaker periphery.

From Table 1 we observe that some ties are activated more often than others and, furthermore, that these ties are of two different types: those between individuals of the same generation (e.g., brothers, brothers-in-law, and male first cousins) and those between adjacent generations (e.g., fathers and sons, uncles and nephews).

Let us first examine the relative number of times particular ties are invoked between individuals on the same generational level.

The average sibling group in the community of Sandur has 4.17 members. Ideally this would give a typical male Ego brothers, brothers-in-law, and male first cousins in a ratio of approximately 1:5:12. However, since about 50 per cent of the women and 25 per cent of the men leave the community, the actual ratio becomes approximately 1:2:5. In other words, for every brother a male Ego has, he will have roughly two brothers-in-law and five male first cousins in the community. Were the rights and obligations between individuals in these three categories of the same order, we would expect that the kith ties between them would be invoked in approximately these proportions. This is not so. Table 1 shows that the ties most commonly activated are, in decreasing order of frequency, those between brothers, brothers-in-law, and first cousins, the number of times they are invoked being 13, 11, and 8 respectively. In other words, the ties of mutual obligations between brothers-in-law are stronger than those between male first cousins but are less strong than those between brothers.

As to adjacent generations, the ties between fathers and sons depend upon domestic residence. As long as a son is a member of his father's household he is under the latter's authority, and the father and son must therefore, for purposes of analysis, be regarded as a single person. When, with this in mind, we examine the eight father-son ties in Table 1, we find that only two of them can be regarded as proper cases of mobilization through the kith obligation between father and son, since the sons in the other six cases were members of their fathers' households.

In the same manner, the ties between uncles and nephews must be evaluated according to the nephew's residence. If a nephew is a member of his father's household, the tie invoked should properly be considered to be that between the father and the uncle, i.e., between brothers or brothers-in-law. We find empirically that six of the nine uncle-nephew ties in Table 1 are cases of mobilization through kith obligations and should be treated as true uncle-nephew relationships. Of the remaining three, on the other hand, one should be listed as a tie between brothers and two as ties between brothers-in-law.

The intensity of kith obligations, as indicated above, is greatest in the central core—i.e., between brothers, brothers-in-law, and male cousins—and declines toward the periphery. The effective limits appear to fall just outside the first-cousin and uncle-nephew ties.

Let me, at this point, make the distinction between the kith category and the kith-based action group quite clear. The kith category is composed of kindred and affines of an Ego, and part of it may be mobilized for specific work tasks, as exemplified in the small action groups working estates of land. A kith-based action group, on the other hand, is not a group drawn from a single kith category but is based on a network of dyadic ties, i.e., on ramifying chains of obligations structured by kith relationships.

Empirically we find that the kith-based action group has the greatest stability when none of its members except the innovator has a disproportionately large number of his kith present in the group. In contrary situations conflict is likely to arise between the innovator, who is in command, and another member with a large number of his kith in the group. It is difficult for the innovator to discipline such a member—or one of his kith with whom he chooses to identify himself —because of the support his kith members are bound to give him. The efficiency of such a group therefore tends to be lowered. In grave cases efforts at discipline may lead to fission, to the severance of the recalcitrant individual and his kith from the action group.

The utility of the kith concept derives logically from a combination of factors in bilateral kinship and sexual differentiation in work tasks. It is therefore likely to have general validity.

NOTES

1. The field work on which this paper is based was carried out in the Faroe Islands in 1960-61 and was supported by a grant from the Norwegian Research Council. I am deeply indebted to Dr. Fredrik Barth for invaluable encouragement and assistance as well as for suggesting the use of the term "kith" to me.
2. Land is also owned by the state, but this type of ownership does not concern us here.
3. The counting of consanguineal and affinal ties was made possible by the fact that, empirically, the crew members were in no case linked by both types of ties except where there was no doubt as to which tie was socially effective. Table 1 does not show 32 crew members not linked by kith ties. These men owed their inclusion to friendship with members of the crew, usually the skipper, or to having applied for the job when it was offered in the open labor market.

BIBLIOGRAPHY

Freeman, J. D. 1961. On the Concept of the Kindred. Journal of the Royal Anthropological Institute 91: 192-220.
Goodenough, W. H. 1961. Review of George P. Murdock, ed., Social Structure in Southeast Asia. American Anthropologist 63: 1341-1347.
——— 1962. Kindred and Hamlet in Lakalai, New Britain. Ethnology 1: 5-12.
Pehrson, R. N. 1954. Bilateral Kin Groupings as a Structural Type: A Preliminary Statement. University of Manila Journal of East Asiatic Studies 3: 199-202.
——— 1957. The Bilateral Network of Social Relations in Könkämä Lapp District. Bloomington.
Williamson, K. 1948. The Atlantic Islands. London.